RADICAL GAMES

Popping the Bubble of 1960s' Architecture

Lara Schrijver

NAi Publishers

Never trust a hippie

\- James Reid

Contents

Acknowledgments

This book is the result of a long trajectory of thinking and retracing questions that in retrospect have been with me since far before I set upon the path to manuscript and publication. Over the course of its development, the work has been facilitated and encouraged by numerous people and institutions.

As with all lengthy projects, my acknowledgments will inevitably be incomplete. Nevertheless, there are a number of people and institutions I would be remiss to not mention here specifically for their contributions to this book.

The initial manuscript for this book was the result of my dissertation research at Eindhoven University of Technology. Funding for archival research was furnished by NWO at a crucial stage in the research process. My dissertation committee fired brilliantly critical questions at me, which later helped to rethink this manuscript towards a book. In particular Christine Boyer, Caroline van Eck and Arie Graafland offered questions and thoughts that drove me to clarify my arguments and specify my conclusions. The dissertation was guided throughout by the stratospheric comments of Gerard van Zeyl. It remained grounded through the daily guidance of Jeroen Boomgaard, highly valued mentor who became deeply valued friend; he knew when to prod and question, and when to simply encourage.

The Academy of Architecture in Rotterdam deserves specific mention for setting me loose on their students with this material. The questions posed to me in the classroom offered guidelines to restructure the manuscript in the interest of clarity.

Within my circle of close colleagues and friends, I have benefited immensely from the range of talks available to me, from quick and sharp comments to extensive discussions. Two people deserve special mention. François Claessens helped me think through steps of the argument in its earliest phases, and has always known the crucial questions to ask. And Deborah Hauptmann, longstanding friend, once teacher, now colleague, has supported my research throughout. She did this not only through discussions, but above all by directing me towards the light at the end of the tunnel when the process seemed no longer to be overseen.

The department of Architecture at Delft University of Technology has given me the space to forge my own path and maintain the delicate balance between rewriting this material and engaging with new research. My students have stoically accepted my occasional detours into the ideas of this book, even when they were not directly connected to the topic at hand.

NAi publishers, in the person of Marcel Witvoet, have been patient with the many delays that set in after my new research and steady teaching duties swallowed up time originally allocated to rewriting.

I chose to end my editorial work with the journal *OASE* before this book was finished in its current form. In my 12 years as editor, the changing constellations of the board formed a constant lifeline of constructive and generous criticism as well as lighthearted chats with nuggets of wisdom. In particular, the insights of Christoph Grafe and Tom Avermaete have been helpful in so many ways that they have led to the kind of collegial friendship that can make academic life rewarding: the warm sense of mutual appreciation and intellectual challenge among peers. D'Laine Camp, indescribably central to *OASE* as managing editor, agreed to edit this book. She not only worked through this manuscript with her usual diligence, but was patient with my many practical questions and offhand reconsiderations of the material at hand.

The last to be named is the central figure throughout this trajectory: my husband, Jasper de Haan. From the dissertation to this book and all the sidelong strands of thought, discussion, observation and perception, his presence, personal and intellectual, built the foundations on which this work became possible.

Revisiting the 1960s

This book is about the legacy of the 1960s and its continuing presence in architecture. This legacy is ambivalent: the time was exciting and its architectural projects reflect this. At the same time, it contained elements of dogmatic thought that continue to leave traces in the contemporary discourse. The architecture discourse (and practice) of the 1960s and its 'radical revolution' form a transitional period, not quite completing the paradigm shifts it attempted to fulfill with respect to modernism. The research is synthetic insofar as it gathers a number of more or less diverse strands that stand for the symbolic sense of an 'era' – the playful and transformative time of the 1960s. I take these transformations, both provocative and incomplete, as symptomatic for their time. The symptoms taken separately show their powerful impact on society and in the architecture debate. Taken as a whole, they demarcate a specific approach to architecture and its role in society, an approach that continues to resound today yet now seems inadequate to the issues at hand, both in architecture and in society in general. This seems to require a rethinking of our own preconceptions and the discourse that arises from it. Architecture could benefit from a new vocabulary as well as a new way of looking that incorporates the insights of the past century while shedding the dogmatic principles it has left us with.

In many ways, this is a personal book. It reflects my sense that the legacy of the 1960s, particularly in architecture, has left us with many ideas that simply are not adequate to address the issues of today. From the very beginning of my studies in architecture, I have felt that something was missing in the architecture discourse – a vocabulary that would allow us to address contemporary conditions and still be talking about architecture. The gap between theory and practice had grown in the years between the 1960s and the early 1990s, making it increasingly difficult to discuss new architectural developments that exceeded the boundaries of theoretical discourse, or to make theory tangible in the cultural conditions of the time. Over time I came to realize that some of the questions that troubled me arose out of a specific form of institutionalization from the 1960s – the institutionalization of theory and the dogmatic positions that accompanied it.[1]

In a field that directly (and often deeply, if not necessarily visibly or explicitly) touches the lives of so many, it seemed not only counterintuitive, but fundamentally wrong that the debate was hermetic and self-interested. That there might be a distinction between the detailed analyses of specific innovations and the public discussion of more general trends was obvious, but that there might be a desire to enclose oneself in the jargon of the surrounding field in order not to address directly the architecture at hand seemed indecent to me, as well as dismissive of the capacities of the public to understand a clearly formulated argument.

At the same time, the responsibility laid at the door of architectural interventions seemed inadmissibly excessive. From the early days of Le Corbusier's polemic statements on 'architecture or revolution', architects have been charged not only with performing well within their chosen specialty, but also with a visionary sensibility, preempting or triggering societal developments through the careful articulation of their buildings. What is the drive behind this exaggerated sense of self-worth? Is it a sense of self-legitimation, justifying the existence of architecture by implying its necessity to transform society? Or is it rather a hope that is indicated by the architect, a desire to transform the world through the built environment? Would it not be wiser to practice some level of humility, presuming that the inhabitants of a building might not utilize it in precise compliance with the intentions of the designer?

Part of the answer to these questions lies in maintaining distinctions between the worlds we envision and the realities we create. This has become increasingly difficult in a time of media saturation, when 'photoshopping' away blemishes on the perfected image seems like the natural course of events. We cannot ignore the conditions of spectacle, nor should we submit to the notion that this world of designer visions is our only reality. On this level, the insights gained over the course of the 1960s should not be trivialized. Through their careful deconstruction of the accepted truths of modernism combined with their visionary drawings, they opened up a new world to us. At the same time, it is time to reconsider their very own position – in light of new times and a changing context.

This period in architecture is diffuse and its boundaries somewhat blurry, but it is nevertheless defined by a few important developments, beginning in 1956 and ending in 1972. These years serve as an 'extended 1960s' framed by significant moments in the architecture discourse.[2] 1956 saw the collapse of the *Congrès Internationale d'Architecture Moderne* (CIAM), the introduction of Pop Art to architecture in the exhibition 'This Is Tomorrow', and the preliminary motions towards the founding of the Situationist International, only a year later. 1972 saw the collapse of the Situationist International and the demolition of the Pruitt-Igoe building, exemplifying the failure of modernism and heralding the new era of postmodernism, according to Charles Jencks. His choice of the word 'postmodernism' implied a critique of modernism, but also grew into a full-fledged architectural style by the mid-1970s. Although various critiques of high modernism were beginning to surface directly after the Second World War, in the 1960s they begin to produce more than just critique or minor transformations of an overall modernist tendency, coalescing into a larger body of (diverse) cultural criticism.

In a sense, the 1960s occupy a unique position: a radical critique of modernism is posed, there is a forceful move towards democratization in the transatlantic world, and the cultural conditions are imbued with a sense of liberation, prosperity and the wonders of technological progress. But this sense of uniqueness should not be exaggerated. By looking closely at the projects of the 1960s, we can also discern some important continuities and responses, often undervalued, that can inform the contemporary discourse and practice. In this book, three crucial areas are traced through the 1960s in its resistance to and continuity with modernism: the city, the image and technology.

These main themes have been chosen for their continuing relevance to architecture today. In recent years there has been a revival of numerous 1960s' themes and the architecture of the time. Exhibitions abounded on the architecture and culture of the 1960s.[3] This revival hints at the importance of the period for contemporary architecture, but by simply framing it as 'radical' or 'pop', some of its significance is lost. This dissertation examines the manifestoes and work of the time to question how the 1960s may be considered radical, and why there was a subsequent failure of its transformative ideals. Understanding this period as underlying contemporary society in its assessment of cultural conditions, mass culture, revolution and democratization may help to better comprehend the position of the critical in architecture, and hopefully find a better balance between the ideals that led to radical critique and the possibility to create an architecture that is neither merely a replication of existing work, nor an embodiment of pure theory. The three main chapters should thus be read not only as a documentation of critiques in the 1960s, but also as an attempt to formulate a different kind of critical practice, which allows for individual agency in the face of mass society, and also for a critical practice within the conditions of capitalism.

The research that has formed this book was undertaken in the Netherlands. Although the primary figures discussed are all part of an international scene, it is the culture of the Netherlands that founds many of the positions taken in this book. Here, many of the ideals of the 1960s were made tangible, in the form of revised management structures, overhauls of schooling and reinterpretations of societal conventions. While in many places the 'flower-power revolution' appeared promising and radical, in the Netherlands it took on a practical form, becoming embedded within the power structures. Because of this, many of the radical ideas that now seem quaint have become part of everyday life. This is what allows their results, and thus their shortcomings to be seen perhaps a little more clearly than elsewhere. Where else was the university truly reconfigured into an anti-authoritarian structure? Where else did the ideas of individuality extend so far as to undermine most social conventions, except those of voicing opinions? It is this cultural baggage of the *kritiese* years of the late twentieth century that have incited me to look at what may have been lost in our determined advances towards a revolutionary society within architecture.[4] Perhaps it would not have been so strongly determined by this legacy if I had not had the sense of being limited by the belief in the work of the 1960s as the final say in how to view the world and architecture's role in it. So ironically, I may owe a note of thanks to those who came before me and believed so strongly in their cause. It may not be my cause, but it certainly clarified why I, as a child of postmodernism, felt uncomfortable in voicing my affinities with both Palladio and the Simpsons, as different but interesting forms of cultural production.

I

Architecture and the Legacy of the 1960s: Crisis or Opportunity?

Pop as 'what's happening': cover of *Newsweek* (April 1966)

Nostalgia for the 'fabulous '60s, '70s and '80s': cover of *Ottagono* (May 2003)

Many projects these days have been reviving a spirit of the 1960s, be it in their style (bubblegum colours, shiny plastic pop, vivacious tongue-in-cheek stylistic references) or in their intent (social commitment, eco-consciousness). And why should they not? Who could possibly resist the sense of optimism and a faith in the future that radiates from 1960s' imagery, especially when it often still strikes a chord? Why should we not look back to a moment in recent history in which the future seemed particularly bright? This retrospective turn is visible in various 'revival' exhibitions: beginning perhaps as early as 1989 with a large exhibition on the Situationist International in Boston, the early years of the twenty-first century extended this with exhibitions such as the 2004 exhibition 'Art and the Sixties: This Was Tomorrow' at the Tate Modern in London, two major exhibitions in the Netherlands in 2007 ('Sixties!' in the Gemeentemuseum Den Haag and an exhibi-

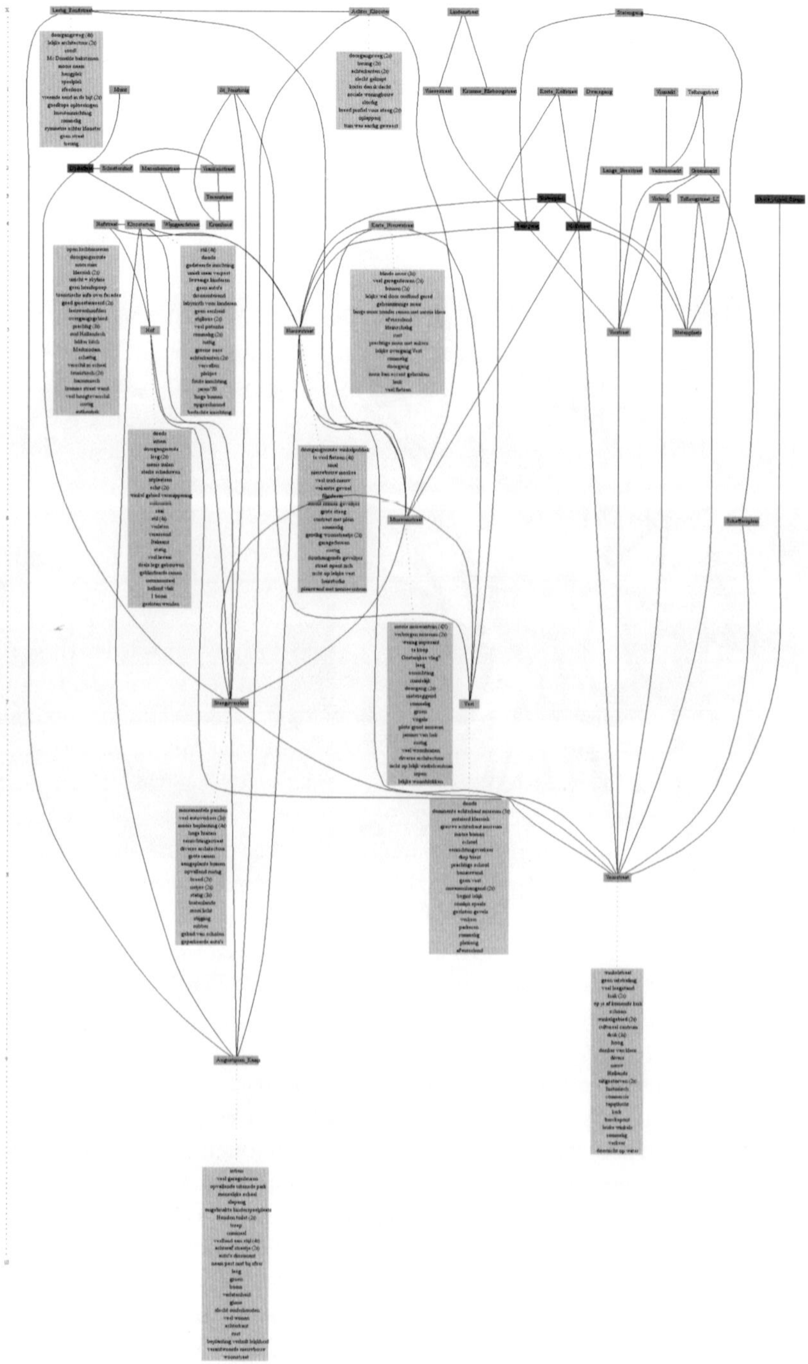

Situationist retracings of contemporary cities enabled by digital technology. Wilfried Houjebek, Psychogeogram of Dordrecht (2003)

tion on the Situationist International at the Centraal Museum Utrecht), as well as the vivid recreation of 'Les Années Pop' at the Centre Pompidou in 2001.

More importantly, this retrospective gaze towards the 1960s has not only derived from an interest in the historical period, but also turned to it for answers in addressing contemporary issues. Just recently, *Arch+* devoted an issue to 'situationist urbanism', while a few years earlier, Dutch artist Wilfried Houjebek held psychogeographic wanderings throughout the world in urban and suburban areas to explore their identity.[1] A large-scale urban renewal project in the Netherlands has recreated an earlier sense of optimism by transforming the well-known phrase 'NiMBY' (Not in My Back Yard) into 'WiMBY!' (Welcome in My Back Yard!). This project in Rotterdam-Hoogvliet has availed itself of the optimistic belief in urban renewal that characterized an earlier era. Moreover, those involved with the project have also utilized the imagery that came out of the 1960s, playing with a campy version of low-culture references. The Venice Biennale of 2006 and the International Architecture Biennale Rotterdam of 2007 both explored the structures of cities in an attempt to reveal underlying agents of power that might help architecture to steer towards revolution and further democratization. All was positioned with the appeal to a social commitment that extended far beyond the 'mere' creation of the physical urban environment.

What precisely is the appeal of the 1960s that has led to these reconsiderations and revivals? For one, the sense of optimism that is intimately connected to the time has remained powerful throughout history. Despite the darker sides of the era (such as the deaths of students involved in riots, the brutal smothering of the oppositional voice in Prague by the Russians in 1968, and the violence that went hand-in-hand with many of the protests), the inherited view of the 1960s has remained primarily a view through the rose-colored glasses of the time. The ideals that were put forward, all imbued with a sense of liberation (freedom of speech, freedom of choice, free love, free bicycles), were full of confidence in a better future. These ideals were also fed by the increasing affluence and vivacious imagery, an 'aesthetics of plenty' following the bleak reality of the Second World War.[2] But perhaps the most important trait of the 1960s, which has continued to define our perception of the time, is the sense of agency: the notion that the revolution may well succeed. The students that ran amok in the streets of Paris might have been little more than post-adolescent troublemakers, they nevertheless managed to communicate a sense of power: that they may well make a difference. The sense of revolutionary potential was powerful, and particularly in France the events turned so quickly that May 1968 became an emblem for the transformations taking place in the1960s. In a recent review of the events of 1968, Sylvère Lotringer comments that the students in France achieved in a month what the Italian movement had been working on for ten years.[3]

Architecture figured prominently in the struggle for a better society. On the one hand it represented the corrupted elite, who kept the working class repressed in the concrete towers that were meant to offer light and air but in reality cut them off from their social networks. On the other it embodied the potential for liberation (much like Le Corbusier had envisioned earlier) by offering a place for individ-

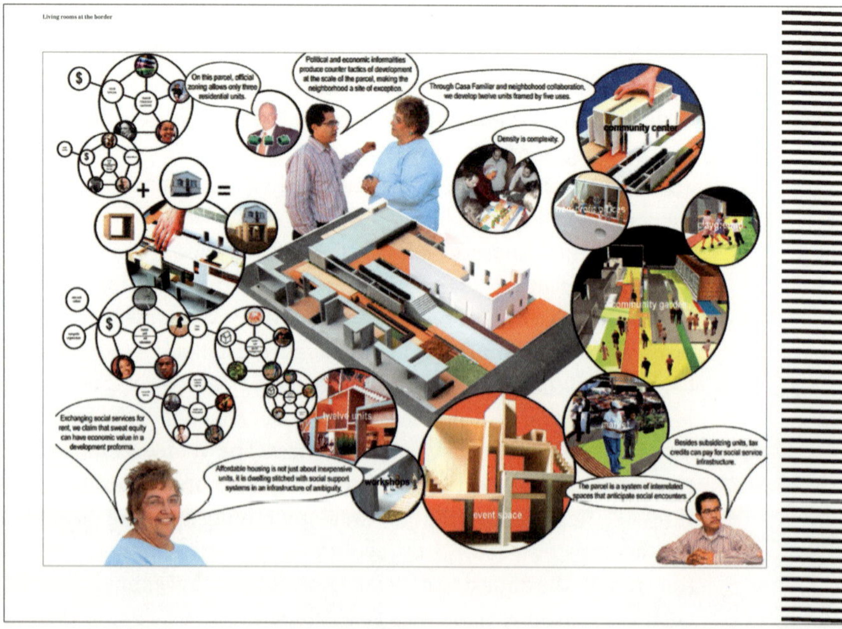

Architecture as social project: 'Living rooms at the border', housing project as political instrument. Project for San Diego, Estudio Cruz. Rotterdam Architecture Biennale (2007).

ual expression and subsequent emancipation from the constraints of society. The project New Babylon could not have been created without a deep sense of the power of architecture to transform the lives of its occupants. In architecture, the critique of existing forms of life was immediately coupled to its capability to instigate a revolution in the form of new societal relations *resulting from* a new built environment.

Perhaps this is why we continue to revisit the 1960s: it offered us a sense of true agency in architecture – the possibility that we may, with a simple plan for a new form of housing, alter the world in a fundamental way, contributing to a quicker realization of the better future that lies just ahead.

If the 1960s will not die, perhaps it is because they shouldn't – at least not entirely. There is a cheerfully naïve optimism underlying these revivals that we can all use in our post-punk, postmodern, poststructuralist, post-critical, post-apocalyptic, media-savvy, eminently cynical and disabused-of-ideals world. The continuing presence of the 1960s is a mirror, or better, the slightly crumpled photograph affectionately kept nearby – something that recalls the image of a better time. It gives us nostalgia to appease our sense of loss – a loss of youth, loss of ideals, loss of conviction. And yet, we might also ask: Whose loss? Whose convictions? Have architects stopped building? This nostalgia, as sweet as it may seem, is also dangerous because it blinds us to the contemporary issues. If we continue to judge everything by how it measures up against the fading photograph, we may easily miss the richness of our surrounding reality.

The 'Post-'60s' Blues'

It is easy to understand the sense of loss when reading both the material of the time and particularly the retrospectives. For example, as Arthur Danto reports on the student uprising at Columbia in 1968: 'It taught me what it was like to live in history, which consists in the sense that something momentous is taking place, without anyone's knowing how it is going to come out.' He recalls the famous Paris graffiti 'l'imagination au pouvoir' and notes that this was a time when 'aesthetics, for once, changed the way we all lived'.[4] The excitement of the time was palpable in its writings and projects as well as in its actions, and it was the moment in time when anything became possible, and nothing unthinkable. It is comparable to the sense of lightness that ran through the 1990s and the early twenty-first century. And yet – the dilemmas facing architects were then, as now, delineated by the 1960s and the sense of being doomed to fail, be always less than one was then.

When contrasted with a contemporary sense of stagnation in architectural thinking (leading some even to speak of a crisis in architectural thinking, in particular around the turn of the century), it should be no wonder that the 1960s have now become a benchmark of what architecture might be or do.[5] The sense of 'crisis' is related to the perception of the 1960s as a revolutionary era, and with our own time as a poor reflection of those inflated ambitions for architecture. As a cultural turn, the period of the 1960s has been getting quite a lot of attention. To some, it becomes a reference for recalling an idealism in architecture or reacting against a wholesale commodification of architecture. In the introduction to a recent issue of *Hunch*, Alejandro Zaera-Polo notes that a desire to recover utopian thinking has resurfaced for the first time since the 1960s.[6] Yet this formulation alone reproduces the kind of dialectic that was central to the work of the 1960s: to engage with society, or to 'sell out'. The question should therefore perhaps be seen as more fundamental. If the work of the 1960s is the standard for societal engagement, why are we trying to re-envision the possibilities of architecture and its agency? And if those possibilities find themselves caught in an unsolvable opposition between ideals and realities, does that mean that there is something we are missing about the 1960s? Is it possible that the architecture of the 1960s introduced certain presumptions that still operate in the architecture discourse today? And if so, is it possible that contemporary practices are offering a different viewpoint that cannot be seen until we revise our understanding of our most recent history?

It is of course easy to turn to the past when confronted with a present that seems incomprehensibly complex. This turn to the 1960s is more than nostalgia, however: many questions addressed in architecture at the time still resonate today.[7] Beyond the sense of loss that this return to the 1960s appeals to, there is also the suggestion of similarity between then and now. The tendency to revisit these earlier solutions is not so much to dismiss them, but to use them again. The cultural conditions facing architects at the time have perhaps become more visible, but not necessarily different. The seeds of today's increasingly visual orientation were certainly present at the time, as were the beginnings of the 'information age', albeit not yet in the form of personal computers and the interface capabilities of the World Wide Web. The technological transformations and cultural conditions being addressed in the 1960s are still relevant to the conditions within which architecture operates today. However, the question remains whether the actual proposals of the time hold answers for contemporary architecture – does Archigram's Cushicle illustrate a potential home-environment, or is it little more than a provocative illustration of the dislocation of a global traveller? Can we perhaps learn some lessons from the failed ideals of the time? In other words, while acknowledging the powerful aspects of the time, we should perhaps be careful to look closely at this period. The pleasure of a nostalgic reconsideration of the 1960s should not prevent us from examining the results of the many plans that seemed at the time destined to succeed in configuring a new and happier world. The endless potential of the individual to create himself, the unlimited possibilities for mass movements to impact their political environment, all were part of a certainty that 'the times they were a-changin' (with apologies to Bob Dylan). In fact, many things did change. On a political level, many battles were fought and won, more or less, in favour of previously unconsidered minorities. On an individual level, choices became more abundant and more self-determined, losing some of their rigorous predetermination. The consumer society we are now so fully embedded in is part and parcel of the need for individual expression. Yet at the same time, the promises of 'peace, love and happiness' were perhaps a little too premature. Moreover, the implications of an endless self-realization seem to have led so easily to an excessive responsibility of the individual to configure his or her own life, no matter what the circumstances. Individual agency can lead too easily to the abrogation of communal responsibility.[8] Nevertheless, the appeal to a similarity in cultural conditions coupled with the nostalgic return to earlier projects not only blinds us to the contemporary, but does something more insidious: it suggests that the contemporary can be approached through a retrieval of history, rather than learning from history in order to approach the contemporary.

Although this book adds to the growing volume of endless reconsiderations of the radical moment of the 1960s, it forms an attempt to use this historical reflection to begin to look forward again. It examines which cultural conditions today still resonate with the 1960s, in order to understand what has continued to be of importance to architecture. At the same time, its intention is to examine the resulting failures, in the hope that we might be able to escape the sense of stagnation. If the architecture of the 1960s has become a benchmark, perhaps by unravelling it a little more, we can begin to formulate new ideals that derive from our own time, rather than coming up short in relation to a historical chimera of radical change. Hence, despite its addition to seemingly endless self-reflections, this book argues that we must look carefully if we are to reflect. Not only at the time that seems to hold so much promise of utopia, of ideals, of powerful revolutions that never came. But also at the presuppositions they have left us with, the oppositional debates that still guide many discussions, and the possibilities that we may have in escaping a repetition of a call to arms that fades into cynicism and neglect.[9] The sense of loss may be real, but it is not merely because ideals have faded. Rather, the results of those ideals were less perfect than the visions of a shiny happy future populated by emancipated individuals seemed to promise. If we are to recall those ideals, we should do so in spirit more than literally. We should first be aware of why it is so easy to see the similarities between then and now, and where the parallels do not suffice. This requires examination in two directions: to learn from our past, we should look at the distinctive features, but to move towards our future it is more helpful to look at the resonances and agreements rather than the differences.

Affluence, the Seeds of the Spectacle, and the Configuration of the Collective

Many of the questions posed in the 1960s have remained valid simply because we do not yet have satisfactory answers, despite all the intellectual and cultural effort that has gone into finding them ever since. In part, this is because some of the strategies of the 1960s fit seamlessly into an age driven by spectacle and mass democracy. And in part it is because there is an appeal to the moral certainty combined with cheerful optimism that seems to have infused the 1960s with a rosy belief that a better world was just around the corner.[10] How then should we view the current results, where all sorts of innovations have become instruments in a public image of commercial veneer, rather than the presumably perfect life of authenticity that we should have attained in our leisure time? More than anything, the diversity of the 1960s as a culturally transformative period allows for the myriad references to the period that we find today. Whether it relates to advertising, mass culture, activism in the city, technology that borders on science fiction, or the position of the individual against a disturbingly homogeneous society, the 1960s have something that can be referred to. Therefore it becomes even more important to isolate those elements that are more fundamental than merely a cheerful nostalgic 1960s' revival, and examine why the need to revive these notions is still so present.

The issues of today are founded on many transformations in the 1960s, and this foundation extends in two directions. On the one hand, the 1960s signalled the turn to a 'condition of postmodernity' (whether we set the beginning of postmodernity in 1968 with the student riots in Paris and the work of Foucault, or in 1972, with the demolition of Pruitt-Igoe, signalling the failure of modernism in architecture, or any other number of boundary conditions, many of the issues we consider as building up postmodernity began to take shape in the 1960s, or as Fredric Jameson proposes, as the cultural logic of late capitalism). In this sense, examining the questions that were raised at an early shift from modernity (defined by speed, technological developments, universal language) to postmodernity (characterized by plurality, the ephemeral, multiplicity, a disbelief in meta-narratives) are still highly relevant today.[11] The underlying issues may have become more clearly delineated, but have not yet been overturned by fundamental changes. Secondly, if we treat the period as one of transition and transformation, many of the changes implemented or intended in the 1960s still function as guides for cultural transformation today. Many of the questions at the time are still relevant to address today, such as the freedom of the individual (and how that relates to the community as a whole), the impact of technological developments (sustainability), and the influence of visual information (and commercial culture).

In general, there are some cultural conditions that have continued to grow over time – most notably, the culture of capitalism and the 'society of the spectacle' (including an increasingly visual culture). The belief in democratization and the concomitant rise of the individual has continued to be of importance: in the 1960s, giving a voice to the 'man in the street' was a revolutionary act, while today it appears that everyone might get Warhol's 'fifteen minutes of fame', whether it is through forums on the Internet or the spectacular rise in television shows that revolve around everyday people. At the same time, there has been a loss of the classic constructions of community within which these individuals would typically be embedded. These have been replaced by Internet forums, or 'light' communities, which are based more on shared interests than shared space.[12] The technological transformations that have been part and parcel of history took a paradigmatic turn, some believe, with the introduction of the personal computer and the Internet. Our sense of place has been fundamentally altered by the simultaneity of contemporary digital, global and urban space.

Consumption and affluence have increased in many parts of the world, and although they seem to form a baseline of contemporary society, some countermovements are also visible within consumer society.[13] Not a wholesale refusal but some level of consumer savvy, such as re-use, purchasing sustainable, 'ethically produced' or local goods. Here, the market finds a way to respond. When viewed cynically, that indicates that there is no 'moral' component to the market, but that profit is the only concern. While this may be true, if the public enforces a conscience upon producers by choosing to purchase some goods over others (and price being one of numerous factors in that choice), the results are not necessarily bad. The TV-programme *Extreme Home Makeover* encompasses a number of different features in this debate. On the one hand, it presumes the desirability of an identity expressed in architectural terms (although primarily on the surface more than in the space). Bedrooms are turned into drive-in movie theatres, incorporate pick-up trucks as beds, have music-themed wall decorations, grass-covered floors – anything is possible, as long as it is based on a particular hobby or interest of the room's occupant. It also offers a 'quick', and sometimes superficial, fix: although wrecking balls and sledgehammers are used extensively, the fundamental structure of the space is not typically transformed. The houses remain recognizable suburban family dwellings. It offers a spectacle: extensive demolition and construction crews are working against the clock with the design team, and the pressure builds as the deadline nears. And it offers the satisfaction of the family returning, who will forget the troubles in their life as they walk through their beautiful new home. We could say: this form of sugar-coated home makeover is no more than a temporary placebo for their problems. Or we could also say: if there is a role for architecture to play in the everyday life of suburban families, this offers a caricature of what architects could be doing – making the home back into a castle.

All in all, a need for a different direction in architecture has been expressed in various forms. The tendency to look back towards the 1960s for a different and inspiring direction is understandable, as it is the most recent period in which a tangible body of ideals was given form and voice. Those who were part of the radical movements at the time might understandably feel that today's forms of resistance or engagement are ephemeral, superficial and inconsistent. However, the fact that contemporary firms are directing their gaze towards sustainability, forms of community, consumer and/or client desires on small levels, is perhaps not so much an indication of fickleness and lack of ideals as it is an indication of their willingness to address issues in small increments. It is precisely these 'small ideologies', the ideals that are expressed and given form with an understanding of compromise and a presumption that they are limited, that offer new ways of examining architecture. And this is why extensive ideas on 'power and the city', which attempt to address a comprehensive condition of urban form, fall flat despite their passionate plea for transformations.

Areas of Critique: City, Image, Technology

These cultural conditions find their specific expressions in the architecture debate. The conditions of capitalism and in particular the increase in a visual foundation for contemporary culture underlie many of the debates on commercial interests in architecture and 'city branding', revealing the tense relationship between architecture and (mass) imagery. The presence of the everyday individual as the primary voice of democracy has remained a crucial issue in the relationship between architecture and the city. Technological progress has always been a part of architecture, but the increasingly intangible nature of many interactions has led to the contradicting desires for architecture to either create a sense of 'place' or become an ephemeral environment defined by new technologies.

To further understand these contemporary issues I trace them back to their roots in the 1960s. This includes looking at how and why some of the projects failed at the time, and why they are in part being resurrected today.[14] The ambiguity in the work of the 1960s has not been adequately examined – it has simply been utilized either to ridicule the unrealistic venture of the utopian project or to hide behind the safety of waiting for the world to change. Although I concur with David Harvey when he states that postmodernism's eclecticism was not a thorough way of engaging with the cultural transformations in perceptions of space and time, I'm not sure that the American Marxist discourse can offer the plurality he considers fundamental to the postmodern condition.[15] As long as a single discourse is considered preferable to others, plurality is by necessity undermined.

A chapter is devoted to each of these three themes: the city, the image and technology, addressing the most radical views of the 1960s. Each one of these areas played a key role in the architecture of the twentieth century: where the city was the primary locus of modern architecture, technology was its driving force, and the image was its manner of (self-)reflection. Not only were these thematics central to the modernist discourse on architecture, but they formed areas of transition in the 1960s and remain relevant to the discourse today. Although other topics are also important to these developments from the 1960s through today, these three are immediately present in the discourse of various journals, and are also circumscribed by both the radicalism and the contemporary revival of the manifestoes discussed in each chapter. Throughout the next chapters I will trace the critical responses in the transatlantic architecture discourse that demonstrate a resonance within these topics. Not only is each critique specific to its context, but it also shares a general sensibility in response to the modernist discourse that has triggered it.[16]

In response to the functionalist city, the needs of its human occupants that went beyond the strictly functional became a key strategy to unseating some of the CIAM precepts. These 'trans-functional' needs became manifest in various ways on both sides of the Atlantic, ranging from radical ideas by the situationists like the *dérive*, to more everyday interpretations such as the social space of the sidewalk introduced by Jane Jacobs. As modern technology began to seem more than merely a useful (and neutral) instrument, diversions were sought through a more people-friendly technology. The introduction of organic forms and individual choice (customization replacing mechanization, prefiguring biotechnology) was reflected throughout the work of Archigram and the Situationist International. In response to the abstraction of modernist architecture, the desire for symbolism and ornamentation was utilized to revise this aesthetic purity. This interest in symbolism ranged from the analysis of the symbolic richness of mass culture by Lawrence Alloway to the extensive documentation by Robert Venturi and Denise Scott Brown of decorative billboard symbolism on the Las Vegas Strip.

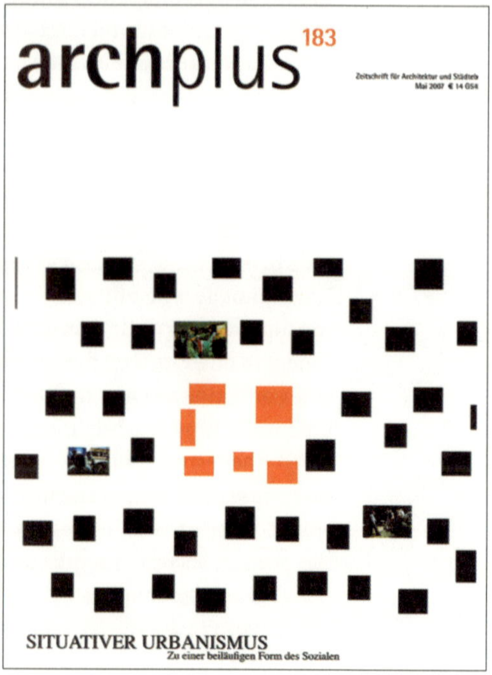

Exploring the potential of situationist thought in the contemporary context. *Archplus* 183, Situationist Urbanism – 'towards a casual form of the social' (2007)

Although the critiques of the failures of modernism pointed to absolutely fundamental problems, they simultaneously replicate some of the underlying assumptions, thus producing a pseudo-revolution. In essence, I argue that the various radical critiques of the 1960s were *both* radical and reactionary. This is particularly visible in the three areas that have been essential to this process of revision in the architecture discourse: the city, the image and technology. Each theme is not treated as an entire topic in itself, but rather for its importance and relevance to the architecture discourse of the time. It is my contention that this discourse reveals a struggle with manifestations of modernism in architecture. This process of analysis and comparison, of individual discussion as well as drawing parallels, has led to an identification of principal strategies of resistance that I discuss at length in each chapter. These are what I would call the basic terms of transformation, or in other words how this 1960s' revolution of the discourse is framed. Most of the words and suggestions involved return throughout various writings and projects, thus indicating that a critique was formed that was more than merely local. Again, these terms (such as 'growth', 'change' and 'flexibility') form the parallels in the transatlantic debate.

Finally, these themes, in particular how they have been addressed over the past 40 years, reveal another underlying question: that of the role of 'critique' in architecture, or the potentially critical role of architecture. The question of 'criticality' underlies the strategy of these transformations. In other words, a fundamental point of resonance throughout the different issues is the necessity, relevance and position of critique. Since the advent of modernism in architecture, its critical role has been of primary importance. Le Corbusier offered a critique of society and the role of architecture within it, and proposed, out of this, a revolutionary architecture. As architecture became less a cultural expression that contained a tradition within it, and more an avant-garde venture, its critical role became paramount.

Roots of Contemporary Discourse: The Failure of Critique

This underlying question is perhaps more difficult to escape: it revolves not around the similarity of cultural conditions we operate within, nor the nostalgia of a loss of ideals, but hides the fact that the very foundations of today rest in the past – not despite but because of our erstwhile revolutionaries. These twin notions, critique and revolution, run throughout the manifestoes of the twentieth century and will be examined in this book for their impact on architectural thinking and the contemporary debate. Defining architecture through the framework of critique and revolution has become more significant than perhaps foreseen at the time. With the responsibility of revolution on the shoulders of architecture, it was given an impossible task, in essence doomed to fail. To transform the world and cure its inadequacies through the act of building placed an inordinate amount of societal responsibility on a discipline that is fundamentally complicit with some of the established inequalities. The primary reason to discuss this issue of critique and theory so extensively is that a revised strategy could aid in escaping some of the 1960s' dichotomies mentioned earlier. The failure of the 1968 revolution deepened

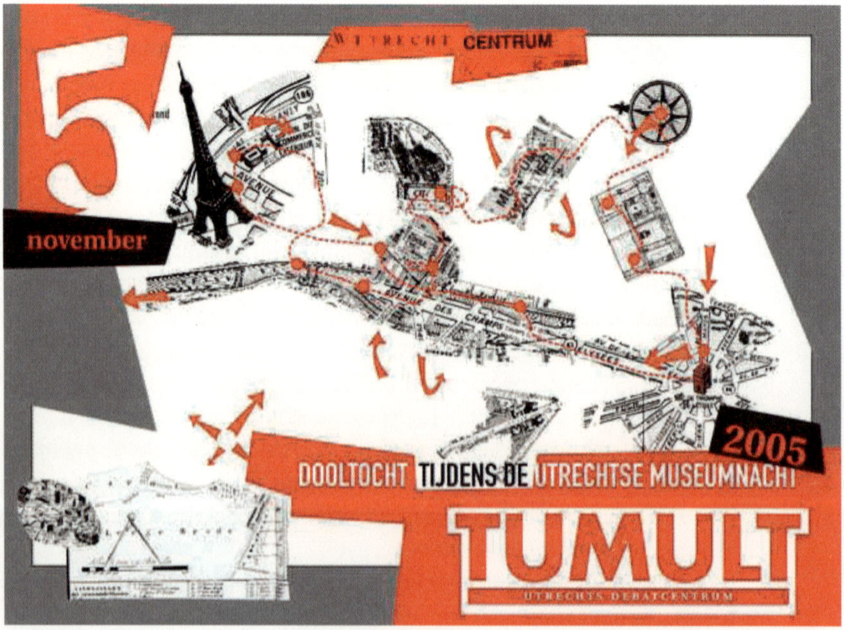

An endless adventure: poster announcing a *dérive* during Utrecht Museum night (2005)

the chasm between the theory and the practice of architecture; by navigating the middle ground and revising the relationship between theory and practice we may find a way to move beyond the polemical reductions of pure radicality. This has become ever more important in the age of late capitalism, where the consumer society has fundamentally transformed conditions of production. According to Michael Hays:

> It may well turn out that a different, younger audience, whose relationship to consumption is altogether altered, whose memories may not include any notions of resistance or negation, may have to produce another kind of theory premised on neither the concept of reification nor the apparatus of the sign, both of which have their ultimate referent in the vexatious territory of reproducibility and commodity consumption.[17]

Note here the key concepts of consumption, resistance, negation, the sign; all of which are omnipresent in the 1960s' discourse on architecture. The roots of what Hays is suggesting as a new direction for theory lie in the 1960s, and before that in the 1920s.

Most of the notions of criticality as handled in contemporary (transatlantic) discourse are founded on a Marxist position embedded in consumer culture. Taking pleasure in consumer culture and various forms of mass culture is accepted, but the analysis of these forms of cultural expression is typically premised on ideas of reification and a need for critical assessment to penetrate beyond the surface affect. The tenuousness of this position is usually emphasized within the text through a discomfort with the slippery conditions of media and commodity culture, often positioning architecture as either hopeless affirmation or the locus of resistance. In the sphere of popular culture, programmes such as *Extreme Home Makeover* may help us at least question whether the divisions are as stark as sketched out in the neo-Marxist discourse.

In fact, the 'altogether altered' relation to consumption suggested by Hays seems a way to sidestep the congealed definitions of revolution that continue to be based on 1968. Revolution now may well be found in culture jamming rather than burning the streets. In architecture, it may well be based on creating the best building for a specific programme. Perhaps the problem is no longer to build a radically different environment (which also, in the forms suggested by Archigram and the Situationist International, embodies a singular logic, negating their own rhetoric of individuality and difference), but rather to build a beautiful environment. Might the 'radically different' today be something that is already embedded in our contemporary culture? If so, is the task of architecture then no longer to offer the radically different, but rather the well-adjusted alternative?

What I am suggesting here, then, is that there is less of a problem with architecture as a whole, and more of a problem with how it is approached. With the underlying intellectual constructions that delineate how we address the success and failure of projects. By conflating critique with negation, and by presuming that critique is the necessary precursor to revolution, it has become all but impossible to see how envisioning (even small and limited) alternatives within the limits of a programme brief can contribute to an environment that is valuable. Its value is not determined by its ability to reveal the great societal conspiracy, but to offer comfort and beauty in the realm of everyday living spaces, and symbolic content that is legible on various levels. Architecture is still struggling with these possibilities, with the idea that architecture may need to be both complicit and critical, and with the idea that the critical itself is not the solution to everything. Bruno Latour was among the first to offer some suggestions on a 'sensibility' that may prove fruitful to architecture.

The notion of the critical has become a strong point of contention in the contemporary architecture discourse. It has led to suggestions such as a 'projective practice' which is understood to incorporate both critical elements and a component of agency.[18] However, I turn here to Latour because he offers a different suggestion for critique.[19] My hope for what we could call an 'embedded critique' is here simply used to reframe our current understanding of critical. As noted above, 'critical' in this discourse is often conflated with negation and resistance. Or, as Latour puts it: 'What if explanations resorting automatically to power, society, discourse had outlived their usefulness and deteriorated to the point of now feeding the most gullible sort of critique?'[20] In the rhetoric of the 1960s, these problems begin to surface in critique not necessarily when it appeals to disbelief (as a mode of scepticism to aid in resisting facile presumptions), but when it appeals to what

Latour calls 'powerful agents hidden in the dark acting always consistently, continuously, relentlessly'.[21] These 'agents hidden in the dark' are continuously lurking at the edges of Debord's critique of the spectacle – the dominance of capitalism is indeed acting relentlessly and consistently, and therefore in a sense already undermines the possibility of critique. This tension between the dependence on critique for liberation, and on the other hand the 'secret powers' that mercilessly define our world is an unproductive illusion that still plagues some ideas about the role of the critical in architecture. It simultaneously posits the need for an active resistance while fatalistically accepting the pointlessness of this resistance. The impasse in this position suggests that perhaps the problem today is not that resistance needs to be reactivated, but rather that critique and agency need to be redefined. Critique in its traditional sense puts everyone in a bind: Are you seeing what you think you see? Is there not another level of reality behind that, controlled by some evil forces of domination? And therefore, is not meaning as you know it completely without value? Agency as defined by a leftist scheme of power and alienation is simply impossible in the society of the spectacle. Yet is it not true that within the spectacle there is also agency? Is a consumer boycott not a form of agency with respect to corporations? And is the act of building by definition not a form of agency?

Although I believe we should look to our own field for the critical questions and the expertise to resolve them, there are perhaps some suggestions we can take

Understanding the forces that make the city. *Power: Producing the Contemporary City*, catalogue, International Architecture Biennale Rotterdam (2007)

from other disciplines for strategy. The examples above of the shifting of architecture theory and the debate are intentionally culled from the architecture debate – they indicate what the issues are *within* the discipline. Moreover, the discussion in this thesis of how we got here is through the architecture debate, albeit framed by mechanisms of mass culture and the media. The knowledge of the history of the discipline and the expertise of the field in its fullest extent – from rhetoric to image to building – is crucial to developing the discipline in a sensible way. Yet since critique itself has become such an important element in this constellation, I also believe it wise to look just over the fence and examine some alternative strategies. Various thinkers such as Douglas Kellner, Douglas Rushkoff and Bruno Latour, diverse as they are, offer possibilities of reframing the arguments, not the content, of architecture production.

The obvious question now is: Where do we go from here? In the 1960s a number of productive questions were posed about the changing relationship between architecture and everyday imagery, or the position of the individual in the city, or the shifts in the relationship to technology. Although each of these problems deserves its own extensive analysis, in this book I concentrate on connections, on resonance in relation to today's practice. I propose a way in which the often-discussed 'paradigm shifts' of the 1960s can become productive today. I hope to demonstrate that there is a distinct connection between how the 'revolution' took place in all these areas, and how this connection offers an opening to a different way of discussing architecture and its mediations, or the practice and its theorizations.

In short: I believe the democratization that took place in the architecture of the 1960s (through such images and mechanisms as a valuation of individual opinion and the everyday life of the street) was significantly indebted to the rise of the mass media and the way they were incorporated in architectural practice. Mass imagery offered a release from the more 'purified' forms of high modernist discourse and introduced a mode of communication with the man in the street. Yet the liberating aspects of this excursion outside the bounds of 'high architecture' also opened a Pandora's box of public relations, complicity with vested commercial interests (replacing traditional power structures), the problems of advertising and the tendency to relinquish expertise in favour of 'what the people want' (uncritical populism).

In other words, what the 1960s left us with is a mixed blessing: the promise of individual freedom is exhilarating when set against the authoritarian society of the 1950s, yet rings hollow when public cohesion seems lost, when there is little communal structure to help define this individuality. The idea that mass imagery and the ephemeral, fleeting quality of the mass media might help form a new aesthetic for a more communicative architecture is admirable, but becomes suspect when architects avoid responsibility for their work by simply replicating mass culture rather than making clear and well-argued choices. Finally, the notion of technology as an instrument of liberation is crucial to the ongoing developments in both the modern and the postmodern, but that does not mean we can close our eyes to the less pleasant consequences of technological progress – in that sense, we cannot hold to a neutral instrumentality of technology, but must acknowledge the autonomy it has also displayed.

These issues are the foundation of the society of the spectacle – they circumscribe the 'paradigm shift' of the 1960s, and indicate the similarities between questions that were raised. Although the Situationist International, Venturi and Scott Brown, and Archigram were all working within extremely different cultural contexts, there was a more globally-oriented, transatlantic debate that had everything to do with the position of the individual in an authoritarian form of modernism and the question of a critical stance at the advent of late capitalism, determined by mass media and commercial interests. This position of the 'critical' is thus defined by resistance against the spectacle, while all else becomes a form of affirmation. On the one hand, we then have complicity with the media spectacle in the form of not only star architects but also celebrity chefs, celebrity fashion designers and even celebrity castaways on Survivor Island. On the other, we have a general form of resistance such as that posed by the Situationist International against the spectacle. Since it is based on resistance as its fundamental strategy, it never takes a stance *for* anything but is always *against*, thus remaining by definition apolitical.[22]

While Guy Debord appeared to believe that there were visual strategies that could undermine the condition of the spectacle (*détournement*), Venturi and Scott Brown suggested that the 'natural' expressions of the spectacle (*Learning from Las Vegas*) perhaps contributed more to the vitality of the everyday than 'high art' could; and Archigram, in its spectacular expressions of futuristic technology, offered a criticism of the purified forms of the machine aesthetic. Each of these strategies implies a revision of modernism and expresses a moment of critique: each one exposes another small piece of the underbelly of rigorously technocratic and progressivist modernism. That critical moment, the discovery of a technique or an aesthetic that can help revise our cultural perceptions, or even only an expression of dissatisfaction, was absolutely crucial to subsequent developments. Yet on reexamination, it seems that each strategy somehow becomes a little too complicit with its own ideology – Debord's Marxist principles undermining the possibility of a critique *within* the society of the spectacle, since to him the revolution needed to be total, or he considered it failed; Venturi and Scott Brown's uncritical populism leading to slightly too smooth replications of mass icons; and Archigram's technological sensibility demonstrating a level of technofetishism that seemed doomed to replicate an earlier machine aesthetic.

Although contemporary architecture may not have as obvious an instrument as the imagery of mass culture was in the 1960s, there are interesting projects to be found, each with its own direction. These are not the ones that subjugate aesthetics to a social goal, or the ones that are so immersed in formalism that they can only be discussed in terms of composition; but rather the ones that hope to offer a micro-intervention: a beautiful building that takes its context into account without presuming it can change the world. Might a building perhaps be both attractive to the general public and inspiring to professionals? Could it potentially offer a space in the city to all the public, even if privately funded? Critique becomes

Ensconcing hippiedom in suburbia. Room with a view, HAP. 'Parasite Paradise', exhibition of various mobile architecture units in Leidsche Rijn (2003, www.skor.nl / photograph by Ralph Kämena)

more difficult when the presumption is that we should discuss things as they are in the world, when we accept that we, too, are embedded in it. But the fluidity and fragmentation of postmodernism should not lead us to think that all can be made uncritically, that an architectural or urban intervention means no more to its inhabitants than the formal discourse we manipulate.

The architecture discourse of the 1960s again utilized 'critique', only in this case its arrows were aimed towards modern architecture. In particular those tenets of modern architecture as disseminated by Le Corbusier and CIAM were seen to be severely lacking in many of their results. Rather than a perfectly clear and rational environment, many people experienced the modern city as increasingly disorienting. The radical nature of modern architecture was seen less as the ultimate expression of man's capabilities, and more as an architecture dissociated from human concerns. The great refusal of ornament as propagated by Adolf Loos was increasingly questioned in relation to the desires of the user. The imminent freedom promised by modern architecture was slowly perceived as a dominant style with little regard for its occupants.

In response, many of these tenets were contested or transformed in the 1960s. Reyner Banham confronted the perceived failure of modern architecture by claiming that its ideas were far more progressive than the available technology. Guy Debord and the situationists developed the idea that the individual was to create

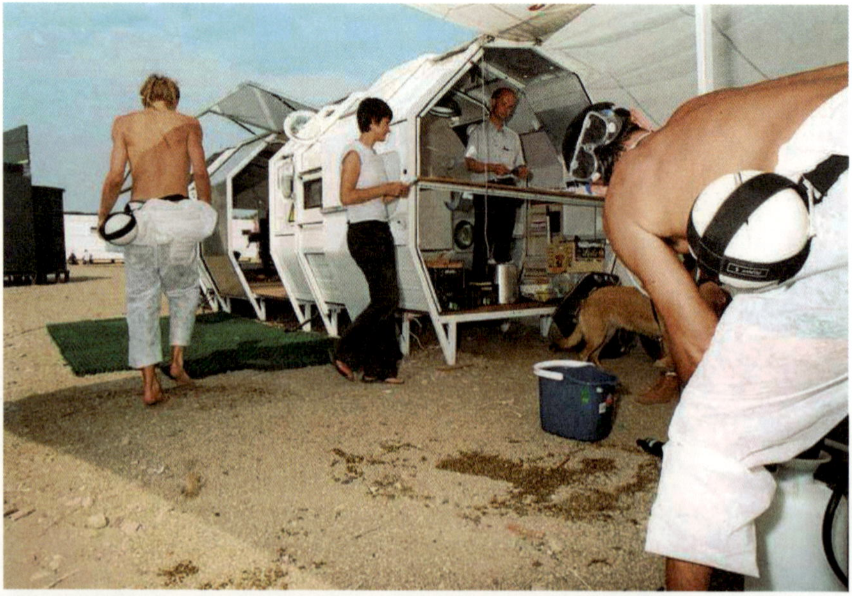

DIY and reuse. Miele Space Station, 2012 architects. 'Parasite Paradise' (2003, www.skor.nl / photograph by Ralph Kämena)

his own environment instead of merely responding to the poverty of the functional city. Robert Venturi and Denise Scott Brown proposed that the everyday environment with its wealth of low-culture symbolism was 'almost all right'. Each of these notions was a radical confrontation with the dominant discourse at the time, and introduced a fundamental revision of some basic principles of architecture.[23]

Of course, the cultural conditions of the late 1950s were beginning to show some fundamental differences with those of the critical years of the 1920s. One of the most explosive changes was the rise of late capitalism, which was linked to what Debord called the society of the spectacle. The high modernism of Le Corbusier that could depend on a reasonably strong (often socialist) government to introduce efficient mass housing that held to high standards, for example, was beginning to be overwhelmed (particularly in the USA) by the driving forces of market capitalism, leading to a cost-efficient version of the same socialist principles – without regard for the community-based qualities underpinning them. The freedom implied in consumer choice also undermined the notion that standardization was appropriate to the industrial era – contemporary forms of industry in the late 1950s, especially in the USA were in fact highly adaptable to 'mass customization'. The freedom of individual expression was slowly beginning to overtake the principle of standardization. With such basic concepts at odds with one another, a revision of some modernist principles in architecture appeared necessary. These revisions came in various forms – from the Independent Group's exploration of new sources of inspiration (the Smithsons' article 'But Today We Collect Ads'), to

Learning from Venturi and Scott Brown: Billboards and historical architecture. FAT architects, Hoogvliet (2001)

Team 10 splitting off from the original CIAM constellation, to Venturi's eloquent plea for complexity and contradiction, set against purity and abstraction.

What is interesting is that these revisions are somehow 'incomplete'. In the crudest formulation: Venturi's complexity became a new kind of purity, as the figural had once been anathema, now the non-figural was virtually forbidden; new sources of inspiration such as the Independent Group's use of ads and popular imagery were simply revalued into high art rather than examined critically.[24] The questions raised in the 1960s in response to modernism are fundamental to what is seen as the postmodern condition. However, the resolutions of these same issues are still embedded in a modernist sense of space and teleology.

The 1960s, on the cusp between modernism and postmodernism, hold the seeds of questions we have today: In the determined search for a contaminated image (mass cultural imagery as used by the Independent Group), have we not mindlessly surrendered the discipline to market forces? Or, by receding into the theory of deconstructivism, have we not denied any social responsibility as architects? Is it not partly the incessant dichotomizing between social responsibility and pure aesthetic pleasure that has left us in this bind? Is it not possible to both be aware of

Signs and symbols in Dutch suburbia: Researching the 'hidden Hoogvlietse style of architecture'. FAT architects, Hoogvliet (2001)

the context we are working in (in accordance with structuralist theory and social responsibility), yet also understand what the limits of this context-dependence are (in accordance with the specificity of an aesthetically-based expertise)?

In the end, although the generation of 1968 formulated some critical questions, it then locked in both the answers and the parameters so tightly that any subsequent gesture was incapacitated from both sides: first, the definition of 'radical' and 'revolutionary' was frozen into a highly specific category, based on a moment in time; second, once the 'truly' radical generation had found themselves well-established in power, they were able to dismiss any other form of revolutionary gesture under the presumption that it was reactionary if it came from any other camp than the established Marxist/leftist one. It is high time we reformulate these categories of art as social critique, of left as progressive and right as reactionary, of establishment as morally wrong, or of traditional society as retrograde, for instance. By constructing oppositions that are treated as mutually exclusive, it becomes easy to overlook a sense of beauty that might also embody critique, or a notion of political progressiveness that might also be pragmatic, or even applicable in today's society rather than a utopian one. Hence my use of a term such as 'embedded critique', which does not presume the falseness or impropriety of reality as it stands, but rather presumes one can be active and critical at the same time.[25] Hence also my move towards contradictory notions such as an 'ideological pragmatism', or perhaps rather 'romantic pragmatism', or maybe an 'aesthetic pragmatism', or 'ideological realism', or 'pragmatic idealism'?

The Praxis/Theory Divide

As the twin notions of critique and revolution delineate a field within which architecture has developed over the course of the twentieth century, so also the relationship between theory and practice forms an undercurrent to the themes explored in this book. The primary products under examination are the manifestoes, the ideas and theories – even if they arise from questions out of practice. Yet the importance of critical theory in architecture has also encouraged theory to recede from practice, beginning with the vast utopian ideals of the 1960s. The radical gestures of the period and the revolutions they aspired to circumscribed a moment in time where the sky was the limit. This is better explored through the most imaginative projects that the realized ones, all the while keeping in mind that reality tends to demand some level of compromise. The ideal image and the built reality will necessarily never be the same. At the same time, when the ideal image is somehow reflected in the built reality, the object itself gains in depth and strength. This book examines the discourse in words and images, concluding that it remained somehow ambivalent by answering revolutionary questions with reactionary responses. In this history of ideas, the discipline itself (both in terms of practice and its theorizations) has shown a tendency towards ideology-based critique and practice. An example is given in chapter 3 in the trajectory from Pevsner's version of modernism (interpreting history to demonstrate the inevitability of modernism) to Banham's reconfiguration of this history by on the one hand reviving crucial but somewhat effaced movements (futurism, for example) and on the other opening up the architecture discourse to mass cultural imagery and influence of (for example) popular design. Similarly, though in a different context, the situationists explored the revolutionary power of everyman through utopian projects like New Babylon and through strategies such as *détournement*. Yet in the case of the situationists, a full-scale revolution was meant to precede any possibility of form, thereby leaving the work far more in the realm of theory than of practice, despite their encouragement to take to the streets.

In the end, although the various critiques in the 1960s explicitly uncovered a number of weak spots in the tradition of high modernism as it had developed in the first half of the twentieth century, the utopian aspects of that very same high modernism were by no means yet exorcized. Although the rhetoric of the 1960s was filled with notions like 'instability', 'flexibility', 'individual expression' and 'freedom', there were obviously totalitarian aspects to many of their designs. And, much like their predecessors, they often showed a blind spot in relation to their own rhetoric. The distinction between text, image and building thus becomes important. We could argue that this is an inevitable condition of the problem of architectural design, relating to the fact that the very practice of architecture has a tendency towards dictating both how one should live and how one should understand space.[26] On the other hand, we can also attempt to untangle the difference between some of the incredibly insightful critiques of this period and the resulting designs. Perhaps there is even a different framework for understanding both design

Technological organisms revisited. Jurgen Bey, Blob Pavilion, Eindhoven University of Technology (2005, www.skor.nl / photograph by Jannes Linders)

Expressive technology. Jurgen Bey, Blob Pavilion, Eindhoven University of Technology (2005, www.skor.nl / photograph by Jannes Linders)

and theory in a semi-autonomous and mutually productive relationship, in the sense of what Stan Allen has called 'material practice'.[27]

What I am aiming at is to find a different conceptual structure here, something that theorists and practitioners will find useful to work with as a new set of ideas, and which may help illuminate forms of practice that are innovative yet underexposed. The basic characteristics of this model are many, but they include a tendency towards plurality rather than the dialectic, and a place for aesthetics as more than just representation or matter of taste, as productive in their own right. It is built on the notion of a 'material practice', encompassing the contamination of reflection and production, as appropriate to a contemporary culture steeped in contamination rather than modern purity. The combination between theory and praxis is viewed as helpful in trying to move beyond cynical reason.[28] The notions of contamination and plurality are essentially postmodern, while the interpretation of aesthetics as productive can be considered modern. The need for interpretation was challenged directly by Susan Sontag in 1964, although she traces it back as far as Plato (and not just as a product of modernity).[29] The notions of material practice and the combination theory/praxis settle this into the contemporary debate, which is seeking a form of engagement with reality.

To look further into the idea of architecture as a material practice, Martijntje Smits' analysis of the theoretical model posed by Mary Douglas is helpful.[30] Smits separates the productive aspects (the idea of contamination, leading to her own proposition of a pragmatic attitude towards technology) of this model from the 'conceptual paradigm' Douglas is locked into. This is what leads Smits to propose a pragmatic approach: according to Douglas, 'contaminated' objects are those that do not fit within a clear conceptual category. This leads to their remaining indefinable. Smits instead suggests that this notion of contamination is more productive when seen as a potential means to reconfigure formerly stable categories. This leads to a continuous process of redefinition, with a mutual influence between transcendent ideas and their specific instantiations. Material practice similarly suggests that there is an autonomy to the practice, but that it is fed by reflection; it is the *mutual* contamination that might revitalize both aspects of architecture. If we can agree that the notion of an 'ocular ontology' or a 'discursive' understanding of vision and/or images is the main conceptual paradigm being taken under fire in the 1960s, then we can perhaps begin to discuss both *why* it needed revision (for instance the serious problems it was producing) and, subsequently, why it was only partially revised.

The reason for proposing a new frame for contemporary work is that it might make some elements visible that cannot be seen when a work is considered through existing categories. Las Vegas was sitting in the desert as it was by the time Denise Scott Brown arrived, but there was no architectural vocabulary that could acknowledge it as something interesting. Scott Brown and Venturi made it possible to incorporate billboard architecture into the discourse. It is this kind of shift in vocabulary and seeing (since words and images work together in mysterious ways) that might be helpful in uncovering some qualities of buildings that may not yet be acknowledged.

In tracing these possible meanings, I follow Banham's notion that it is more about a 'sensibility' than an 'aesthetic'. I believe that still holds true today, though in retrospect a slight question may be put to the work of Banham. To him, the idea of a 'sensibility' was a way to open up a restricted understanding of 'aesthetics'. Yet in some ways it also allowed him to hide his own preferences, since his 'technological sensibility' was not yet a well-defined category and had no specific aesthetic rules. His own aesthetic preferences (such as American car designs) thus become theorized through this idea of a 'sensibility'.[31] Aesthetics are a critical aspect of architectural practice. A 'sensibility' should not preclude an aesthetic judgment. Most of the examples I will discuss here are set in the margins of architecture; they do, however, involve all forms of the visual and of city space. Most examples revolve around collectivity and cultural significance, and the complex forms in which they become manifest. Another point of interest might be the ethics of hackers, with their belief in equality on the Internet, while at the same time subverting power structures by targeting Microsoft in its position as a powerful corporation. Furthermore, in many areas of aesthetic production there is a revaluation of craft, expertise and beauty as a form of resistance to overly politicized work, possibly since overpoliticization offers only a single interpretation. In this sense, private reflection is productive, and contemporary imagery possibly allows that by being less linear or direct.[32] Moreover, high technology and new materials are also being utilized as more than a mere image of functionalism or of modernity, and instead are seen as experimental steps in a continual reconfiguration of the architectural environment and what is required of it.

Directions forward are now perhaps not for theory to define – but it is up to theorists and intellectuals to carefully examine the products of architecture for their value beyond the singular case study. This is not meant to generate a new theoretical framework within which alternative positions can again be discarded, but rather to follow Latour's suggestion that our models are often insufficient. Only by bridging the practice/theory divide will we be able to maintain the ideals of perfection while simultaneously appreciating the full breadth of reality. Moving beyond a 'tactics of resistance' is a first step in this process, as is taking the time to listen, see and feel the products of sustained effort – be they in music, architecture or otherwise. The depths of understanding are perhaps an intellectual endeavour but cannot be explored without the time spent in honing a skill. If there is anything left to resist, it should be the urge to reduce reality to a model that does not do it justice. We can model many things in the world (these days, even the beauty of a face), and yet it takes a special talent and a well-trained skill to *create* what we can so easily *analyse.*

Constraining Critique

In architecture, critique is in fact a problematic notion: by extending the avant-garde idea of a principally *critical* function of the visual, of symbols and of imagery, the 1960s' discourse presented a problem in addressing the visual. The aesthetics of visual production are not reducible to only a critical function, nor does a critical attitude encompass only one strategy: it may have as much to do with transforming aesthetic convention as it does with social liberation, or with questioning contemporary developments. The continuous *mutual* influence of tradition and innovation is important in creating a productive interplay between the conventional and the critical. In this sense, the radicality of the 1960s' revolution was ambiguous: it presented tradition and vernacular as a revolutionary intervention in the discourse, yet its radical quality was reminiscent of an earlier revolutionary position which was opposed to an embedding in tradition. On that level the 'purity' (again for lack of a better word) is very much at the heart of today's problematic: if the everyday and the pragmatic and the real were somehow more incorporated in a discourse, the general rules of revolution and return could be modified to a point of specificity. This would mean accepting that innovation takes place on a small scale equal to the large (and mediagenic) scale of manifestoes and publications.

The critiques I trace out in this book are simply moments, and perhaps that indicates precisely that some of the grand narratives have disappeared: instead of critique leading to a stable or defined reality, it is now a moment in time. This does allow it to retain its historical dimension, but not in the Hegelian or (following him) the Marxist sense, where there is a discernible progression in the course of history. The notion that revolution is a lead-in to a permanent state, and that it is a

Re-presenting the individual city: drawings by audience members of their paths to the Arcam evening debate on the situationists. Project conceived by Jan Rothuizen (29 October 2008)

pure process, divorced from the reality of its roots, no longer seems tenable (even if only judged by its own premises). Throughout the following chapters, a typical pattern will begin to emerge: the critique that is ever so important at a certain moment in time, in a certain situation, will begin to extract itself from the history, time and culture it is embedded in. During this process of extraction, it will begin to form general rules, as guidelines to follow in order to create a better world than the one it is faced with. And slowly, as it emerges into a general system, it will begin to form a new status quo that will necessitate a new, fresh vision in order to expose its flaws and contingencies. Critique can be a powerful tool, but when it becomes a set of rules or guidelines, it often creates a world no better than the one it forced us to depart from. In and of itself this might be construed as a natural process, something akin to a Darwinian evolution of thought, leaving the best ideas standing. Nevertheless, at times the critique is so thorough and so powerful that its sheer presence hides underlying ideas that should be equally exposed and questioned. These ideas, when left in the shadow, can begin to acquire the status of inevitable truths merely by having been left alone, while they, too, might benefit from some critical assessment.

In the end, maybe the spectacle can do little more than teach us that critique itself is ephemeral. That when it does its job well it will be superseded by transformed conditions and need or seek a new target. The critical moment is fleeting but also a permanent condition. Is contemporary architecture indeed primed for this awareness and the ability to operate within the ephemeral? Judging from some journals of architecture (*Archis, Grey Room, Architectural Design*) the ephemeral moment is still treated as something that can be given eternal form (as in blob architecture). Diller and Scofidio are perhaps the only firm who have made an ephemeral form in their Blur Building, even though the notion of the ephemeral is avidly sought. Is theory even ready to be aware that each critique will soon be superseded or no longer relevant, yet also remain conscious of the absolute necessity of agency? Permanence and architecture are at odds with the revolutionary programme of critique, and have been for some time. Is it perhaps time to revise our approach to critique rather than the form of architecture? Rather than continue to search for a critical and revolutionary architecture, should we perhaps consider that the very framework of critique and revolution might be obsolete in architecture?

In order to explore these possibilities, this book discusses a number of diverse phenomena that are intimately connected, such as the media spectacle, the idea that passivity is concomitant to the spectacle, and the difficult position of the critical within an image-based culture. These are all issues that are rooted in the 1960s, and have become increasingly crucial to contemporary discourse. Each theme is interesting in itself, but the book is intended primarily to delineate and understand the resonance between these phenomena. As a result, one of the concluding questions remains: Is agency absolutely pointless in the society of the spectacle? Are we doomed to create only some kind of constructed public relations for capitalism? Or is there a mode of 'critical practice', of 'praxis' that can be *in* the world yet critical? Is a 'critical realism' as described by Latour possible, and does 'projective practice' escape the constrictions of pure commodification? This position would attempt to hold a median between critique and idealism, yet to do so with the context as a given.

This requires some adjustments – though nothing necessarily drastic. A re-examination of where we stand today – and a refusal to play purely formal games, yet also a refusal to subjugate aesthetics to social rhetoric. This proposal is close in spirit to notions like 'material practice' and 'projective practice'. Yet what I argue here is not radical, and therefore not necessarily attractive as a media representation. It is not clean, clear-cut. But it goes into details, asks more questions that it can provide answers. I am also trying to connect here to tendencies in other disciplines, and to draw a line from developments begun in the 1960s (such as freedom of the individual and critical thinking) and to find the limits of these ideas as well as their potential. All this within the media spectacle, both *despite* the influence of the media, of the image, of the spectacle, and *because* of it.

Although my suggestions here have not yet found material form (this does remain, after all, a theory) I hope that a more subtle negotiation of the conditions of late capitalism, of the spectacle, of commodity culture, a strategy that is not based on radical revolution but rather on a form of embedded critical view, will bring architecture both closer to its own discipline (in terms of building) and remain true to the notion of not being purely affirmative (in the sense of merely replicating existing conditions). Should we be afraid that media will overtake the meaning of architecture? Or should we be afraid that the media have offered a new platform for architects to replicate their manifestoes more effectively? Or should we be 'slipping in and out' of the logic of the spectacle, looking for the gaps where the confrontation between architecture and its image produce new meanings, new forms of independence for its users and (maybe even above all) new moments of beauty in the world at large?

In conclusion, Latour describes a new potential role for the critic, which I believe resonates with the notions of projective practice and embedded critique:

> The critic is not the one who debunks, but the one who assembles. The critic is not the one who lifts the rugs from under the feet of the naïve believers, but the one who offers the participants arenas in which to gather. The critic is not the one who alternates haphazardly between antifetishism and positivism like the drunk iconoclast drawn by Goya, but the one for whom, if something is constructed, then it means it is fragile and thus in need of great care and caution.[33]

It is this care and caution that need to be exercised today, in contrast to earlier manifestoes. In order to do so, we must look carefully at the ideas that have been put forward in favour of a revolutionary transformation in architecture during the 1960s.

II

The City: From Modernist Battlefield to Situationist Playground

The Situationist International and the Reinvention of the City

The work of the Situationist International has been periodically revived since the 1960s as a way to come to terms with the city. It offers the most outspoken thought experiments and manners of contesting or engaging the mid-twentieth-century city, particularly in its modernist form. The radically subversive ideas that directly countered the CIAM-grid of the city, combined with the provocative rhetoric of neo-Marxism, offer a revolutionary sensibility that these days strikes a chord with many. At a time when efficiency was becoming crucial to the development of the city, when the speed of modern life was increasing, the situationists spoke of dreams, desires and wasting time. They countered every argument for rationality with a plea for creativity. The shield that the metropolitan individual had developed according to Simmel was replaced by a desire to engage with unknown others. The issues raised by the situationists, combined with their somewhat obscure

'Discours sur les passions d'amour': the psychogeographic map of Paris as exploration of urban sensations rather than the traditional map. Guy Debord, *Guide Psychogeographique de Paris* (probably 1957)

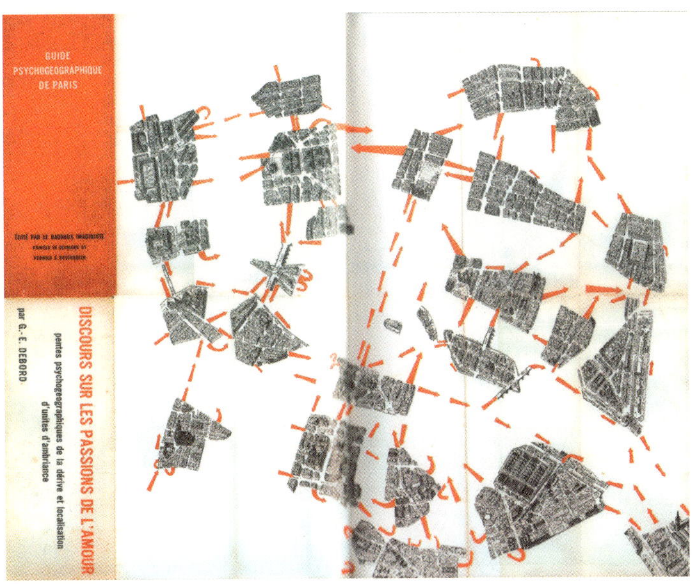

and suggestive ideas, offer a rich ground for a contemporary sense of discomfort with modern life to be filtered through.

This has also resulted in a rather steady revival of situationist thought. As recently as May 2007 a theme issue of *Arch+* was devoted to 'situationist urbanism', which explores various parallels for situationist ideas in the contemporary city. Yet the various revivals of the 1960s also beg the question: Why do we return to these ideas rather than address contemporary urbanism with contemporary ideas? Have groups such as the situationists created such a fundamental reference point that we cannot escape their influence? Did they hit upon such basic questions that their work has become inescapable?

To understand the importance of the critique posed by the Situationist International and its reconceptualization of the modern city, we also need to understand the position of the city in the architecture discourse. Modernity itself is framed by the city; grown out of the industrial era, the city becomes the environment for modern life. The very imagery of modernism grows out of the rise of the industrial city, as for example Dziga Vertov's *Man with a Movie Camera* (1929) shows so well. Although the approaches to the city from within the architecture discourse have been diverse, there are a number of characteristic features shared among the various critiques. This chapter examines the position of the city in the architecture discourse and practice of the 1960s as a response to the crisis of the functional city. Perceived problems with the functional city were its focus on efficiency rather than comfort, its anonymity and the lack of symbolism that appealed to its users, its lack of 'unprogrammed' space (as a result of the efficient use of space), and therefore a lack of the unexpected. Even within CIAM itself, the bastion of the functional city, an internal conflict arose that led to its collapse in 1956. The critique came from a young group of architects who would eventually form Team 10, and was focused on the absence of convention, tradition and the everyday. These absences were seen as a direct reflection of the shortcomings of rationality and mechanical functionality as defining features of the modernist city.[1]

The sterility of Le Corbusier's city for 3 million inhabitants.

Critique on the modernist environment: the *banlieues* in Paris formed the backdrop for Jean-Luc Godard's *Alphaville* (1965)

As a group, the Situationist International lasted from 1957 to 1972. The main people involved with its inception were the artists Constant Nieuwenhuijs (1920-2005) and Asger Jorn (1914-1973), and the political theorist Guy Debord (1931-1994).[2] The Situationist International was rooted primarily in two movements from the early 1950s: it combined the conceptual tendency of the Lettrist International and the expressionist artistic values of the International Movement for an Imaginist Bauhaus. After its founding, the Situationist International consisted of various, ever-shifting groupings of artists and intellectuals. Its membership and subgroupings extended throughout Europe, but the centre of the movement remained in Paris, where self-proclaimed leader Debord lived. The propositions of the Situationist International, incorporating influences from many disciplines, were published in the 12 issues of its journal *Internationale Situationniste*, published intermittently from 1958 to 1969, on average once a year. Although many different members contributed to situationist theses on the city, the work of Debord and Constant has remained the most influential to architecture discourse. The situationist critique of the urban condition can be seen as not only the most radical critique of the modern city, but also as exemplary for the ideas of the time. It incorporates the two fundamental problems facing the city in the 1960s: the position of the individual in the anonymous modern city, and the exponential increase in mass imagery that led Debord to write on the 'society of the spectacle' as a new condition. On the most basic level, resistance against the functionalist modern city was framed in terms of 'human relations.' The functionalist city was seen as too mechanical and anonymous to incorporate such things as children playing in fountains (Robert Venturi), ever-changing conditions of life (Alison and Peter Smithson), everyday informal social relations (Jane Jacobs), and the passion of human life (Guy Debord). In each of the critical views on the modernist city, the presence of the human being was at the centre of the city. This human being was now no longer an expression of rational and modern life, but rather an individual entity longing for human contact, a sense of place, and, especially in situationist thought, adventure.

Following in the tradition of the early twentieth-century avant-garde, Guy Debord envisioned a totality of art and life, where each person was involved in a continual and passionate creation of his own life and its surroundings. This was something he claimed 'can only materialize at the level of urbanism'.[3] Here,

The urban environment made to encourage the 'continual and passionate creation of his own life and surroundings'. Constant, New Babylon, plan view of group sectors (1959)

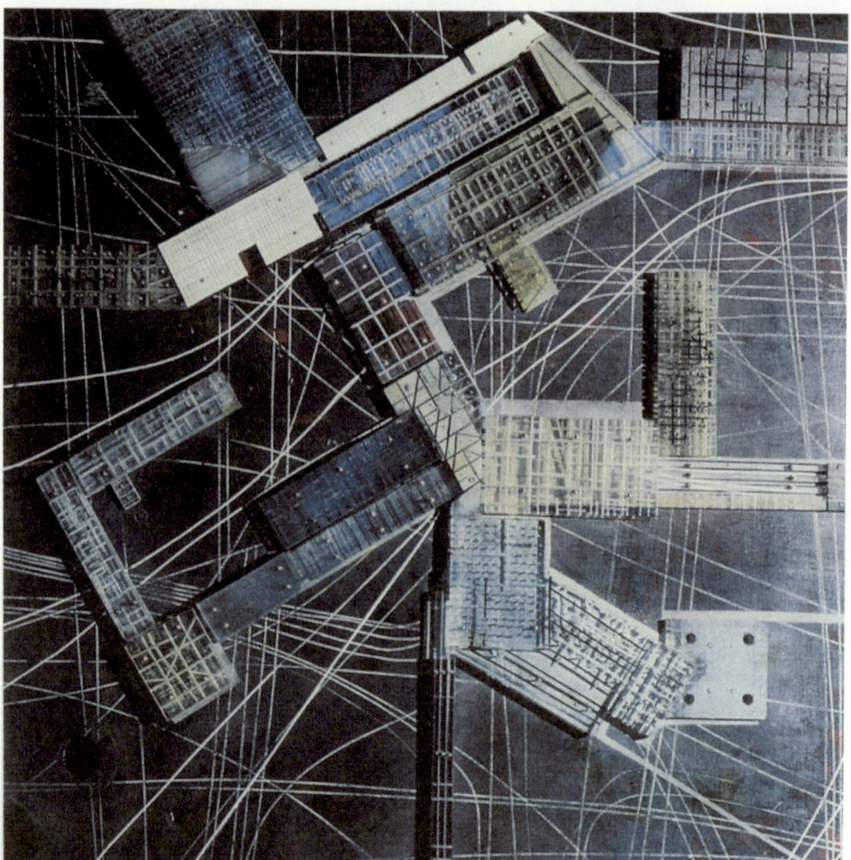

as in many manifestoes of the high modern period, the urban environment remained central. The structure of the functionalist city as proposed by CIAM in the 1933 *Charter of Athens* was attacked directly by Debord and his colleagues of the Situationist International. However, the importance of the city as a place for life was never challenged, indicating that not the city itself, but rather its form and structure were a problem. Henri Lefebvre (1901-1991), a sociologist briefly involved with the Situationist International, even wrote of people's *droit à la ville*, or 'right to the city'.[4] Although his relationship with the Situationist International was brief, lasting only until 1962, Lefebvre made an essential contribution to the early development of situationist ideas and an alternative understanding of the city.[5]

Mass Culture and the City: Founding the Society of the Spectacle

Lefebvre's formulation of a 'right' to the city is based on a critical mass of people and communal facilities. The influence of a rising mass culture underlies all the architectural positions on the city. Whether it is treated as a problem (as in Frank Lloyd Wright's comparison to an overpopulation of rats, biting each other to death) or a blessing (as in Jane Jacobs' notion that the bustle and diversity of a city street offers the full breadth of life), the very presence of a mass population contributed to the rise of the modern city. These 'masses' and 'mass culture' are present in the poetry of Charles Baudelaire, the sociology of Georg Simmel and Ferdinand Tönnies, the essays of Walter Benjamin and the philosophy of Theodor Adorno. Works such as 'Die Grosstädte und das Geistesleben' by Simmel show the relevance of finding a new mode of interaction in the face of anonymous masses of people,[6] as opposed to the traditional rural model of *Gemeinschaft*, where interaction is formed by social relations.[7]

The twentieth-century city's quantitative expansion in sheer numbers also had its repercussions on the form of the city, on its representations and on the human interactions within it. The latter two in particular begin to play a critical role in the 1960s, in a general rethinking of the social aspects of the city and the omissions of earlier, abstracted modernist representations. The massiveness of the twentieth-century metropolis takes form both as a social and a cultural phenomenon. As an opposition to the individual, the masses only present a problem when the individual is no longer seen as a self-evident element within the larger whole. This reaches back a little earlier to the Romantic era's focus on the individual and his innermost drives. Whether it is the protagonist feeling anxiety about the faceless gray mass of people in T.S. Eliot's 'The Wasteland', or the excessive focus on individual expression found in the work of Oscar Wilde: the individual steadily gains more ground over the course of the nineteenth century. Simmel's metropolitan individual must maintain his individuality in the face of anonymous masses while being severed from the natural social order that is present in rural societies. This lays the groundwork for the explosive focus on individuality that will later inform the situationists. At the same time, the masses themselves merit attention in themselves, not only as a counterfoil to the individual. The twentieth-century city saw a rise in population that necessitated a study of 'the masses'. Sociologists such as Simmel and Robert Park began studying 'the crowd', and Charles Baudelaire and Walter Benjamin offered literary and cultural reflections on the crowds in urban spaces. Whether 'the urban masses' are treated as a social class destined for revolution or a cultural class with different aesthetic sensibilities, the masses have a significant impact upon the architecture discourse of the time. Although these issues resonate throughout the transatlantic context, the specific natures of the American, English and French contexts also help illuminate the different forms each critique takes. This results in, for example, a French discourse that attempts to engage the urban masses in social revolution (in the form of the Situationist International), and on the other an English discourse that takes up the symbolic language of mass culture as signifying liberation from architecture as an élite institution (the Independent Group). The complexity of this two-sided nature of mass culture became increasingly apparent in the 1960s, when there was a further extension of the influence of mass culture through the mechanisms of what Debord calls the 'spectacle'. The imagery of consumer capitalism introduced a new level of mass imagery, and the mass media helped transmit it. This phenomenon, based

High art reconfigured through mass cultural imagery: collages of commercial symbolism. Eduardo Paolozzi, *Meet the People* (1948)

The masses that keep the city running: factory workers change shifts. Fritz Lang, *Metropolis* (1927)

LA FIN DE LA TRANQUILLITÉ

The urban revolution begins with the masses in the streets: Paris student revolts, 1968.
Image published in *Internationale Situationniste* 12 (1969)

on recognizable imagery (thus also transcending cultural boundaries) also contributed to the homogenization of public space.

Furthermore, we can argue that the overwhelming massiveness of the 1960s' city (such as the Parisian *banlieues*) is not only about the actual number of people living in the city, but also about the dissolution of the city borders in an era of growing global sensibility. In part this is related to the increase in travel and communications. The increasing sophistication of media technologies had an enormous influence as well: the city became not only a physical object, but is now also related to the global village, the digital community and other virtual constructions of community. This development is not only one of expansion: though the space of the city and its confrontations with difference have on the one hand multiplied (in the global lines of migration), there is also a diminished sense of community (in the narrow orientation of online digital communities). In architecture discourse the global sensibility is also compounded in the modernist notion of a universal form, by which cultural differences are transcended by the general applicability of an industrial form. This idea of universal form allowed the debates on appropriate architectural form to no longer be bound by local traditions and cultural differences, but rather by the ostensibly 'neutral' issues of programme and industrial fabrication.

The radical critique of the functionalist city as posed by the Situationist International reveals a particular focus that resonates with other critiques such as those of Team 10 and Jane Jacobs: the notion of individual resistance against a perceived 'machinery' of domination. Although there are important distinctions between the various movements to be discussed, especially in what form this 'machinery' takes and how the 'individual' is framed, the idea that resistance is to be found from within individual freedom and creativity is a cornerstone of the new directions in architecture in the 1960s. The position of the individual in relation to a collective body (anonymous in the case of the city) can be traced throughout the twentieth century, whether in the idea of *Gemeinschaft* as opposed to *Gesellschaft*, or in the work of Simmel on the individual in the metropolis. It is precisely through its radical position that the Situationist International offers insights. There is an ambivalence in its treatment of the 'creative individual', propagating a strong belief in the liberating power of the free and conscious will of each (romanticized) individual. It also claims the need at this moment in history to guide these imminently self-sufficient individuals towards their utopian destiny. The situationist theory of liberation is based on purely individual resistance, yet still claims the need for leadership by a vanguard (namely the situationists) until the new society is realized. This ambiguity is critical to the treatment of the city in the latter half of the twentieth century, and will be discussed at length in this chapter. Situationist thought also embodies another ambiguity in the situationists' incorporation of individuality within a larger critique, while at the same time maintaining an emphasis on the individual. This ambiguity is only possible since they maintain an implicit distinction between themselves as individuals and the collective individual that will arise through situationist practice.

The Situationist International and the Spectacle of Urbanism

During the years of the Situationist International, many different viewpoints were espoused under the large umbrella of situationism as a general condition of resistance, but the most consistent three points revolved around the city, the spectacle and everyday life.[8] The city and conditions of everyday life featured prominently as central concerns in the early issues of *Internationale Situationniste.* To the Situationist International, the environment of the contemporary city did not offer sufficient conditions for all aspects of life, especially since the functionalist tenets of the CIAM *Charter of Athens* (presented in 1933, though not published until 1943) had reduced life to three activities: work, dwelling and leisure, which were connected by a fourth: travel. This separation of zones negated the importance of

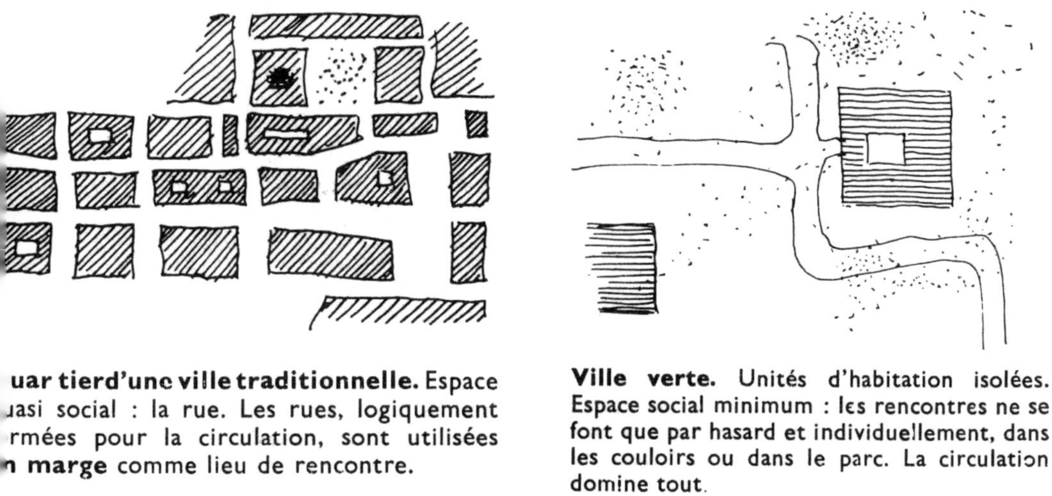

Diagram showing the lack of space for unexpected social encounters in modern city planning.
Constant, 'A Different City for a Different Life', *Internationale Situationniste* 3 (1959)

unexpected encounters in the city. The critique of the spectacle became increasingly important in later years of the Situationist International, coming to fruition in Debord's *La Société du Spectacle* in 1967. The spectacle, as 'capital accumulated to the point where it becomes image', added to the poverty of the physical environment by denying its importance and simply shifting attention to consumption and imagery as the primary activities in life, transforming everyone into a passive spectator.[9] In other words, the working class might be miserable, but the cheerful imagery and ads of desirable consumer goods could distract them from their misery, and also encourage them to work harder in order to obtain those goods. The spectacle was thus also a means of maintaining dominance in a capitalist society. The problems of everyday life were exacerbated by the poverty of the environment and the domination of the spectacle. The anaemic version of everyday life in this city

The spectacle of modern dwellings. Jacques Tati, *Playtime* (1967)

'Subconscious publicity', image accompanying the editorial of *Internationale Situationniste* 8 (1963)

La publicité inconsciente.

dominated by spectacle was precisely where the situationist transformation was to take place. The Situationist International believed that only an active engagement with the everyday environment would finally lead to a transformation in all spheres of life. This emphasis on active engagement and wholesale transformation does show its specific deployment of the idea of the spectacle: in the situationists' view, it has replaced everyday life rather than become an extra dimension incorporated in everyday life.

In the early years, the city was central to situationist thought, both as an existing environment to be mined for as yet unrecognized significance and as a conceptual problem due to the failure of the modernist city. At this time, their treatment of the city still had some relation to 'form', in the sense that the sterile forms of the functionalist city were critiqued, and a major component of their work towards a 'unitary urbanism', aimed at 'l'emploi d'ensemble des arts et techniques concourant à la construction intégrale d'un milieu',[10] took shape in the design of the future city New Babylon by Constant. Although the city remained an important part of situationist critique, the possibility of designing the future at all slowly became a problem for Debord, and the combination of critique and design made way for pure critique.[11] These are also the years (1961-1967) when the tension between words and images become more and more visible in Debord's work. His critical views become increasingly oriented towards a Marxist interpretation of the power structures embodied in the city, explaining, for example, how 'the history of cities . . . is also a history of tyranny, of State administration controlling not only the country but also the city itself'.[12] He also discusses urbanism as 'the mode of appropriation of the natural and human environment by capitalism'.[13] This almost off-the-cuff subsuming of urbanism under capitalism ignores the complexity of the mutual influence between capitalism and urbanism. It becomes increasingly difficult for Debord to envision the city of the future until

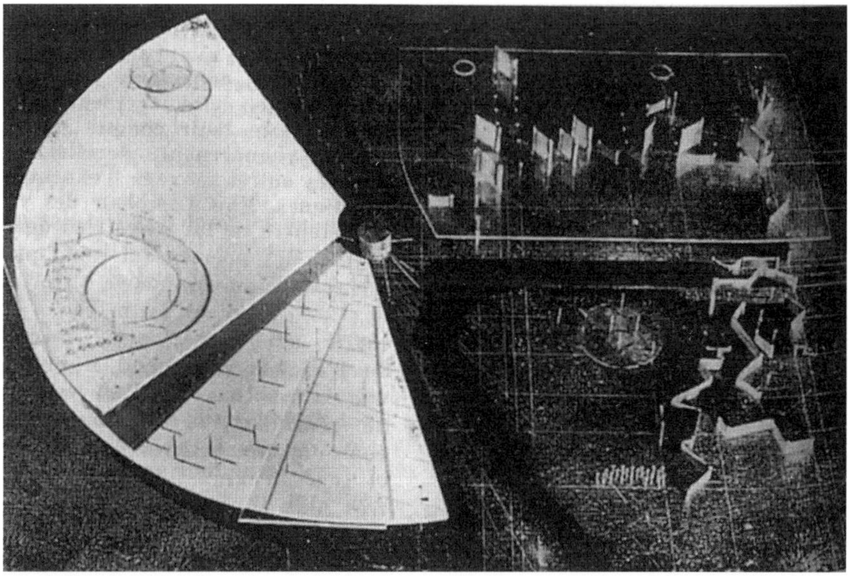

The unitary urban environment, meant to trigger total creativity in configuring life and urban surroundings. Model of what would later become New Babylon as published in *Internationale Situationniste* 3 (1959)

the revolution has happened. However, he still firmly believes that an active class struggle in the city will lead us beyond the congealed forms of domination now ever-present in the urban environment. This active struggle is aimed specifically at opposing the passivity inherent in the spectacle, which underlies the analysis he offers in his 1967 *Society of the Spectacle*, shortly before the student revolts in Paris. From then until the disbanding of the Situationist International, situationist engagement with the city seems to become ever more dependent on active

LES OCCUPANTS DE L'UNIVERSITÉ CORNELL L'ÉVACUENT AVEC LEURS ARMES

The radical break as the only way forward: armed revolt at Cornell.
Image published in *Internationale Situationniste* 12 (1969)

revolt (such as the events in Paris in May 1968) and on a radical break with the existing societal structure of the spectacle.

The actual influence of the situationists in the 1960s (and especially on the events of May '68) is still debated, among others because of the limited dissemination of their ideas.[14] Their texts have become more accessible in the digital age, and have attracted many people through their focus on the ephemeral world of the spectacle. Their (early) critique of the city shows a number of traits that resonate with other critiques of the time. Parallels are to be found throughout the transatlantic discourse. Therefore, despite its status as a subculture, the Situationist International exemplifies a combination of features that might be said to define not only the break with the modern city in the 1960s, but also the contemporary understanding of this time as a period of revolutionary resistance. It is the radical nature of situationist critique that makes it an ideal mirror to hold up to the period in general, as it magnifies the more subtle issues at hand in the debates on the city in the 1960s that still underlie the contemporary discourse.

Situationist Practice: Strategies of Resistance

One of the goals of the Situationist International was to open up a space of resistance in the city, a resistance to the dominant progressivist thought of high modernism and to the overwhelming developments of a post-war budding capitalist society. The way it hoped to do so was primarily through individual action: on the one hand by simply using the city – walking through it, reclaiming what was interesting, remapping it and editing out what it considered uninteresting (mostly the modernist developments). On the other hand by subverting the mass imagery that was part and parcel of an increasingly affluent post-war society. In this revaluation of the inhabitant of the city as a productive element in the creation of space, the situationists are deeply indebted to the work of Henri Lefebvre and connected with the later work of Michel De Certeau. Lefebvre's work in particular offered an exploration of the everyday (the *vie quotidienne*) which would become important in their critique of the abstracted modern city, as well as a theory of moments, which to the Situationist International was related to its theory of situations.[15] His later thoughts on the people's *droit à la ville* agree with situationist thought in the emphasis on the social needs of people as opposed to the pure functionality offered by architects and urbanists. The importance of sociology to the situationist critique of the modernist city is visible throughout the early texts, but they transformed the sociological analyses of the city and everyday life into a call to action.[16] Thus the situationists introduced techniques of 'drifting' and other forms of 'mapping' as a conceptual tool, critical of existing ways of understanding urban space. At the same time, their strategies were dependent on action, on the actual use of the city (and not on its image or their passive reception of it) thus forming a praxis intended both to engage and perceive that space in a different way.

The situationists introduced two fundamental ideas that demonstrate their belief in individual agency, the *dérive* and *détournement*. These two correspond to the situationist critique of the urban environment and of the spectacle. The *dérive* is a form of reappropriating urban space and rediscovering its qualities, while *détournement* is directed at the proliferating imagery in the city, and the potential to transform it into something more meaningful. Both terms are explained in the first issue of *Internationale Situationniste* in 1958, along with a number of other definitions, each of which are significant in their relationship to the terminology of high modernism.[17] All of them are also a guide to situationist praxis: they are not only a way of understanding the ephemeral conditions of the city, they are also a critique as well as a call to action. In a sense, the other definitions of situationism simply draw from the two primary situationist inventions, the *dérive* and *détournement*. For example, psychogeography is an extrapolation of the *dérive* which would eventually result in psychogeography as a scientific study of 'the exact laws and precise effects of the geographical environment, consciously organized or not, acting directly on the affective deportment of individuals'.[18] It implicitly refers to techniques of social geography, insofar as it examines the relation between the social and physical environment and also lays claim to an aspect of scientific research. Unitary urbanism is the most concrete idea to result out of situationism, and was originally seen as the ultimate answer to the problem of the 'urban spectacle'. It offered an infrastructure for *dérives* while simultaneously transcending the separation inherent in the spectacle. As such, it became the ideal environment for the totality of art and life.

The *dérive* is literally a 'drifting' through the city, a practice intentionally construed to investigate aspects of the city repressed by functionalism, in which 'one or more persons during a certain period drop their relations, their work and leisure activities, and all their other usual motives for movement and action, and let themselves be drawn by the attractions of the terrain and the encounters they find there'.[19] In this process of dropping their usual motives for movement, the people involved in a *dérive* were moving against the intent of the functionalist city. Rather than moving from point A to point B in the most efficient manner, they were letting themselves drift along on the flow of 'ambiances' (not a word typically used in modernist discourse) they encountered in the city. Rather than a strictly quantitative definition of their movement based on an efficient use of time, they were 'wasting' time by following intuitions that were not determinable within the framework of functionalism.

Visual record of a *dérive* through Venice by Ralph Rumney (1957)

Yet the situationists were not trying to obliterate the idea of functions as important to city form, but rather the 'absolute functionalism' of CIAM. In their view, this absolute functionalism had destroyed much of the traditional fabric of the city. Their use of the *dérive* to map out the 'feeling' or the 'ambiance' of neighbourhoods was aimed explicitly at clarifying which zones of the city were critical to an urban experience without necessarily following the CIAM divisions of the functional city into the four categories of work, dwelling, traffic and leisure. The position of the situationists revolved around finding 'passion' on the one hand to undermine the notion of 'function' as the only gauge of whether a city is well-constructed. On the other hand, they were also looking for the 'psychological functions' that had not been addressed in modernist discourse. Perhaps this is why the *dérive* has continued to be present in contemporary debates on the city. It still appeals to a sense of resistance in the face of a highly rationalized and efficient society, and attempts to address the psychological impact of urban spaces. For example, the Dutch artist Wilfried Houjebek has organized *dérives* through the new Vinex neighbourhoods in the Netherlands, which are typically criticized for their lack of 'ambiance'. His *dérives* were meant to explore whether this criticism is based on reality or whether it is more of a preconceived notion that is strengthened in media coverage, thus becoming a self-fulfilling prophecy.

Détournement is perhaps the only definition still related to the artistic invention that would later cause the rift between Debord and Constant. It is an abbreviation for:

> Short for '*détournement* of preexisting aesthetic elements'. The integration of present or past artistic productions into a superior construction of a milieu. In this sense there can be no situationist painting or music, but only a situationist use of those means. In a more elementary sense, *détournement* within the old cultural spheres is a method of propaganda, a method which reveals the wearing out and loss of importance of those spheres.[20]

By using prefabricated aesthetic elements in a non-conventional way, *détournement* ensures that they no longer affirm existing conditions, but critique them and contribute to a 'superior' environment. It proposes that creative appropriation of the environment (not unlike the intention of New Babylon) will also temporarily shatter the preconceptions that keep people blind to the oppressive power of the spectacle. These ideas are not unfamiliar: early avant-garde movements such as the Dadaists, for example, believed that using 'shock' in the form of jarring com-

'C'est un jeu de la vie et du milieu': collage of map sections, texts and quotes by Guy Debord. At right, page as published with painting by Asger Jorn. Guy Debord with Asger Jorn, *Mémoires* (1959).

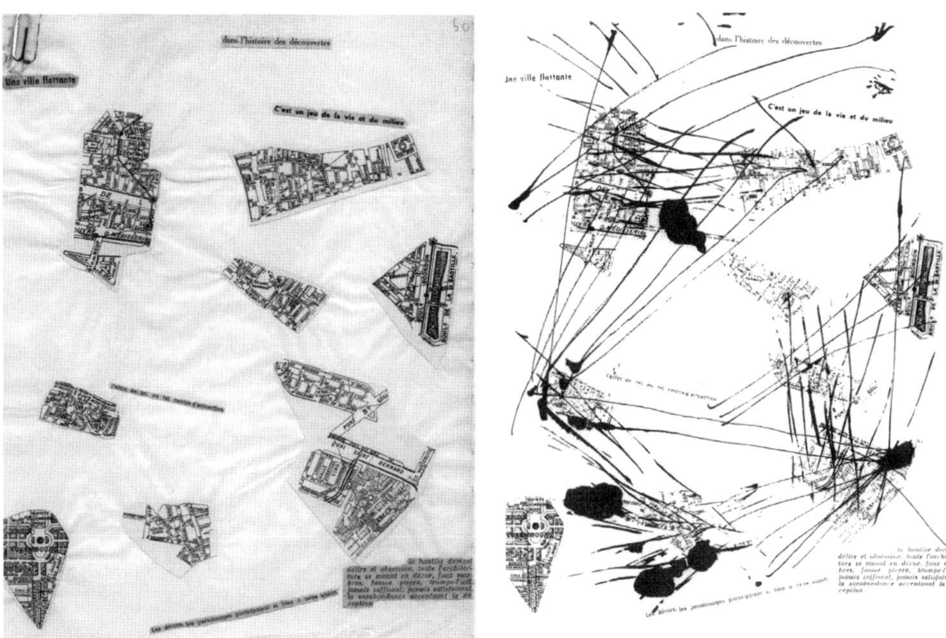

binations or unexpected juxtapositions could trigger a heightened consciousness in the observer. The idea of *détournement* prefigures Debord's later critique of the spectacle, which he will eventually define as 'a social relationship between people that is mediated by images'.[21] This relatively cryptic definition is often quoted to refer to a permanent state of illusion we are all somehow trapped in.[22] Although ideas leading to the spectacle such as examinations of advertising and mass culture are present in the early discourse of the Situationist International, as an object of critique, the spectacle becomes of primary importance much later, when the Situationist International has taken leave of the idea of being able to offer a formal definition for a future society. To Debord, the society of the spectacle poses a particular problem because it leaves everyone in a terminal state of passivity, unable to truly intervene in their own lives. The final goal of situationist strategies is to shatter the spectacle, yet the alternative they offer remains unclear. Perhaps the typical drunken revelry of the *dérives* unlocked a mystical understanding of the 'totality' of art and life, but the only visual definition of the principles of the *dérive* is to be found in the psychogeographical maps of Paris by Debord and Jorn, and the design for New Babylon by Constant.[23] These projects begin early in the course of the Situationist International, with New Babylon first taking form in 1956, and the psychogeographies beginning in 1957.

New Babylon is the most fully developed architectural and urban proposal to come out of the Situationist International. At first, the project is also treated as the only example of 'unitary urbanism' as discussed in early issues of *Internationale Situationniste*.[24] The third and fourth issues of *Internationale Situationniste* contain images of what will later be called New Babylon to support the critique of the modernist city and demonstrate the possible environment of unitary urbanism.[25] Until Debord finally denies any possibility of imagining a future form, New Babylon takes up a prominent place in the discussions of the Situationist International. 'Unitary urbanism . . . aims to form a unitary human milieu in which separations such as work/leisure or public/private will finally be dissolved.'[26] Unitary urbanism will create the situationist city, where everyone can continually be engaged in transforming their own environment and creating situations, in other words, in living the totality of art and life. In New Babylon, there will be no spectacle, only lived experience.[27] Separation is truly dissolved in New Babylon because its environment is not static – every conceivable boundary can be reconfigured depending on the needs and desires of its occupants. In its emphasis on authentic 'lived' experience (as the way to produce continual change), New Babylon also prefigures Debord's later critique of the spectacle.

The *dérive* as practiced by the situationists was perhaps flawed in its dependence on individual creativity and sensibility, yet it did reveal a major gap in the modernist utopia: the absence of human qualities such as desire, intuition and feeling. Although these may not be quantifiable or directly applicable to a design, their absence in the modernist city could clarify why the perfectly designed open parks and playgrounds were not being efficiently utilized as expected. There was something missing in these designs, something that ran counter to rational understand-

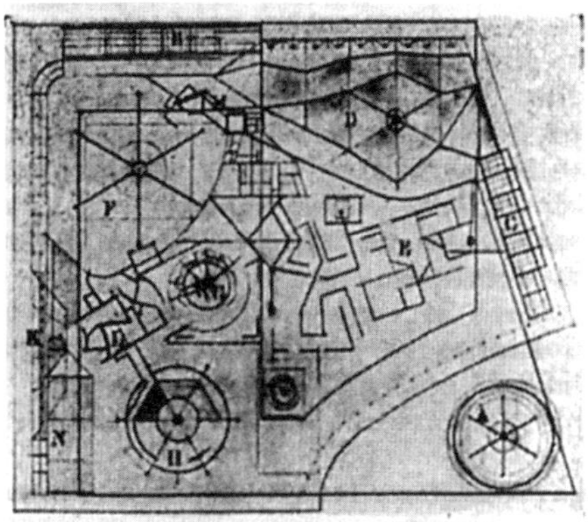

Plan général de la zone jaune.

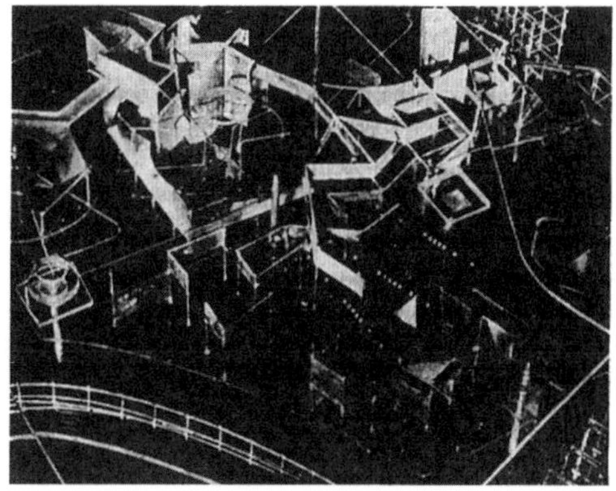

Vue rapprochée des secteurs G et E.

Plan and view of the 'zone jaune' (the yellow sector). Project still called 'Walks to New Babylon'. Constant, 'Description de la zone jaune', *Internationale Situationniste* 4 (1960)

ing. This missing piece of the puzzle was to be found precisely in the traditional and conventional understanding of the city that had been dismissed by the modernists. Since the modern era demanded of everyone that they live accordingly, they simply denied that societal convention was part of that modern era – that the *Gesellschaftliche* metropolis described by Simmel was not only modern, but incorporated all the conflicting tendencies of the rural and the urban, the individual and the collective, the private and the public. By claiming that the order of the modern city must by necessity acknowledge the non-quantifiable, non-functional aspects of human behaviour in a collective environment, the situationists brought something new and critical to the surface.

As a praxis based on drifting and use, the *dérive* is one of the most provocative ideas of the situationists: it was a conceptual form of mapping inscribed within a practice that was meant to influence reality. Urban drifting introduces a form of liberation by occupying space counter to the architectural intentions associated with it. The habits of everyday use attach to the existing structures of the city, representing a formal manifestation of longstanding traditions. New Babylon incorporated the potential for continuous change within its very fabric. This environment, subject to continual transformation, is radically anti-functionalist. Rather than the clear, stable surroundings where each space is devoted to a certain aspect of life (working, dwelling, leisure), unitary urbanism proposes a radical dissolution of all separations. This is a vision against efficiency, against a predetermined use of space and against the programmatic boundaries sketched out in the *Charter of Athens*.

The situationist city is simultaneously a forward-looking utopian idea of a progressive society based on leisure and individual agency, and a return to the traditional European city, which more than anything is defined by the multiplicity of its spaces. The chaos of the traditional city that caused Le Corbusier to propose a separation of functions is precisely what attracted the Situationist International to the traditional city. The unexpected was to be enjoyed, especially if it was inefficient. In terms of Lefebvre's *droit à la ville* the city potentially had so much diversity and culture to offer, yet it remained unfulfilled because of the reductive nature of the modern city. Instead of the functional determination of the modernist city, urban needs would entail 'those of qualified places, places of simultaneity and encounters'.[28] Although Lefebvre and the Situationist International claim that the traditional city itself is not the answer to this need for a richer environment, they both return to traditional spaces in the city as more meaningful. This ambiguity in the Situationist International's anti-functionalist strategies is illustrated in the psychogeographic maps of Paris generated by Debord and Jorn. As noted above, their maps show a vast amount of white space, indicating places that have no 'ambiance', and otherwise consist of islands of 'attractive' city spaces, usually the more traditional neighbourhoods. These maps show the traditional sides of the city in the clippings of existing maps while presenting a radically different totality. They prefigure later ideas on the rhizome in their non-hierarchical relations, and imply a city constructed of heterotopias, with its visually distinct and simultaneously present clusters of city spaces. The environments mapped out by Debord and Jorn exist alongside one another, yet are not necessarily connected.

Situationist thought on the city will continue to straddle these two treatments of the urban environment. In this aspect, it embodies an eternal dilemma of architecture that was exacerbated by the radically progressive force of modernism: the complicated decisions that underlie architecture take place in a field circumscribed by both the need for an as yet unformed future, and the delicacy of the existing environment as a container of inhabited history. Situationist thought maintains this dilemma: on the one hand it embodies the progressive idea of a liberating city, or a radical city that cannot yet be given form. On the other, it uses and examines the material of the traditional city, it allows for the possibility of finding elements in the existing spaces that critique the sterility of Le Corbusier's utopian city. Until the idea that a future city could by definition not yet be designed took hold, Constant's design for New Babylon was an important part of the progressive theories on the city. It was radically new, and in this it still followed certain principles of the modern: it did not refer to traditional form and it was premised on technological progress. What it did not subscribe to was the clarity and order espoused by Le Corbusier, which was a common theme among critiques of the city. The general sense that the four purely delineated functions of working, dwelling, leisure and travel were simply insufficient to house the full breadth of human life was shared among contemporaries such as the members of the Independent Group in England and the journalist Jane Jacobs in the USA. This turn to the existing conditions of the traditional city forms a critique of the tenets of functionalism. Radical solutions such as New Babylon were proposed in opposition to the sterile city of Le Corbusier, yet a careful study of the traditional city fabric held the same kind of significance. The *dérive* mapped out what functionalism could not address, and Jacobs described the views of the city that Le Corbusier's eyes could not see.

Despite the resistance against a functionalist perception of the city, the progressive beliefs of the situationist city still affirm the teleology of modernism. Even in the vastly different formal expression of New Babylon and psychogeography from the earlier machine aesthetic models, there is a belief that progression is still possible. The activism proclaimed by the Situationist International has as its task to tempt the creative individual into transforming his or her environment. The belief that this would somehow create that 'totality of art and life' implies that, despite its movable forms, unitary urbanism then creates a finalized totality. This reveals the fault line along which the differences between Constant and Debord became irreconcilable. The battle lines were drawn along the opposition between words that signify an as yet unformed future and the images of New Babylon that Debord found too definitive, and immediately implicated the machine of abstraction that he considered modernity to be.

Modern Abstraction: The Tension between Model and Reality

The problem of abstraction and its relation with reality goes to the heart of the situationist critique of the modern condition, and by extension the city as its environment. Modernism itself stands as a formal metaphor for alienation: modern abstraction has taken away the communicative symbols of our environment, has stripped our environment of the richness of everyday life.[29] The modernist city serves to illustrate this alienation, since it equates a conceptual notion of rationalization with the Cartesian visual order of a rectilinear grid. In the words of Peter Smithson: '"Rational" in this case meaning right-angled buildings parallel to one another' or, more critically: 'More like filing cabinets that have been built by mediaeval techniques rather than places where people actually have to live.'[30] Note in the latter comment the use of 'actually' – implying that the modernists had more of an eye for the models they had conceived than for reality. The rectilinearity first proposed by Le Corbusier as the expression of the rationality and clarity of modernist man is now seen as 'arbitrary and inhuman'.[31] Yet Smithson himself is not entirely free of this type of conflation: he notes that a 'discipline of growth' should be developed which is 'pragmatic – not Cartesian'.[32] The implication in this statement would seem to be that a structure will only allow growth if it is not Cartesian, and that pragmatism and a Cartesian grid are mutually exclusive.

According to Debord, at the heart of modern conditions of construction we find 'an authoritarian decision-making process that abstractly develops any environment into an environment of abstraction'.[33] It is the commodity structure of the spectacle itself that precludes the possibility of lived space.[34] Debord implies two definitions of 'lived space': visibly occupied (or not abstract) and active (though not necessarily in formal expression). He propagates the need for the people themselves to create their world. His neo-Marxist beliefs surface in a radical shift of the premises of urban planning from the formal to the political:

> The most revolutionary idea concerning city planning derives neither from urbanism, nor from technology, nor from aesthetics. I refer to the decision to reconstruct the entire environment in accordance with the needs of the power of established workers' councils – the needs, in other words, of the anti-State dictatorship of the proletariat, the needs of dialogue invested with executive power.[35]

In one manoeuvre, he has replaced the formal abstraction of modernism with a conceptual abstraction. Although the appeal to (presumably 'real') needs is based on an engagement with everyday reality, the radical nature of situationist critique continues to follow a modern scheme of total revolution:

> Differentiating itself from extreme-leftist groups, the Situationist International particularly distinguished itself through the radical and total critique of the modern world that it formulates. Throughout the works of Debord and Vaneigem, but also throughout the articles that appeared in the pamphlet *Internationale Situationniste*, it adheres to above all critiquing new forms of alienation, thus offering a revolutionary theory that is incontestably modern.[36]

The situationists replace modern alienation with a neo-Marxist form of alienation based on power structures, which only they can see past to distinguish 'reality' from abstractions. Their ideas are built on the belief that they are already enlightened and (not unlike the rhetoric of Le Corbusier) that they are necessary to guide the proletariat.[37] Their models, even when premised on the reality of everyday life, too easily transform into a new abstraction. Even New Babylon, with its notion of the 'great game to come' and the potential for every occupant to transform the space, becomes an almost overwhelming apparatus.

In her famous book *The Death and Life of Great American Cities*, of 1961, Jane Jacobs also criticizes the tendency to 'replace' reality with a model.[38] She comments on the modernist tendency to posit a planning principle purely from ideas, and not from day-to-day observation. She discusses the tendency of urban planners to state 'how cities *ought* to work and what *ought* to be good for people and businesses in them' and how they believe this so fiercely that 'when contradictory reality intrudes... they must shrug reality aside'.[39] She discusses the traffic problem of Le Corbusier's Ville Radieuse as an example. Parking space was vastly underestimated, as was the sheer volume of car traffic: in this case the model came first, was locked down into a formal plan, and its reality remained of lesser importance.[40] Jacobs addresses both the intention of the modernist city and the resulting reality. She opens up the abstract structure of the Corbusian panoramic city to the complexity of the local, particular and everyday. As such, her understanding of the qualities of the everyday bears some resemblance to the work produced by Henri Lefebvre in France.[41] In contrast to the French (and Marxist) tradition of the intellectual leading the masses however, it is sometimes noted as a qualification that Jane Jacobs has no degree in planning, but simply works from her own personal experience.

Modern abstraction from plan to reality. Frank van der Salm, Panorama (2004). Le Corbusier, Plan Voisin (1925) and Lefrak City (1961-1967) as published in James Wines' *De-Architecture*

Le Corbusier and Pierre Jeanneret, Plan Voisin proposal for Paris, model, 1925.

Lefrak City, Queens, New York, 1961–67.

Perhaps this is why she resists the idea that reality can be captured at all in a model: 'We are all accustomed to believe that maps and reality are necessarily related, or that if they are not, we can make them so *by altering reality*.'[42] Yet in her resistance to models, she also turns back to traditional urban environments or notes the presence of what is, and does not necessarily have viable alternatives. The explicit suggestions and scathing analysis of high modernist repetition and economic design precisely fit the stereotypical model of the 1960s: in search of a more individualized understanding of space and a glimpse of the everyday, the banal, rather than just the regimented performativity of modern life. Her writing suits the 'grassroots' style of 1960s' rhetoric in the sense that she extrapolates her ideas from the 'mere' observation of her direct environment in Greenwich Village: 'In setting forth different principles, I shall mainly be writing about common, ordinary things.'[43] This process of extrapolation from individual everyday experience is what leaves her open to criticism.[44] Yet it is also what makes this work relevant today: her empathetic understanding of the direct environment sees it as *possibly* indicative of larger questions, without presuming to hold the final answer.[45] In a gesture that resounds with the 1960s' faith that individuals hold the key to fundamental changes in society, she, too, holds stock in the idea that the individual people of the neighbourhood, as a community, offer more viable alternatives to urban renewal than the planners.

Common to many of these echoing criticisms is the 'fallacy of physical determinism' pointed out by American sociologist Herbert Gans in 1962. This fallacy does not only underlie a significant number of modernist proposals on the city, but remains present in many of the counterproposals of the 1960s, including those of Debord and Constant.[46] The idea that people's behaviour is unequivocally determined by the form of their environment neglects to take the various influences on human behaviour into consideration. To Gans, social ills are primarily to be cured by social tools. The environment may certainly influence the occupant's behaviour, but it is by no means always as the architect intended.

The relationship between the map or the model and reality remains a source of conflict in the 1960s. This too goes back to an aspect of modernist rationality, based on a linear understanding of relationships such as cause and effect. For example, in the 'fallacy of physical determinism', Gans is not attacking the idea that the physical environment has an effect on people. He is only attacking the simplicity of the planners' understanding of cause and effect: changing one element (the physical environment) in a multitude of factors (income, education, family life, social network, and so forth) will not transform an entire society. The typical 1960s' resistance to this simplicity rests on the conflation of, for example, moral and aesthetic values in the rhetoric of modernism: the notion that 'ugly' equals 'ethically bad' or that 'good' architecture can create 'good' people. This type of behaviourist interpretation of architecture becomes problematic in the late 1950s when people realize that the *banlieues* in Paris, built to 'light and air' specifications, are not functioning at all the way they were planned. The ease with which different things are conflated is related to a level of abstraction, and an idealized perception built on models.[47] In the

1960s, the complexity of reality begins to be acknowledged and the model becomes less powerful. There is a growing understanding that the relationships between different things may not be as linear or direct as presumed under modernism: more technology did not lead to more leisure time for the labour class, nor did it lead directly to an overall increase in wealth.

Jacobs' interest in empirical study illustrates a general interest in sociological methods in the 1960s. But it also offers a direction to escape the fallacy posited by Gans. The empirical studies of sociologists are reminiscent of the different models that the situationists hoped to generate with their psychogeography, but these studies are based more on everyday practices than on the radical practice of the *dérive*. These investigations into plurality and diversity, alongside the distinction between a model and its reality, and the understanding that some relationships are more complex than we can capture in a single gesture, helped in the search for a vital urban environment, as well as in the definition of what was so lacking in modernist design and planning that a counterforce seemed necessary. The desire remained to understand and define reality, however, and sociology seemed to hold the promise of a better understanding of everyday reality through its empirical study and extrapolation of collective knowledge from individual experience.

Sociology and the Scientific Definition of Reality

Although sociology had played a role in the architecture discourse since the work of Simmel, it gains more ground in the 1960s, when the rationalized and mechanical view of humanity underlying the functional city begins to give way to alternative interpretations. The turn to sociology reflects an interest in a broader view of everyday life, while maintaining a belief in the need for scientific study. Its study of what is already present in the city becomes a form of resistance to the doctrine of functionalism. Sociological insights allow architecture to acknowledge the vitality of the traditional city while framing the social relations within the city in a historical and objective manner.

The scientific study of complex patterns of human behaviour took on many forms at the time. In *The Image of the City* (1960) by Kevin Lynch, it comprises a study of how people mentally map their own environment. This resulted in a primarily symbolic interpretation of the environment, with paths, nodes and landmarks determining a city's appearance. In analogy to the intentions of the *dérive*, Lynch was trying to understand the collective perception of the urban environment by exploring individual experiences. The methods of sociology seemed to promise an objectivity through the combination of interviews and statistical data. In taking many different individual viewpoints into account and subsequently combining them with quantifiable data, something approaching an objective, collective perception could be achieved. The situationists take a more radical approach by projecting individual trajectories onto the urban map in the form of the *dérive* and extrapolating them into psychogeographic maps. As representations of everyday human behaviour, these maps attempt to scientifically represent the 'sensibility' of a neighbourhood rather than its traffic flow or programmed activity.

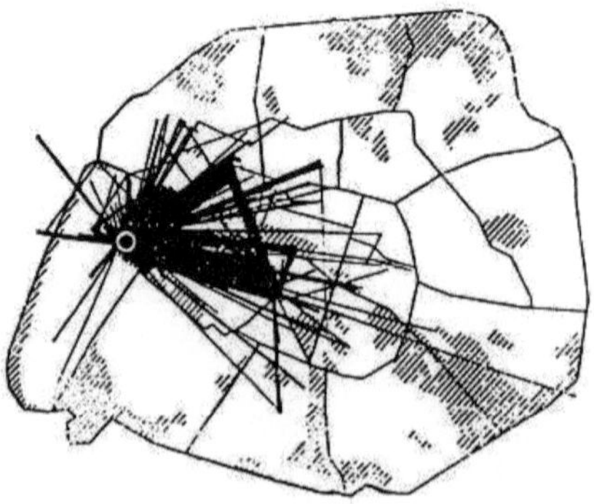

Scientific study of individual city experience: limited range of movement as mapped out by Chombart de Lauwe. Published in *Internationale Situationniste* 1 (1957)

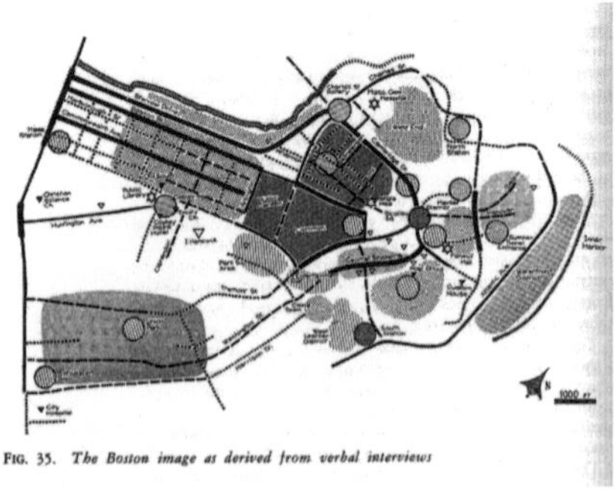

Sociological study of city perception: 'mental mapping' derived from interviews with city inhabitants. Kevin Lynch, *The Image of the City* (1960)

The technique of mapping offers a way to connect the perceptions of the city to a more overall scientific understanding of the urban environment, thereby forming an image of a city different from the functionally defined city of CIAM. Although psychogeography incorporated new qualifications such as the emotional response to certain streets, its emphasis on objectifying information reveals the continuing belief in the scientific analysis of reality. It is in this context that we should understand the use of Chombart de Lauwe's diagrams, which illustrate one person's use of the city.[48] The Situationist International intended this as a method of critique, however, as a way to move beyond everyday perceptions, which were seen as reflecting the dominance of the spectacle. Lynch was more interested in simply understanding the common perception of the city, and subsequently learning to utilize these perceptions and preferences. Although the work of Kevin Lynch does not involve a radical concept like psychogeography, it does enumerate and catalogue the various images that people use to map and identify their urban environment.

Sociology also helps to analyse the underlying programme of architecture in the city and to understand the mass networks of social relations that comprise the urban environment. In England, Alison and Peter Smithson turned to the work of Young and Wilmott, who had done studies of East-London that helped define some of the existing issues on social networks in the city population of the late 1950s. In an article exploring the relationship between 'pop' and architecture, Charles Jencks also mentions the importance of sociology in the ideas the Smithsons were putting forth at CIAM meetings.[49] Sociology helps to define the everyday and to map it, laying a (pseudo-)scientific basis for a new interpretation of city space. The discipline of sociology was thought to reveal as yet undiscovered qualities of the city. It contributed to identifying the everyday as a site for resistance against the reductive schemes of modernism.[50] Lefebvre illustrated this in his distinction between 'conceived space', as the idealized model of space in the architectural drawing, and 'lived space', as the occupant's experience of that same space. His discussions of the everyday introduce a sensitivity towards patterns of spatial appropriation that are not acknowledged in modernist city models. The Situationist International was able to utilize these distinctions to clarify and identify what it perceived as missing in the work of Le Corbusier. Instead of the purely spatial quantification of the Modulor (how tall, what space is needed to sit, to swing arms, to sleep), sociology now offered an opportunity to measure or qualify people in a new way.

For the Situationist International, the process of mapping the everyday and understanding it more fully helped to identify it as a site of resistance. An early CoBrA statement (1948) emphasizes the richness of the everyday: 'Ce qui caractérise un art populaire est une expression vitale, directe et collective.' This is indeed what the 1960s' artistic and intellectual revolutions hoped to achieve. Yet in the totalitarian schemes of situationist engagement and urbanism in the form of New Babylon, the everyman had no choice but to be enlightened – and was thus placed in the same position as in the earlier schemes of modernist thought. The 'vital, direct, collective' expression referred to above is certainly premised on everyday life. But it is hard to see how, if this becomes the revolutionary endeavour so conceived, it can remain either 'direct' (and not instrumental to revolution) or 'collective' (if it is to follow Debord's vision). In the end, the images presented by the Situationist International as a crystallization of its own 'sociological' experiments in the space of the city are still traditional plans, albeit transformed by eliminating some parts and adding images and texts.

The turn to sociology suggests that the architecture debate on the city was shifting from a mechanical paradigm to a social paradigm. Perhaps it is more accurate to say that the idea of the city shifted from the mechanical city to the living city.[51] Notions of growth and change are explored both visually (through non-linear imagery, assemblages, specificity) and conceptually (in open-ended city plans, flexibility), replacing the static city image with a dynamic one. The living city is seen

Diagram by Walter Gropius, as published in *Architectural Design* 6 (1957)

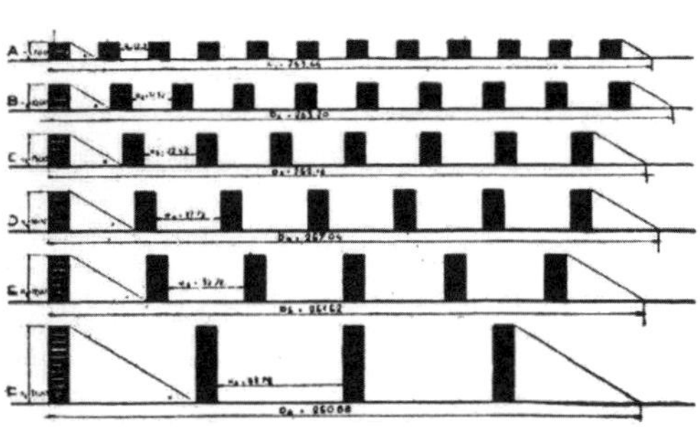

Diagrams by Walter Gropius showing how height of, and space between, blocks, can be regulated to allow for adequate sun penetration and cross ventilation

Movement diagram as published in *Internationale Situationniste* 6 (1961)

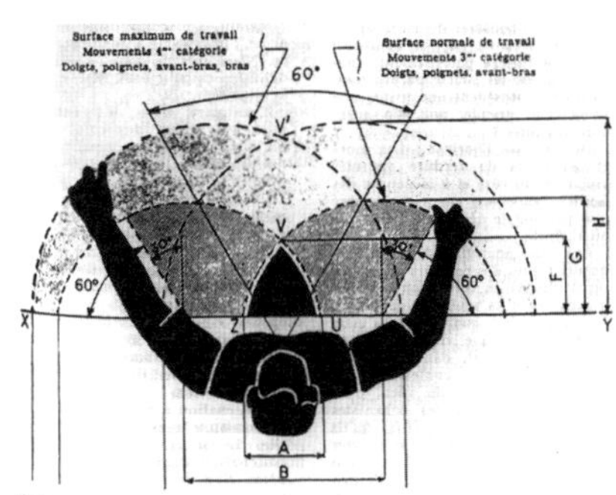

Surfaces maxima et normales de travail dans le plan horizontal.

35

The city as perceived by its inhabitants: dynamic, contingent and fragmented views.
Archigram, The Living City (1963)

as an organism whose systems are interdependent and cannot be treated as entirely separate entities. The vitality of this organism manifests itself throughout patterns of sociability. We can therefore argue that this is the first step towards *Gemeinschaft* in the city, as transforming the rationalized and regulated forms of *Gesellschaft*.[52] Furthermore, by treating the city as a 'living' organism, historical continuity gains importance, thereby reinforcing the value of exploring the historical and social significance of the urban fabric, along a similar line to Lefebvre's 'lived space'.

This transformation is particularly visible in the representation of the ideal occupant, which has shifted from being a mechanical metaphor (rational, functional, efficient) to being a sociopsychological metaphor (desiring, creative, free). This is not only manifest in the permanent desire and creativity that the situationists hope to unleash, but also in the rhetoric of social interaction used by the Independent Group. The 1960s' turn to the social, to the level of 'human' rather than 'machine' manifests itself in two main tendencies: one oriented towards the individual human (psychology, individual expression) and one oriented towards the socialized human (community, tradition). Most work incorporates both tendencies to some degree. For example, the Independent Group is concerned with the psychology of the individual, but also with exploring the possibilities for community in the massiveness of a city.[53]

The imagery used to explore these sociological issues not only 'represents' some kind of 'truth' (in the way we would typically associate with modernism) but gives a *presence* to these underlying thematics, and in giving them presence, they also become part of the world around us. The importance of the individual presents itself in the increasing focus on reception. Eduardo Paolozzi and Richard Hamilton use found imagery in their work, exploring its visual pleasure as artists while also acknowledging that the audience adds their own network of personal connotations. As Lawrence Alloway points out, the conventions of mass culture are democratic and should be treated differently from those of high art. In appropriating mass imagery, these artists are on some level also appropriating the shift in conventions that accompanies these new images. This is a crucial difference with Debord's idea that first the world must change, and then its visual and physical forms will follow. While he maintains a linguistic orientation, placing conceptual thought above visual manifestation, the innovative use of imagery by Paolozzi and Hamilton contains a possibility that progress is not linear – that ordinary images may also subvert conceptual thought or demonstrate something as yet unthought. Debord's use of existing imagery remains oriented towards the ultimate goal of pressuring the individual to express his authentic self while the work of the Independent Group and later work on the Living City by Archigram also explore collective identities that are construed through existing imagery. The relationship between the individual and the community is not only explored through the images of mass culture, but also defined by them.

Imaging the City in the Age of the Spectacle

Architecture set itself a difficult task regarding the 1960s' city: it was forming a critique of the modern city, which was still being realized, it was trying to address the imagery and spectacle that was rapidly becoming part of the urban environment, and it was trying to find appropriate visual representations that would offer both a critique of the modern city and a form for the future city. In 1957, William Whyte noted:

> But what is the image of the city of the future? In the plans for the huge redevelopment projects to come, we are being shown a new image of the city – and it is sterile and lifeless. Gone are the dirt and the noise – and the variety and the excitement and the spirit. That it is an ideal makes it all the worse; these bleak new utopias are not bleak because they have to be; they are the concrete manifestation – and how literally – of a deep, and at times arrogant, misunderstanding of the function of the city.[54]

This is the crisis of the modernist city, and the central issue facing architecture in the 1960s.[55]

The introduction of 'variety, excitement and spirit' found an expression both in the use of the city and its representations. Although these two aspects usually represent different approaches, it is at the intersection of the everyday images of mass culture and the city as the site of everyday life that the force of a new vitality begins to recuperate the urban environment. The new, vibrant proposals for the city often incorporated a fragmentation that both represented and arose from a sense of plurality. They also made extensive use of found imagery, referring to the everyday visual environment of the city dweller. The Independent Group presented this new spirit in the profusion of mass imagery it experimented with. The Situationist International on the other hand, hoped to find the same spirit in the unexpected (and not yet visually determined) actions of the people in the city.

The cheerful radiance of ordinary images was of primary interest to a number of collaborations, including the Independent Group, Team 10, and Venturi and Scott Brown. The Independent Group, coalescing in 1952, was a loosely organized group of artists and architects that held occasional gatherings at the London Institute for Contemporary Arts to discuss contemporary developments and their ramifications for architecture. The Independent Group included, among others, Eduardo Paolozzi (1924-2005), Richard Hamilton (b. 1922) and Alison (1928-1993) and Peter (1923-2003) Smithson, all of whom were struggling with issues of mass culture and advertising. The images and rhetoric used by the Independent Group reflect their belief that the intersection between mass culture and everyday life is an important element in the break with the modern city. Team 10 originated from CIAM, finally breaking with it in 1956, and formulated precise critiques of the functionalist city. The Smithsons were involved with Team 10, as were Aldo van Eyck, Candilis Josic Woods and many others.[56] The connection between the city and mass culture is explicitly articulated by Lawrence Alloway, a central figure in the Independent Group. He writes both on developments in contemporary film and on the contemporary city, noting for example that 'mass art is urban and democratic'.[57] This democratic nature of mass culture would become a focal point in the work of Robert Venturi and Denise Scott Brown ten years later, when they began exploring the ordinary environment of American main streets, suburbs, and the Las Vegas strip in an effort to understand the communicative quality of everyday imagery.

The situationists took the critical potential of found imagery a step further in their belief that when properly utilized, *détournement* could undermine the existing conditions of the spectacle. Debord's critique did not extend merely to the visual sterility of the modern city, but also to the all-encompassing nature of the spectacle as a repressive structure. In the eyes of Debord, there was a fine line between *détournement* as a critical intervention using everyday imagery, and the affirmative quality of imagery that is uncritically presented, thus reflecting the dominance of the spectacle. The Independent Group did not subscribe to this idea of the 'false consciousness' of the spectacle, leaving room for their imagery to be

The vitality of communication: photographs of Las Vegas billboards. Robert Venturi and Denise Scott Brown, *Learning from Las Vegas* (1972)

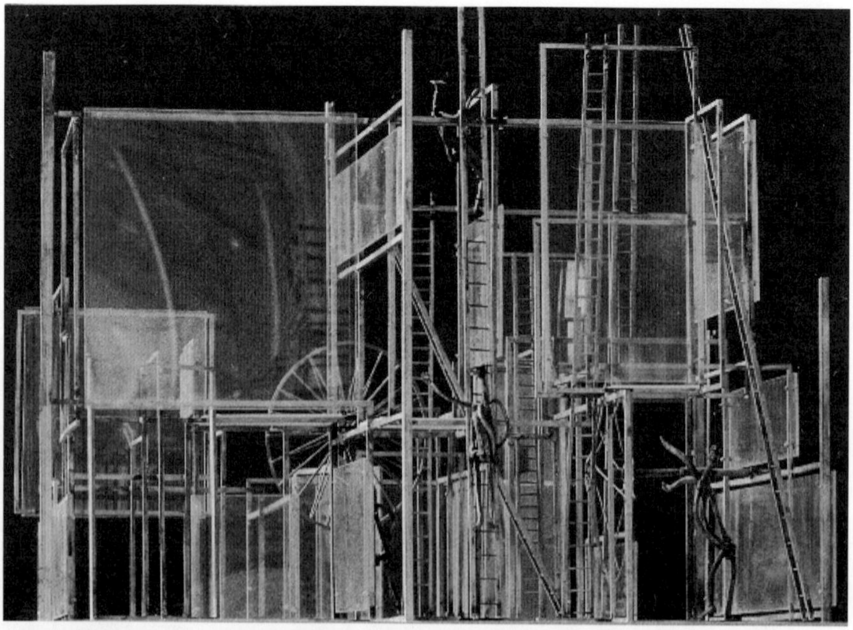

A sense of instability in the depiction of movement. Constant, New Babylon (1967)

simultaneously communicative and critical. Their use and adaptation of everyday imagery to construe a new image of a future city was informed more by the idea that pop imagery was able to communicate with the people in the street. Here, no *détournement* of these images was necessary to instigate a revolution – their presence itself was radical enough.

The fragmentation introduced by the situationists is another step in breaking through the smooth totality of the spectacle. When the fragments are dislocated from their normal context, they become more vivid and begin to form a new consciousness of their presence. In the representations of New Babylon, the notions 'unexpected', 'flux' and 'individual agency' are expressed in the design precisely through its resistance to singular defining images, the lack of a stable grid, the variations in viewpoints and depictions. This expresses the fragmentation of a city based on individual intervention, which immediately elicits a sense of instability. This fragmentation returns throughout the drawings of Constant, just as it is visible in the collages Debord and Jorn made of Paris. The fragments themselves are often constructed out of found images. The title page of the *Mémoires* for example, notes that 'cet ouvrage est entièrement composé d'éléments préfabriqués'.[58] The use of prefabricated imagery is significant to the Situationist International in its negation of artistic production (thus going against the idea of the expressive genius of the creative artist). And at the same time, it still utilizes imagery as some form of symbolic expression that reflects a sense of community, since the symbols must be to some extent legible. Might the city and its people find their way to liberation through reflecting on these found images, consciously *détourned* by Debord and Jorn? If so, does that not imply that there is still an 'artistic endeavour' at work here to demonstrate a more appropriate way of looking at things?

Debord's ambivalence towards images is visible in the first two issues of *Internationale Situationniste*, where the visual material on the city is restricted to plans and mappings of routes or borders. In issue 3, photos are included of the models for New Babylon, as well as sketches by Constant accompanying his article 'Une autre ville pour une autre vie'. In *Internationale Situationniste* 4, the world is still treated as a visual labyrinth in a discussion of the incomplete situationist intervention at the Stedelijk Museum in Amsterdam in 1959.[59] The description of the yellow zone in New Babylon is also inserted in this issue. Issue 5 already announces the rupture between the Situationist International and Constant, thus initiating the dissociation from a visual manifestation of the situationist city. Although the creative force of the individual is crucial to the 'great game to come', the situationists maintain a problematic relationship with all forms of imagery. The 'constructed situation' is not visually defined, but it has the power to trigger the development of the creative (non-artistic, non-elite) individual, while ordinary, everyday images must be *détourned* if they are not to be implicated in the mechanisms of the spectacle. Each definite image becomes suspect: where the Plan Voisin represents an ideal to be attained, Debord's Naked City simply demonstrates the problem of the existing city, showing its shortcomings and absences. Thus the imagery of Le Corbusier projects an ideal, where that of Debord presents a critique, or at least so he believes. Apparently Debord sees the visual designs made by Le Corbusier, and later Constant, as *prescriptive* merely by virtue of their visual definition – as if Debord's creative individual has no imagination that can interpret or go beyond what Constant has already sketched out. Apparently, the words describing a possible situationist city are less restrictive than a visual suggestion towards the same. Although Debord is articulate in his critique of representation and the spectacular, it quickly becomes impossible for him to see visual material as anything other than the representation or embodiment of a status quo. Similar to Adorno's understanding of art as negation and mass culture as affirmation, Debord maintains a highly intellectual, not to mention linguistic approach to art and imagery. Ironically, this approach is based on the 'sterile' modernity he so dismisses. For Debord, the potential of his notion of *détournement*, which utilizes prefabricated imagery, is fully dependent on active intervention by means of language and text, either to reveal new meanings or the uselessness of old meanings. It is this dependence on words that undercuts the truly revolutionary potential of some of his ideas.

In the end, the activist urban practice advocated by the situationists is posed in direct opposition to the reception of the city as spectacle. This increasingly absolute contrast strengthens the problems with the visual, as it is demoted from a potentially critical endeavour, or the possibility of imagining something as yet unknown, to an affirmation of existing conditions, which according to Debord feeds the machinery of capitalism and bourgeois power. He does not offer a place for an 'autonomous' or productive form of visuality and use, like Lefebvre seems to imply with his notion of 'lived space'. In the use of the space it is transformed, but meaning is also accorded to it from within tradition. Of course, in neither is there a direct visual manifestation of these ideas; we must still look to the artistic production of the time for possibilities in the realm of the visual. Returning to thesis 1 of *Society of the Spectacle*, we are reminded that the spectacle is in opposition to directly lived experience. The everyday (as the locus of directly lived experience) is the site of active resistance to this spectacle. In England, the more light-hearted approach to the 'ordinary' indicates a vitality not so much to be conquered through resistance, but already present in the fabric of the everyday environment. This vitality resides not only in the domain of the creative individual, but is also present in the manifestations of spectacular culture, such as science-fiction films and advertising. The intersection of the urban environment and mass culture is a reflection of the ordinary environment of 'the man in the street'.

Taking It to the Streets

Looking at all these new realities and ideas, one physical element is strikingly central: the street. The voice of the man in the street, the style of the street, the imagery along the streets, the space of the street all become emblems for the failure of modernism. No longer merely an efficient connection between the spaces of the city, the street now becomes a space of occupation where unexpected encounters can take place, and a space of resistance when the barricades are set up against the authorities. In the 1960s, the street is where alternative realities are evoked, be it through a physical presence (mass demonstrations) or through new signs and symbols (billboards and graffiti). These new urban gestures are gathered in and along the streets. The everyday experience of the urban inhabitant, neglected in the modernist city, is visible in the description of the sidewalk as a space of encounter by Jane Jacobs, but also in the situationist perception of the street as a space of dreaming and *dérives*. As a form of everyday, communicative symbolism, the billboards along the street lead Venturi and Scott Brown to claim that 'main street is almost all right'. The powerful presence of people in the streets is seen in peaceful demonstrations like the 1963 March on Washington, and in the form of revolts like the Paris student riots in May 1968. Despite the increasing proliferation of the spectacle and the visual already signalled by Debord, the street is the space where transformations take place, where voices are heard. In architecture, the street is given a new meaning: it is no longer the space of separation between the different functions of the city, but a space of encounter, of collective activity and social interaction.

As such, the importance of the street to the sense of change in the 1960s can hardly be underestimated. The crisis of the modern city necessitated a reconsideration of the street. The social spaces of the city, embodied in early modernism by the *flâneur* and the blasé metropolitan individual, were primarily located in the street. Yet CIAM's reduction of the street to a traffic artery did not allot a significance to the street as a space, but rather as a metaphorical space of transition and speed. The streets, conceived of as corridors of mobility, became a means of separation, a hard

LA RÉCUPÉRATION VULGAIRE (affiche pour un film commercial, automne 1968).

'La poesie dans la rue', *International Situationniste* 12 (1969)

Presence and power of the street as gathering space and as visual reference. March on Washington (1963)

boundary between one city space and another. The social identity of the street resurfaces in the 1960s, when it is seen as a space of diffusion and blurring. The street was about mixing the different functions of the city, and about the unexpected, which could take the form of social encounters, but also of riots. The street, as a critical space in the modern city, became transformed not so much in its design as in its significance to the new analyses and designs in the city. The primary transformation in the social significance of the street is that the *flâneur* remains at a distance to observe the crowd in the city, while the 1960s' models follow the lines of active engagement.[60] This creates a new relationship between the traffic of the city and the presence of the urban dweller. While New Babylon echoes the modernist removal of traffic from the zones of activity by placing traffic below the space of occupation, for the

Programme préalable au mouvement situationniste.

Cette inscription, sur un mur de la rue de Seine, remonte aux premiers mois de **1953** (une inscription voisine qui relève de la politique traditionnelle aide à dater avec la plus sûre objectivité le tracé de celle qui nous intéresse : appelant à une manifestation contre le général Ridgway, elle ne peut donc être postérieure à mai 1952). L'inscription que nous reproduisons ici semble être la plus importante trace jamais relevée sur le site de Saint-Germain-des-Prés, comme témoignage du mode de vie particulier qui a tenté de s'affirmer là.

'Ne travaillez jamais', chalk graffiti from 1953 in the Rue de Seine, Paris. Presented as a preamble to situationist thought, later claimed to have been written by Guy Debord himself. Guy Debord, *Mémoires*, afterword (1993)

Smithsons and Jane Jacobs some of the traffic space becomes a space of occupation as well. It becomes a site of informal interaction, not purely of mobility.

The situationist practice of mobility takes place in the street, becoming an occupation of the city, not a means of getting from one place to another. The street itself is lined with the signs of individual resistance in the form of graffiti. In the situationist *dérive*, the street offers a space of unexpected encounter and of physical attractions, directing those involved in the *dérive* to psychologically interesting spaces in the city. The situationist texts and images on the *dérive* embody a street-level experience of the city, incorporating the fragmentation they see as part of the modern city. The new position of the street is already prefigured in the images of the Naked City and the *Mémoires.* As a collection of fragments, there are comments drifting throughout that prefigure the ideas of the *dérive* and psychogeographic maps ('dans la décor réel des rues', 'l'exploration systématique des cartes d'autrefois', 'ambiances nouvelles', 'comportements nouveaux', 'ce petit monde en dérive', along with fragments of the Paris map). Although the position of the street is not specifically addressed, Debord's collages and the painterly interventions by Jorn already show the many fragments that will be published in a larger body of situationist thought in the pamphlets.[61] For the situationists, the street represented a space

'Reclaim the Streets', street party on Broadway, New York (1998)

of freedom, and as such it had the potential to become the space of revolution. They hoped that eventually people would tear up the pavement to discover the beach underneath. The *dérive* was thus meant to appropriate the space of the street as a space for the life of the city, where encounters could take place and people would actually engage with their environment. This notion has remained throughout the remainder of the twentieth century, echoing through 'street fashions' as truly cutting edge, but also in urban movements such as 'Reclaim the Streets'.

Of particular interest on the role of the street in New Babylon and situationist thought is the 1959 article by Constant 'A Different City for a Different Life'. He describes the street both as a desolate space of separation in the modern city, and as a potential space for renewed pleasure in the urban environment. To Constant, the street has been deprived of any social role in the city.

> In old neighborhoods, streets have degenerated into highways, and leisure is commercialized and adulterated by tourism. Social relations there become impossible. Newly built neighborhoods have only two themes, which govern everything: traffic circulation and household comfort. They are the meager expressions of bourgeois happiness and lack any concern for play.[62]

The fundamental character of separation in the functionalist city is conceived of as built up of two components: traffic circulation (which becomes an experience of non-space as it is merely a transition between one space and another) and household comfort (where the spectacle holds sway, since all sense of unhappiness is alleviated by the material comforts of the home). Even in the Covered City, the early incarnation of New Babylon, traffic was directed to the lower and upper levels, and the pedestrian occupation of the street within the fabric of the city went so far as to make the street as such be completely incorporated in the urban fabric, making it disappear altogether as a separate entity. Constant offers a radical transformation of the street from a space of transition (neither here nor there) into a space of occupation. The streets as such are done away with:

> Our concept of urbanism is thus a social one.... Instead of the idea of a garden city, which most modern architects have adopted, we set up the image of the covered city, where the layout of thoroughfares and isolated buildings has given way to a continuous spatial construction, elevated above the ground, and which will include groups of dwellings as well as public spaces (permitting modifications of purpose depending on the needs of the moment). Since all traffic, in the functional sense, will pass underneath or on overhead terraces, streets can be done away with. The great number of different traversable spaces of which the city is composed form a vast and complex social space.[63]

The ordinary social space of the street. Photograph of Beacon Hill, Boston. Image as published in *Architectural Forum* 1 (1962)

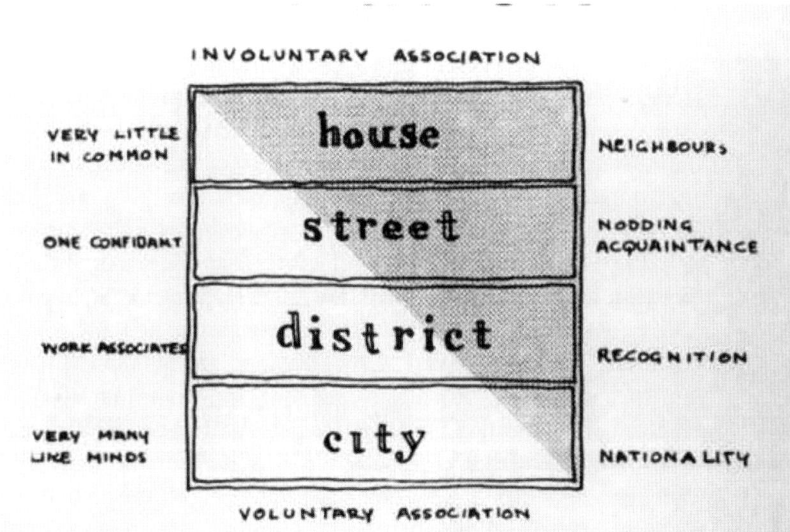

Scale of Association, diagram by Alison and Peter Smithson (1956)

The street becomes urban fabric, defined less by its form than by the social interactions of those who occupy it.

In a similar vein, Jane Jacobs pays specific attention to the street as a social space and its role in facilitating communication within the urban neighbourhood. She introduces the idea of formal versus informal interaction in her chapters on the uses of sidewalk space.[64] One aspect of her careful analysis of the use of the sidewalk is the introduction of the living, breathing, everyday occupant of city space, and with this, the reintroduction of an ordinary image of the city. The sidewalk is the place where informal interaction is encouraged by its place outside the private space of the home, but within its sphere of influence, thanks to the windows overlooking the street. In a healthy and busy neighbourhood, the sidewalk is where invisible forms of social control are manifest simply in the many eyes that are trained on the street.[65] Wide sidewalks help to assimilate children in urban neighbourhoods, who are better off playing under the supervision of parents and neighbours than at a specially designed but isolated playground. Her descriptions of children playing in the street and the social relations that are generated by the presence of people in the street and in the windows overlooking it echo early situationist ideas on the importance of being in the streets.

The Smithsons also acknowledge the social function of the sidewalk in their projects, most pointedly in their 1952 design for the Golden Lane Housing competition with its street decks that have ample space for interaction.[66] In this design, the 'informal social interaction' Jacobs sees as fundamental to the social cohesion of a community is given a place above ground level. For the other members of Team 10 as well, the street was a social space, not merely a space for traffic. In the by now familiar diagram by the Smithsons illustrating the 'Scale of Association' in the city, the spaces of the city are defined by social interaction. The street holds a middle ground between house and city. It mediates between the private space of the home and the public space of the city, with the district forming another level of association, as a smaller unit of community than the city. This space of mediation to the Smithsons was the site of the social, precisely as Jane Jacobs describes the significance of the sidewalk. Although the Smithsons maintain a more traditional form of street and sidewalk than the entirely dissipated form in New Babylon, theirs is still a far cry from the modernist lines of traffic structure, meant to allow efficient travel between separate zones. In their Network City infrastructure becomes a primary focus, since everything in between the basic infrastructure can be left to the interventions of individual occupants. To the situationists, this space of the social not only enriched urban life, but it represented something more radical: as a social space that could not be controlled, the street was potentially revolutionary. In New Babylon, the importance of the street caused it to dissolve into the urban fabric, spreading throughout the city and creating 'the urban network, the natural expression of a collective creativity'.[67] In a grand gesture appealing to the potential of the individual to transform his or her environment, New Babylon was meant to embody a sense of individuality, growth and change within the very fabric of the city.

An Architecture of Growth and Change

A new direction is given to the city of the 1960s through the intention to encourage vitality in the spaces of the city and to leave room for change. The network of New Babylon incorporates change and allows for multiplicity (of different psychological 'ambiances', for example) by allowing the environment itself to be determined by individual psychology and modified at the whim of the inhabitants. The Smithsons, on the other hand, see a stable infrastructure as a strategy to

Incorporating development and change in the city, *Architectural Design* 7 (1956)

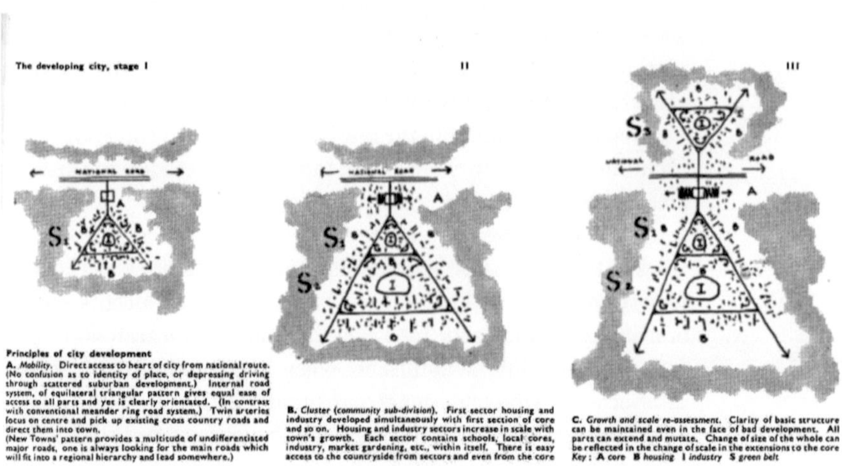

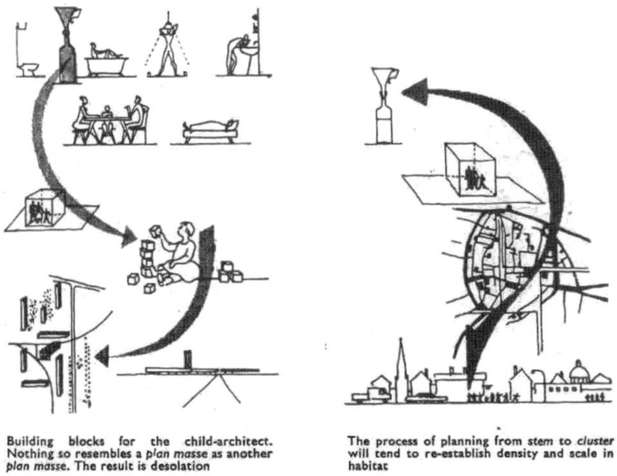

Rethinking the city through organic growth: 'the process of planning from stem to cluster', *Architectural Design* 5 (1960)

ensure room for change and diversity, maintaining the traditional functions of the city but adding an explicit concern for the function of human association. Again, these plans contain specific responses to the modernist city that demonstrate its shortcomings while also responding to societal changes. The Smithsons were perhaps most direct in their rebuttal, being both part of the CIAM conferences and the later internal critique of Team 10. The critiques were directed at the static nature of the modernist city, perceiving its clearly defined order as restrictive. The modernist city forced the individual occupant into a straitjacket of rationalized and mechanical behaviour that had nothing to do with traditional patterns or convention. The slow sedimentation of historical patterns that allowed the traditional city to grow over time had been interrupted by the radical insertion of modernist principles. These critiques found their expression in metaphors of growth and change, which play an important role in defining the character of the city in the 1960s. 'Growth' was present in the many references to natural forms (the city as a 'tree' or a 'leaf'), offering a counterpoint to the mechanical nature of the modernist city. By incorporating the possibility of change, the urban environment is given a strategy to embrace transformations over time.

The increasing concern for the urban fabric as a whole can be seen in the work of the Smithsons, which develops an emphasis on networks from an earlier focus on the street.[68] The increasing presence of networks in the city plans of the Smithsons facilitates the interpenetration of the separate CIAM spheres, and helps to group individual elements into clusters.[69] The cluster itself embodies a sense of association which is crucial to the reintroduction of human interaction in the city, while the process of clustering implies growth and change. In the case of the Smithsons, the presence of the street in the Golden Lane project becomes increas-

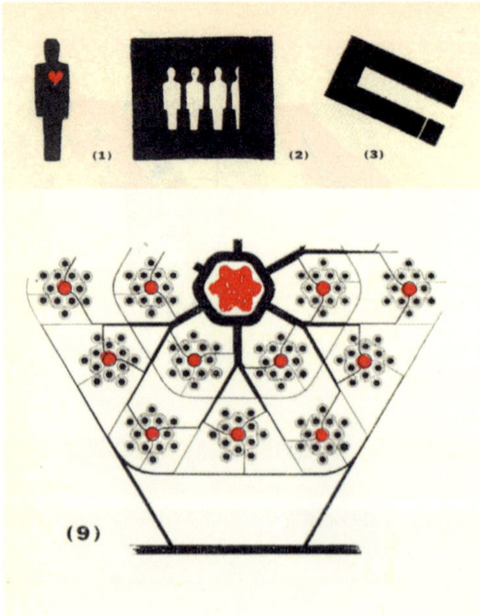

The cluster city as more amenable to inhabitants.
Diagram by Victor Gruen (1956)

ingly networked and connected to emerge as a full-fledged pedestrian circulation deck (or 'precinct' to follow Eisenman's terminology) in the Hauptstadt Berlin project of 1958.

There are undeniable similarities between Golden Lane, Hauptstadt Berlin, the various presentations of cluster cities and New Babylon.[70] In particular, they all share an emphasis on different levels and connections, and are organized around networks of infrastructure, with pedestrian movement generally a level removed from the ground which is devoted to motorized traffic. These networks incorporate the idea of endlessness while simultaneously representing flexibility. The flexibility of these networks is founded on the idea that cities can be made more responsive to their inhabitants by incorporating the potential for change. Nevertheless, there are distinctions between how the Smithsons and Constant handle their respective infrastructure and networks. Many of the 1960s' proposals for new cities (including those of Archigram and the metabolists, for example) follow the model of the Smithsons, which is to offer a relatively stable infrastructure that can be expanded and also accommodate change within. Constant takes this a step further by elevating the notion of 'flux' to the very essence of his city order (where the formal expression of the city is dependent on the actions of its occupants). To him, an ever-changing life necessitated an ever-changing environment: the instability of his city was a great adventure that would encourage the *homo ludens* to emerge.

Various forms of growth and change would continue to be important to the treatment of the city in the 1960s as can be seen in *Archigram* issue 5, which was devoted solely to the new metropolis: the growth-based crystalline city as proposed by the Japanese metabolists, cluster cities, network cities, Yona Friedman's spatial city – the issue is full of visual manifestations of the idea of growth and change. These projects, as well as the additive infrastructure in the work of the Smithsons no longer form a closed system. Their cities can grow to whatever dimensions and in whatever direction necessary, unlike the more rigorous formal boundaries of the Corbusian city. Although the Corbusian grid is in principle endless, in his images he shows virtually no possibility of variation within the assigned scheme. In the 1960s, terms such as 'flux', 'flexibility' and 'freedom' are introduced in opposition to the rigid forms of the modernist city. They represent a need to manifest individuality (as opposed to the mechanical collectivity of the modernist city), as well as the need to address the failure of universal form (thought possible by modernism) and the desire to replace a static and permanent design with space for changing conditions. Yet both approaches are still based on what Gans called the fallacy of physical determinism, whether that is expressed in a need for clarity through 'rational' architecture or a need for change through 'flexible' architecture.

The ideas of growth and change play a similar role to the modern idea of the 'ephemeral' in defining both a critique and a societal condition. In the early twentieth century, the 'ephemeral' offered a counterweight to the stifling heaviness of bourgeois European culture. The 'ephemeral' expressed the transparency and speed of the modern age, and became a metaphor for the modern condition. It was used to emphasize the importance of new forms and materials in architecture, always echoing the very essence of modernity. The 'growth' and 'change' of the 1960s confirmed the continuing speed of societal transformations, but also opposed the mechanical orientation of modernism by inserting a reference to the natural and human world in particular. The idea of change resonated with the need for individual expression and the potential to transform. The idea of growth offered a metaphor that might make the city less rigid and more amenable to its inhabitants. Nevertheless, the metaphors of growth and change proved no insurance against a final definition of city form. More importantly, an underlying question remained unanswered: Is it the role of architecture to express the psychological conditions of society, or of its occupants? Can architecture evoke behaviour through form, and is this desirable?

The City as a Negotiation between the Individual and the Collective

The endless promises of the 1960s in the form of play, liberation and emancipation seem to ignore the complexity of incompatible desires within the larger urban whole. Some conflicts can only lead to imperfect compromise, and some issues by definition will require a prioritizing of conflicting interests. The perfectly collective individuation of the situationists denies this problem entirely.

Ultimately, the situationists placed the responsibility for the vitality of everyday life with the individual. The flux that would indicate the possibility of change and the vitality of the urban neighbourhood was possible thanks to individual agency. Yet this physical manifestation of growth and flux could not yet be formally defined, since it must await the rise of the new city inhabitant. Before 1961, New Babylon was seen to have a role in encouraging the transformation of the urban dweller, but later the new societal structures were thought to be a first priority, which would only later be reflected in its artistic productions. The situationist dependence on words rather than images, and a linear narrative that precluded the alternative interpretations they hoped to encourage indicates the fundamental schism underlying the transformation of the city in the 1960s. Although the unexpected and undefined potentials of the city were to be introduced, it became part of a totalizing argument that ran counter to its own premises. The limitations of the individual were not taken into account, nor was the tension between individual and communal concerns.

Where the European city of the twentieth century is predominantly social, or has always been defined by some kind of societal discourse, the American city has less of an underlying social agenda.[71] Or perhaps it is more appropriate to say that the American libertarian tradition limits the discussion of communities, since 'community' is generally placed below individual freedom. Conceivably then, invoking 'tradition' in the American city discourse is more about a nostalgic image than about a structural understanding of societal tradition. At the same time, there is a somewhat useful pragmatic result in just 'accepting' social context, as opposed to fashioning a brave new world. In the US context, critiques of the modern city reflected concerns similar to their European counterparts, yet also illustrate the specific American condition of a society steeped in capitalism and individual freedom.

The key to the Situationist International's proposals and reconfigurations of the city, in the end, is the individual. This precedes everything, even pre-empting the need to define an architectural space. Again, in terms of the position of the individual, the work of the situationists proves itself more radical than that of their contemporaries struggling to address similar problems. The Smithsons, as mentioned above, leave room for change within a stable infrastructure, thereby positioning themselves as designers of an environment that simply leaves some details up to its inhabitants. The infrastructure itself is still treated as a concrete design problem, and the architect is still seen to have a certain relevance in shaping collective space.

Although the same could be said of New Babylon, in the sense that it is an actual design proposal and has a form given to it by Constant, there is a very different premise here. In New Babylon, the final form will always be determined by the sum total of individual actions. This is both a reiteration and an inversion of Le Corbusier's city. It inverts the idea that a city's form can determine the behaviour of its inhabitants (in other words, that a rational city form will cause people to occupy their environment and behave in a rational way). In New Babylon, it is the occupants that determine the final form, not the other way around. Yet the forms are presumed to 'trigger' a creative use of the environment, indicating some level of determination through architectural form. Thus New Babylon places a similar de-

'Labyrismen': The creative individual in the labyrinth of New Babylon. Constant (1968)

mand of self-realization on the individual that Le Corbusier does. Only now, rather than achieving the heights of rationality, people are required to continually express their inner creativity and manifest themselves as individuals. Instead of being the perfect expression of a collective (mechanical) humanity, they now become the inevitable collective of an individually expressive humanity.

The universal treatment of the form appropriate to this individual agency can be said to tend towards modernism, although Constant was always quick to point out that his was not to be considered a definitive form. This is an inevitable problem between proposing a design and leaving room for individual intervention. One end of the spectrum would consist of the methodical data collection of all individual expressions without design intervention, as done by Venturi and Scott Brown in their work on Levittown;[72] the other end of the spectrum is to design a possible world while acknowledging that this is one of many possible solutions, as Constant to some degree did.

The radically creative individual underlies all the situationist theories on the city. Although their critique of the city was also a Marxist one, involving the uprising of the working class, their conception of the working class was a romanticized one of a group of repressed individuals, all waiting for the opportunity to manifest their creativity. As Vidler has already pointed out, this implies a Nietzschean conception of the individual that is exhausting: the inhabitant is required to transform the environment continually to manifest his or her individual creativity.[73] The notion that every moment, every action must be engaged towards a radical transformation of the environment is easily as totalitarian as the repressive mechanical nature of the Corbusian city. It is precisely this radical nature of the critique coupled with the purity of the solution (instead of pure mechanical collectivity, there will be pure individual creativity) that seems to predict the failure of the situationist city. As they themselves critique the functionalist city, not for being entirely wrong but for neglecting some important aspects of life; so they, too, are not entirely off the mark, but forget that there are moments when their hyperactive individual might want to just be passive. The relationship between individual and collective is one of compromise and negotiation. As the modernists (notably Le Corbusier) forget the importance of individuation, so the situationists seem to bypass the fact that collectivity will not always be the perfect expression of their romantic conception of the individual.

As early as 1947, Henri Lefebvre proclaims the importance of the city in terms of amenities and more than anything, *community life* as a fundamental aspect of everyday experience.[74] Although the transformations in the understanding of community make it difficult to offer a general definition of the qualities of community life, the importance attributed to community is prevalent in most of the debates. In architecture, various definitions of community play a role throughout the twentieth century. There is the traditional village ideal we are familiar with from Heidegger's *Building Dwelling Thinking*, where there is a naturalized relation between man and his environment, man and his soil, and thus the

The desolation of the new creative city: New Babylon as 'ville couverte'. Constant, New Babylon (1971)

community extends out through a shared sense of the relation with the landscape (which is also defined in opposition to the city). Tönnies' rural *Gemeinschaft* follows along similar lines, but is embedded more in the social relations of the rural community than the relation with the land and nature. There is also a modernist (or techno-progressivist) nearly mechanical sense of community, where community life is both organized (through leisure time, shared labour and universal standards) and rationalized – a more urban ideal. This hints more at the ideas of *Gesellschaft*, where regulations determine interaction, yet the naturalization of this mechanical community, where each inhabitant at last becomes the idealized efficient inhabitant still resoundingly echoes with the sense of a collective body of people.

Tactical Resistance

In the end, it is by drawing the lines along a 'tactics of resistance' that the situationists failed in producing their utopia.[75] Each moment of resistance against the dominant discourse held a key to seeing the problems inherent in the modern city. Yet by continually positioning themselves in opposition, they unintentionally replicated the problems of the modernist city. When the street disappeared as a highway but became the space of resistance, it also seemed to lose its innocence. Although the abstraction of the modern city was defied, it became imbued with a new sense of instrumental abstraction. Although incorporating growth and transformation was seen as progress from the static images of the modern city, the ultimate result was a forced representation of growth that would lead to equally static and metaphorical embodiments of flexibility.

What we have now seen of a 'global' resistance to high modernism (and by this I mean the widespread resistance in the transatlantic debate) shows the problems beginning to surface as many cities were reconstructed according to CIAM tenets. The modernist city was perhaps not all it had promised, and as already noted the reactions were extremely varied, although their points of critique were resoundingly similar, focusing on the lack of social space, the lack of traditional city fabric, and its visual sterility. One of the many texts of the period that illuminates the problems of the modernist city well is 'Planning Today', a conversation published in *Architectural Design* between Peter Smithson, William Holford and Arthur Ling.[76] Peter Smithson, in particular, defines the issues well. Moreover, many of the phrases used show a startling resonance among the transatlantic critiques of the modernist city.

It is clear that some of the most prominent, original and radical ideas of the 1960s were formulated explicitly as a position of resistance against a dominant modernist ideology. Criticisms echo one another throughout the transatlantic debate, referring to the lack of visible identity, the sterile character of modern cities and their lack of traditional city fabric. The main points of criticism can be categorized as: abstraction (as a denial of reality), mechanization and rationalization (as a fixation on quantitative definitions over qualitative assessments), and massiveness. Each of these in their own way contributed to the sense of constraint – that the individual living in the city had been stripped of choices.

The alternatives, or strategies of resistance, revolve around a number of specific themes, each of which reveals a specific shortcoming. Each aims at regaining some kind of social cohesion and value (however loosely defined) through its strategies. These critiques are produced over an extended period of time, from the late 1950s to the early 1970s. While the Situationist International shifts gradually from the aesthetic to the political, the trajectory opened up by Jacobs' work moves towards the aesthetic in the work of Venturi and Scott Brown. They are all, however, seeking ways to transform the sterile city of abstracted form into something more human and vital, be it through collective action or collective symbolism. One issue that remains problematic, however, is the limited interaction between the social and the formal. Although it is true that neither can determine the other, denying any mutual influence is also counterproductive. Identification through signs and symbols is reasonably universal and to think that modern man would have no need of this is presumptuous, as is the hierarchy between 'authentic' symbols and those of the mass media.

One of the primary modes of critique of the modern city was a formal one. In response to an overly mechanized environment that was deemed inhuman, the designs of the time proposed organic forms. Since abstraction was considered to not be communicative enough, it was replaced with figuration. These formal reactions did liberate the general design tendencies from a rigorous dependence on clarity, rectilinear form and visual purity. However, in their rigorous application, they began to form a new aesthetic that was no less demanding than its predecessor.

The conceptual innovations of the 1960s were principally engaged with replacing the idealist tendency of modern designs by a more realist version. Rather than offering only the perfected vision of their future city, these critics were also examining the fabric of the existing city to find its beauty. In theory, the 1960s were all about the intersection of the ideal and the real. Yet in practice they often so reduced the reality they were examining that little was left of the multiplicity they were seeking.

Each of these critiques of modernism points to perceived failures, which derive in part from the tenets of modernism, in part from transformations towards a late capitalist society and in part from the experience of modernity itself (and the inadequacy of modernism's response to it). The question remains whether the counterreactions offered viable alternative solutions for the problems thus perceived.

In a sense, modernism never did address the schism of modernity: the discombobulation of living in a time determined by conditions beyond our control. The hope inherent in modernism, its promise, was that Reason would inevitably resolve the problems of modernity. This promise had however been shattered by the Second World War, when rationality also proved to be a very efficient means towards destructive ends. The dependence on reason derives directly from Enlightenment thought, but in the modern era lost the spiritual stability of religion that Kant and Descartes were still able to lay claim to. Without an external universal determinant of value, the ephemerality of modernity becomes troubling, if not downright traumatic. Self-realization taken to the extreme also means that any twists of 'fate' are our own fault. This is the Nietzschean conception of the individual that still plagues the 1960s. The alienation created by an environment of modernist architecture became not only visible but also a tangible part of everyday reality once it had been built. A pointed example here is the Parisian *banlieues*, which served as the disturbing décor for *Alphaville*, a 1965 film-noir science-fiction film by Jean-Luc Godard. He found precisely the dark, disorienting and unfamiliar setting he was looking for in the modernist building blocks on the edges of Paris. Once this built environment had left the domain of utopian plans and speculations and entered the world in built form, its shortcomings became more apparent. Rather than the promised land of efficiency and the perfectly rational city inhabitant, there was disillusionment with the disorientation arising from uniformity. The contrast between the model and the reality is one of the problems here. This follows on Jacobs' critique of 'how things ought to be'. Where Le Corbusier was designing how he felt the world ought to be, public housing projects such as Lefrak City in Queens were clashing with reality, and showing that the world was not yet (and may never be) ready to become as idealized as he thought. Use tended towards the familiar (parks, sidewalks), not the new forms of the completely modern environment.

Furthermore, the basic societal parameters of the modern city had also changed, rapidly becoming more amassed than ever before.[77] The massiveness already present at the dawn of the modern metropolis (Simmel) took another leap in scale in the 1960s. Here, the problems facing the 1960s might be construed as an exacerbated form of the modern condition. Mass had now been further compounded with plurality; alienation with the disappearance of traditional public space (in the CIAM city); loss of 'place' with the uniformity of architecture. Additionally, Alloway comments that mass culture is by its nature urban.[78] The place and importance of the city in the society of spectacle is testimony to this.

In a way, the 1960s were not as directly opposed to modernism as the statements of the time imply. Many of the critical strategies proposed in the 1960s are also already present in modernism – and even acknowledged as such. There is, for example, the situationists' comment that Frank Lloyd Wright was heading in the right direction but not yet radical enough. Broadacre had a diffuse structure and was based on individual freedom of action, similar to New Babylon as a network of active engagement.

The crucial role of the individual becomes apparent through the distinctions between the American and European treatment of the city. The work of Jane Jacobs and Henri Lefebvre demonstrates some shared underlying ideas and a general critique of modernism, such that these two theorists seem to be aiming at the same goal: a revaluation of the city as it stands, a renewed sense of place and importance for the individual living in that city, and a carefully weighed critique of what modernity has brought us and what modernism has perhaps also taken away. At the same time, a clear distinction can be made between the two that reflects the very different cultural backgrounds they operate within. Whereas Jacobs can be said to operate from a pragmatist position, following American thinkers such as William James and John Dewey, Lefebvre is firmly rooted in a Marxist tradition.

The pragmatic position (in theory) does not presume an ideal, or a greater good, outside of everyday reality. What it does presume is not dissimilar to Aristotle's notion of the median: the appropriate response within a given situation, taking into account the individual subject and his context. Marxism, on the other hand, presumes a certain attainable ideal society based on a redistribution of capital and above all removing the alienation inherent in the labour process in capitalist society. The workers are responsible for this revolution themselves, but there is still an important place for the intellectual in Marxist thought. In the Situationist International, the artist and the intellectual are seen as essential to instigating the revolution, but will no longer be necessary once life has become truly 'authentic' for everyone. Interestingly, the work of Jacobs is probably closer in spirit to Marx's idea of the revolutionary labourer, since she does not presume the necessity of an intellectual leader. On the other hand, there is a unique place reserved for the artist in the Marxist-based neo-avant-garde, since the artist has the power to break through the 'false consciousness' of the spectacle and 'see' beyond it to a better world long before the creative individual can. This is reminiscent of Le Corbusier's position for the architect-engineer, though it incorporates a shift from rational to personal expression.

The parallels between Jacobs and Lefebvre are indicative of some of the points of resonance in the transatlantic critique of modernism, such as this introduction of the everyday in its various forms. At the same time, their contrasts illustrate some of the cultural specificities within these responses. The American tendency towards liberal pragmatism results in an almost 'naturalized' acceptance of the world as it is, and the belief that, as such, one should explore the qualities of existing conditions. The European-bound versions of Marxist emancipation see this same condition of the ordinary and everyday as an instrument to overthrow an authoritarian government – demonstrating how saturated the Marxist critique is with a consciousness of a bourgeois ruling class.

What they do share is a fondness for the word 'actual' and various synonyms, which are favourites in the writings of the 1960s – as in the work of Jacobs, Lynch and also Lefebvre, taking stock of a reality that is less ideal than the future that Le Corbusier's Plan Voisin projects, is the indication of a critical stance. Where the modernists rebelled against the 'actual' reality they faced in the nineteenth-century city, this same condition now became the instrument of resistance. 'Reality' was the place critics were turning to find the vitality they found lacking in modernist developments.

Again, the words and images of the 1960s' projects point to specific shortcomings in the work of their predecessors. The continuous use of 'actual' and 'real' indicate that somehow the modernist city was not 'real' enough. Although the modernist city had attempted to project a future reality, by the time the Parisian *banlieues* were constructed and a large part of the European mainland was beginning to be filled with what Peter Smithson called 'filing cabinets', there was a disjunction between everyday reality, which was filled with tangible and specific architectural and visual form, and an environment determined by smoothly abstracted building blocks.

Although abstraction was a useful tool around the turn of the century to reduce the clutter of the Victorian city to manageable proportions, this resulted in a form of Platonic thinking in (potentially) perfected models, which often negated the good qualities of the existing fabric. This problem with a model *abstracted from* reality, then *projected onto* that same reality, is reiterated time and again, as is noted above in relation to the work of Jane Jacobs, in her distinction between 'ought to' and 'does'. In the 'Planning Today' article, Smithson comments: 'And by "society" I mean an actual group of people, rather than generalized "man".'[79] The process of abstraction (and deduction from a model) in itself is not the problem: Smithson, too, discusses the possible benefits of being able to 'deduce from its existing structure a possible further structure' as long as we keep in mind 'that any society is in constant change'. The problem with abstraction arises when it is held as a formal principle, rather than a strategy that understands its own contingency. In a society that is, as Smithson states, continually changing, taking an abstracted notion of that society to be ideal and permanent is in direct contradiction with its very premises. The understanding of modern life as changing or developing is thwarted by the retreat into abstract models. This problem is very much one of form, and is often handled as such by (re)introducing everyday symbolism (Venturi and Scott Brown, Lynch), or everyday visual material (the Independent Group). Yet here too, the role of abstraction or figuration is just touched upon.

In the end, modernism also negates its own premise of designing for a new era, which is half determined by ephemerality: by seeing its planning as a 'permanently valid form of architecture'.[80] In response to this sense of a form that is too restrictive and understood as universally valid, the notions of change and flexibility are incorporated in architectural form. There is a strange condition here, however: 'change' is often framed as a time-based condition, and linked to the idea of impermanence, yet often translated into a static form that remains little more than the representation of flexibility. Archigram perhaps takes this idea to its most logical conclusion, almost allowing architecture to disappear entirely in favour of 'space suits' or mobile capsule-like environments.

Here we should perhaps recall Lefebvre's critique of architects in general, that they somehow presume that their drawings represent the actual space, while these are necessarily abstractions, and can in no way seen to be universally valid for every time and culture.

As indicated, there was a huge leap in scale of the metropolis in the 1960s. This resulted in further disorientation, since first the traditional symbols of architecture had disappeared with CIAM. Yet also, as Holford notes, the 'efficient' modern city became surprisingly 'inefficient when the scale grew past the point where it was easily comprehensible'.[81] The massiveness of the modern metropolis was complex, yet the CIAM tenets seemed not to acknowledge that. Nor did they acknowledge that the complexity of the modern metropolis might require a different formal approach – incorporating signs and symbols to navigate its complexity. This is addressed quite early in the work of Lawrence Alloway, and later more radically in *Learning from Las Vegas*.

Furthermore, the city was conducive to, or perhaps even caused the rise of a mass culture. As Gans argues, it is the transition from a primarily rural peasantry to an urban one that initiates a mass culture to replace the earlier (rural) folk culture.[82] The problem of mass continually returns throughout the 1960s, and is most succinctly phrased as 'democracy face to face with hugeness'.[83] The inherent tension between the individual and the community becomes exacerbated when the 'community' becomes an anonymous mass population as in the late twentieth-century metropolis.

Yet this is also what allows the potential for individual agency and mass culture to become the instruments of reform. The overall critiques of the modernist city share a need for individuation in the face of an overwhelming 'machinery' of the functionalist city on the one hand, and the use of mass culture is seen as a potential tool in the general revaluation of the modernist city. This indicates two general issues that follow opposing directions. Individual agency moves further into a sense of specificity and the uniqueness of each person within the larger environment of the city. In contrast, mass culture becomes a new level of communication that brings a sense of cohesion, of being a part of society and understanding its symbols.

The Situationist International places the creative individual at the centre of its urban critique; the spaces of the modernist city are to be critiqued and transformed by means of interventions such as the *dérive*, organized around individual desire and interpretation. The situationists' acknowledgement of mass culture is coupled with a theory of creative, subversive intervention by the individual in the notion of *détournement*. In the UK, the Independent Group and Archigram wrote less on individual intervention as a creative tool, but saw freedom for the individual available in the new conditions of mass culture and consumerism. Their utilization of mass culture transcends the boundaries between modern architecture and the vernacular. Jane Jacobs similarly saw some freedom available in symbolic expression, although hers tended more towards a traditional view. Later, with the introduction of the vernacular American landscape by Venturi and Scott Brown, the qualities of mass culture as posed by the Independent Group will find more footholds in the American discourse. Jacobs' ideas on the city do offer a strong place for the idea of a collective, and her ideas are less radical than those of the Situationist International, but incorporate more of an examination of the social.

In the work of the 1960s, valuable questions are asked about the relationship between people and their environment, and which position architects might take. Yet the critiques circumscribe areas of 'incomplete revolution': they were both insightful in their questions and simplistic in their answers. By seeing to what extent the 'radical' critiques of the 1960s recapitulated and confirmed some of the modernist distinctions they struggled against, we might put them to better use today. This is why I refer to the 'incomplete' paradigm shifts of the 1960s. Although there was a clear understanding of the insufficiencies of modernist thought with respect to the complexity and vitality of the city, the way this was handled resembled very closely the emancipatory project of the moderns. The impossibility of universal solutions and definitions was acknowledged in the projects (text and image) of the 1960s by questioning modernist utopias. Yet they consequently reiterated the modernist position by proving incapable of truly incorporating the uncertainty of a postmodern plurality while still retaining a belief in the need for judgment.

Therefore, it is important to be aware of some of the dualities that were cast in place during the heyday of modernism and survived the radical critiques of the 1960s. By making the resemblance between strategies visible, we may find some possibilities rather than the impasse so often proclaimed these days ('the death of public space' for example).

The first and foremost duality in debates on the city is that between the desires of the individual and the needs of the collective. While Le Corbusier presumed that by defining the function of a mechanical collective the perfect individual would arise, the situationists hoped that unleashing the creativity of a romanticized individual would shape the collective into something expressing an ideal passion for human life. Either way, the understanding of a necessary tension between the two seems to have given way to a hope that by perfecting one or the other, there will be a final state of harmony. This is what I mean when defining this as an 'emancipatory project of the moderns' – the goal is still a transcendent state of perfection, rather than an understanding that there is a continuous state of development. Every moment of emancipation brings with it a transformation, therefore necessitating a renegotiation.

The continuous construction of social space in the city, which floats above the 'functional traffic' zone. Constant, New Babylon (1970)

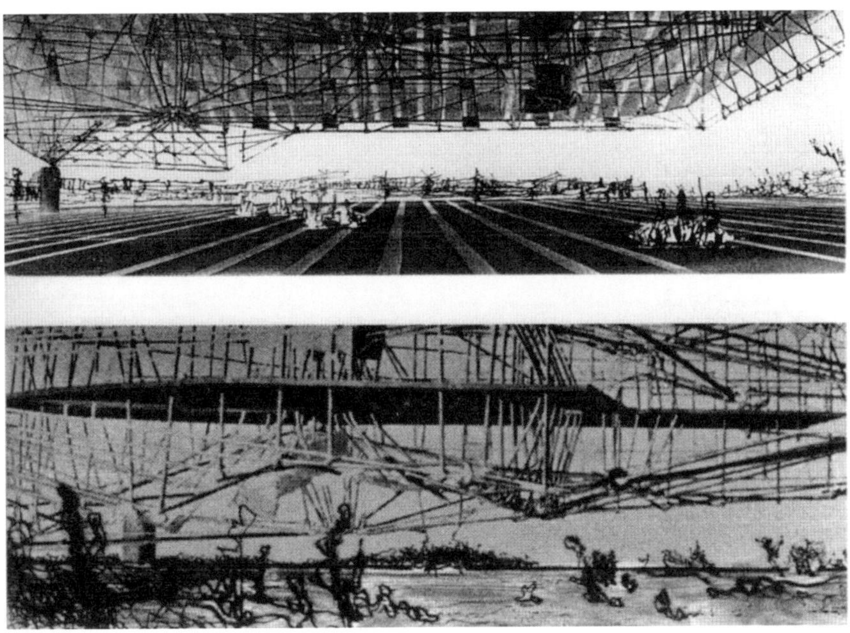

In that sense, understanding that the relationship between the individual and the collective will always be subject to negotiation is perhaps more productive than attempting to design a system that presumes the perfection of either. This leads to one of the most divisive problems in architecture: How much is to be designed? And to what extent can we presume an impact of architecture on behaviour? To Constant, New Babylon would somehow instigate people to play with their environment and transform it. To Le Corbusier, the Plan Voisin would encourage people to become the rational and efficient beings a modern society needed. Neither of these basic premises allows the conceptual room for a counter-use of their spaces. Even when a counter-use is envisioned, it is immediately given form as space for 'subversion'.[84] Each element was designed to a certain effect, and this effect was presumed to be attainable. For the situationists, unitary urbanism was not so much a utopia as a state yet to be achieved. To counterbalance this definitive understanding of the city environment, we might hope that presuming individual autonomy while projecting an ideal environment could bridge the gap. In other words, this means going back to the craft of design. Rather than creating a metaphorical future city (a mechanical city, a walking city, a living city), this would mean looking at the public spaces (the conjunction of individual and collective) and making them work on an architectural level rather than a metaphorical one. This entails functionality (the modern ideal), but also proportion (formal aspects of architecture) and visual information (aesthetics).

There is a problem inherent in Le Corbusier's conflation of 'good design' with 'good morals', and the problems it caused for 1960s' critiques. This original conflation was perhaps not even so much a conflation as the presumed universality of modernist morals and design.[85] The underlying promise of modernist utopias was that society would function perfectly and properly. The underlying message of 'ornament and crime' was that bad design showed a lack of moral fibre (rather than an imperfect eye). The 1960s began to see the shortcomings of these principles in terms of repression of 'otherness' or 'diversity'. Yet in placing so much emphasis on the meaning of form (sterile equals repressive; rectilinear equals oppressive; organic form equals freedom), the work of the 1960s produced the inverse problem: ethical architecture could only have one form, and aesthetic form must necessarily be unethical. The figurehead of Dutch post-war architecture, Aldo van Eyck, takes this problem of physical determinism to its logical conclusion: in his designs (such as the municipal orphanage in Amsterdam) he envisioned *everything* that should take place, including the 'subversive' activities (such as illicitly smoking a cigarette), and attempted to allot a spatial intervention for everything. This excessive attention to individual actions ultimately leads to its counterpart: a complete denial of individual agency.

In the end, it is necessary to recognize the specificity of architecture. Not as Kenneth Frampton's critical regionalism, which romanticizes the *genius loci*, but as a profession that addresses a single programme on a single site at a single point in time. Even if the programme is more universal (such as a basic concept for a generic design – say McDonald's), this is tied to a need of this time (globalization), and the critique of a space should address the success or failure of a design in those terms. Also, the symbolic value of architecture is different than that of art and visual culture, as well as its timeframe. In architecture, both the use of a space and its reception (supported by its symbolic expression) need to be incorporated – the strength of the critiques written by Jacobs and Lefebvre is in their discussions of specific and successful spaces. Yet there is also a fundamental need for what Vittorio Magnago Lampugnani calls 'tolerant normality'.[86] The spaces Lefebvre and Jacobs appeal to may be constructed out of individual elements, yet they do not scream out their individuality. It is precisely because they are part of a larger and relatively unobtrusive fabric that they do not call attention to themselves specifically but are rather present in the whole, that they work. The logical conclusion of the ideas of the Situationist International, though it seems in opposition, is precisely the constructed individuality of the Guggenheim Bilbao, or other projects that lay claim to a uniqueness that can be utilized as an iconic gesture.

Careful Reconsiderations

In general, the 1960s addressed a critical failing in the modernist city – in its purified design, it failed to make space for the extra-rational aspects of human life and association, while at the same time it left little room for the individual. The above excerpts and projects show a forthright concern with this, and break open the rigid structure of the discourse. Yet in turn, the work of the 1960s, too, failed to fully comprehend or address the *plurality* it was propagating in its words. Through the radicalization of these theories and their operation on the basis of models (of, for example, the creative worker suppressed by capitalism) they likewise failed to offer a 'real' space for the people they hoped to liberate, as their modernist fathers before them, only now from the mechanical city of the 1930s rather than the diseased city of the 1900s.

At the same time, with these critical notes in mind, it is clear that so many of these issues still resonate today, presumably because the rhetoric at the very least addressed questions now facing us, such as how to maintain individuality in an increasingly massive and technological world. Therefore, despite the failure of these radical critiques, the fundamental issues should remain under critical scrutiny. The best lesson we might learn from the above examples is to remember to accept the limitations of architecture; to understand that it is a field with so many variables that simply designing a space for an ideal occupant will not make that ideal human come to life. Furthermore, keeping both eyes open to the different facets of the discourse, from image to text and built form, is important. Architecture as a public image is not the same as architecture described towards a utopian society, nor is it the same as the building in the experience of the everyday user. All of these issues were raised in the manifestoes of the 1960s, yet seem to have been forgotten in the heat of revolution.

In part, this is about reception. How have we taken up the ideas of the situationists, and do we indeed need them to stage a city that is amenable to contemporary urbanism, and that also subverts the power structures that keep us mired in a system of labour and consumption? In fact, the Situationist International identified a number of considerations that are crucial to the contemporary city, not only in the 1960s, but today as well. The opposition of more individual and notably *Gemeinschaft*-oriented ideas such as identity and place against the universalist CIAM ideas is one of the key shifts. At the same time, the situationists' radical critique of the city set up an inescapable opposition between the creative individual and collective interests that prevents us from moving beyond the modernist oppositions they so fiercely battled. According to Lefebvre, the right to the city 'manifests itself as a superior form of rights: right to freedom, to individualization in swon, to habitat and to inhabit'.[87] We are still waiting for Lefebvre's individualization in socialization to take shape – let us hope that the spectacle can contribute rather than detract from it, if we learn to inhabit the contemporary city in a more considered and cohesive way.

III

Technology in Architecture: The Ghost in the Machine

Archigram: Re-Envisioning the Potential of Technology

The most radical expressions of a revised relation between architecture and technology came from Archigram, a group of recently graduated architecture students who worked together in London from 1961 to 1974. The group consisted of Warren Chalk (1927-1987), Peter Cook (b. 1936), Dennis Crompton (b. 1935), David Greene (b. 1937), Ron Herron (1930-1994) and Mike Webb (b. 1937). Their first pamphlet appeared in 1961, the last one in 1970. Not only did they completely rethink future technology and visualize its possible impact on architecture, they posed important questions to the strictly mechanical technology that had become such an important visual metaphor in modernist architecture. Archigram critiqued the modernists not for their attention to technology, but for how they utilized it. The failure in modernism to offer a truly comfortable environment was based on the presentation of a 'machine aesthetic', forcing the user to comply with the machine rather than rethinking the architectural environment through the potential of technology.

The proposals of Archigram circumscribe a spectrum of architectural transformations based on new technologies, revolving around themes such as architectural flexibility and the virtual environment. Yet the implicit understanding remains that technology is an instrument that can be utilized in a direct fashion. Its unexpected ramifications find little place in the new environments proposed by Archigram.

The connection between the rise of mass culture and an increasingly technological society is continually present within Archigram's visions of technology.[1] Basic premises of consumer culture such as obsolescence and freedom of choice were seen as relevant to a new understanding of technology in architecture.[2] The most famous comment on this comes from Peter Cook, who wrote: 'The pre-packaged frozen lunch is more important than Palladio. For one thing it is more basic. It is an expression of human requirement and the symbol of an efficient interpretation of that requirement that optimizes the available technology and economy.'[3] In contrast to the modernist use of the machine as a formal and symbolic metaphor for transcendent values such as efficiency and rationalization, the members of Archigram joined their contemporaries in examining what was already present and visible in the world. In their predilection for mass culture, they also demonstrate their indebtedness to the Independent Group, who preceded them in their affinity with commercial culture. It seems that the slight difference in timeframe

Architecture meets pop collage. Ron Herron, Holographic Scene Setter (1969)

somehow allowed Archigram a looser approach to technology, more saturated in the mass culture that the Independent Group was interested in. Although technology was important to many of the Independent Group writings on the contemporary environment, within the group, Reyner Banham (1922-1988) is primarily the one encouraging an explicit reconsideration of the role of technology in architecture. As an independent visual theme this pop-saturated version of technology truly came to the forefront in the work of Archigram in the early 1960s, and was promptly championed by Banham.

The young architects of the Archigram group are the obvious choice on which to centre this question of a revised relationship between architecture and technology. Not only did they display a boyish enthusiasm for technological innovations, but their choice of platform to distribute their work was also dependent on technology.[4] From 1961 to 1974 they published their work in small pamphlets, their name deriving from *archi*tecture tele*gram*. These pamphlets, selling about 300 copies of the first issue and reaching a sale of 5000 by their ninth and final issue in 1970, contained the final student projects of a number of their members, small manifestoes in the same style as the *Internationale Situationniste* or *L'Esprit Nouveau* before them, and various collaged images intended to provoke reactions or express questions related to a postmodernist (in the literal sense of 'after modernist') architecture.

The platform of the 'little magazine' allowed for a flexible positioning in the architecture debate; before needing to execute its ideas, Archigram was able to build up a solid repertoire of designs and provocative essays, creating an oeuvre of unbuilt work that was nevertheless influential. Furthermore, Archigram was deeply embedded in the London scene coming out of the Architectural Association, and exposed to the work of the Independent Group and the lectures of Reyner Banham. The importance of Banham to this small circle can hardly be underestimated, and his interest in American design was influential. As discussed in the previous chapter, the Independent Group was already incorporating the imagery of a popular culture in order to question the purity of a modernist aesthetic.

Archigram in its own fashion was doing something similar in undermining the purity of engineering aesthetics as Le Corbusier had presented them, and turning towards the expressions of technology as they were found in science-fiction movies, comics and other mass-cultural expressions of technology and its relationship to society. Furthermore, Le Corbusier had proposed that an aesthetic based on technological, functional and rational requirements would embody the perfection of a rational humanity; he also deemed it necessary to create architecture as the perfect environment – the house as a 'machine for living in'.[5] Archigram was more intent on examining other conditions technology made possible, such as planned obsolescence and disposability, as well as nomadic forms of dwelling. Moreover, Le Corbusier's maxim of the machine for living in may have been taken to an extreme: Mike Webb's Cushicle certainly served no purpose beyond providing shelter for the nomad. Living became not the Corbusian experience of a rationalized life, but rather the freedom to be wherever one wanted to be.

As with other groundbreaking architects of the 1960s, the members of Archigram maintained a strained relationship with modernism. On the one hand they raised critical issues that would appear to shatter the foundations of modernism. Projects such as Webb's Suitaloon destroyed the notion of an architectural space by transforming the stable space of the home into a flexible piece of clothing. Issue 5 of *Archigram*, 'Metropolis', was primarily interested in completely re-envisioning the ideal city on the basis of flexibility, freedom and choice, with little regard for ideal forms. This makes it possible for Isozaki to see the work of

From architectural space to nomadic space suit: a home on the go. Mike Webb, The Suitaloon (1968)

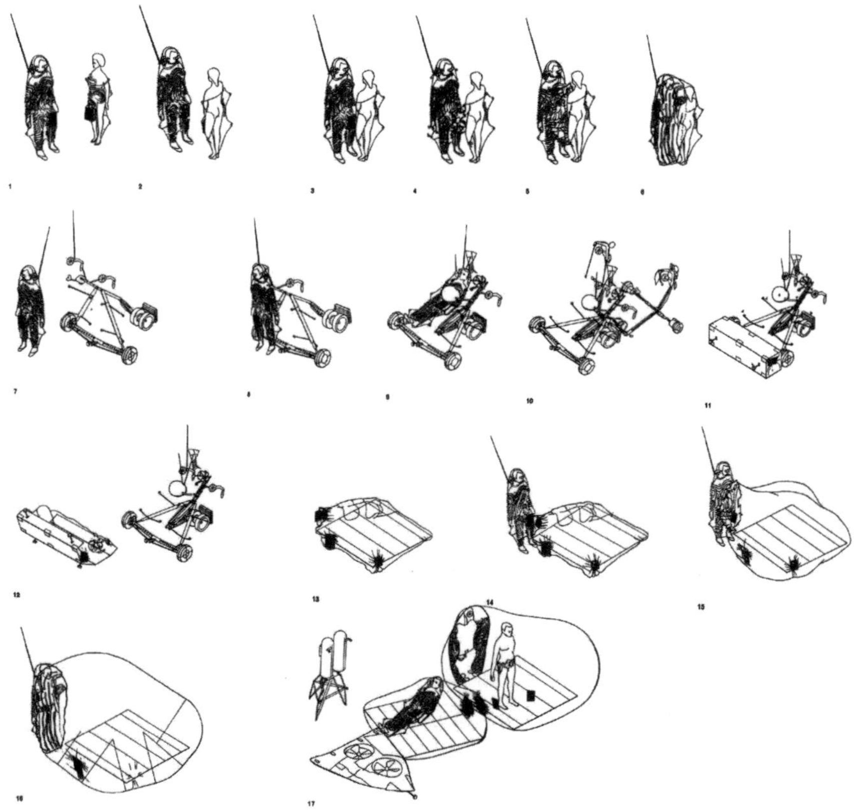

Archigram as truly dismantling modern architecture.[6] Yet to what degree the group actually set out to *dismantle* modern architecture remains a question; in many ways, they were simply revising (and revisualizing) some traditional modern beliefs; updating a modern architecture they still believed in. In fact, a piece of text by David Greene in the first issue of *Archigram* expresses this position of ambiguity: 'A new generation of architecture must arise with forms and spaces which seems to reject the precepts of "Modern" yet in fact retains these precepts. WE HAVE CHOSEN TO BYPASS THE DECAYING BAUHAUS IMAGE WHICH IS AN INSULT TO FUNCTIONALISM.'[7] The first piece (about rejecting 'modern') is reiterated on the main page of the broadsheet, giving it additional emphasis, and is interspersed with comments such as 'a rich, vital, organic whole' and 'flow', all arranged in a free-flowing collage of student projects and spiralling commentary.

This also demonstrates the distinction between the premises of modernism and functionalism they did believe in as evidenced by their tendency towards a technocratic scientific ideal, and the reception and manifestation of those same ideals by the late 1950s, which was the target of their critique. In other words, Archigram can be more accurately positioned in between affirmation and negation: it questioned and re-examined modernism by raising questions crucial to the

Updating the beliefs of modern architecture into a 'rich, vital, organic whole'. Collage, *Archigram* 1 (1961)

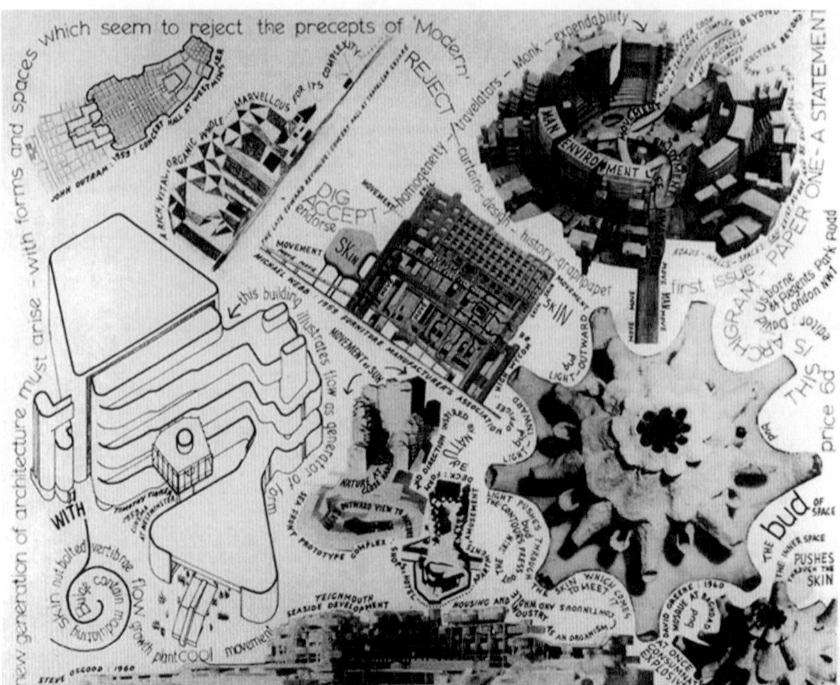

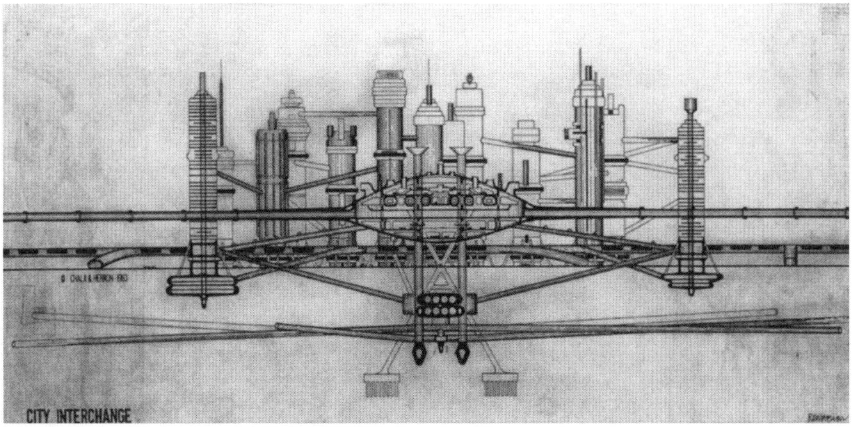

Expressionist technology. Ron Herron and Warren Chalk, City Interchange (1963)

experience of modernity which remain unresolved, such as issues of standardization and mass society. Yet it simultaneously reaffirmed the utopian ideals of modernism in other ways, remaining certain that someday in the future there would be more leisure time and much pleasure to be had due primarily to the wonders of modern technology. Especially this last belief is visible not only in the modernists, but also in the situationist notion that unlocking everyman's creativity was the way forward. As noted earlier in relation to the city, modernity itself encompasses certain conditions that may be seen as premises for 'being modern', and technology, like the urban condition, is one of these formative premises.

Archigram thus offered possibilities of resistance to high modernism and saw opportunities in contemporary design. In the work of its members, this became manifest through their exploration of many aspects of technological developments: the technology in and of the city, obsolescence, networks and computerized environments. Their technology was instrumental (much as it was in New Babylon), enabling people to control and transform their environment or live in the environment of their choice. At the same time it was also thematic: they took the possibilities of technology to extremes. A project such as the 1963 Interchange by Ron Herron and Warren Chalk took the technological potential of new forms of mobility and designed a complex interchange between monorails and self-guided transport systems. The Instant City offered a technology-supported travelling metropolis, which would temporarily offer all the amenities and the excitement of urban life to out-of-the-way sleepy villages. The Cushicle (Webb, 1966-1967) was the ultimate high-tech backpack, providing the future nomad with food and shelter. In this way, both Archigram's enormous collective city projections like the Plug-In City, the Walking City (Herron, 1964) and the Instant City (Crompton, 1968), and the extremely individual projects like the Suitaloon (Webb, 1968) and the Living Pod (Greene, 1965), offered a radical utilization of technology in order to reconfigure the perception and experience of architectural space.

Bringing the metropolitan experience to everyone: Instant City (1969)

Furthermore, to Archigram technology was not an image or a static example of human development. Rather, it had the potential to facilitate growth and change. Instead of opposing technology to an organic and developing human society, Archigram saw notions such as growth and change as also built into the technology itself. This forms the premise for the Plug-In City.[8] Keywords used throughout the debates in the 1960s such as continuity, connection and change are here not only applied to human society in opposition to machinery, but also to future technological developments.

The crux of this approach is that it takes a broader view of technology, not as something static to fulfil a certain function, but as an integral part of human society, destined to be transformed in equal measure. In this belief, Archigram perhaps moved beyond the modernist approach to technology. However, at the same time, an unwavering faith in the ability of technology to overcome all obstacles is reminiscent of an earlier confidence in the liberating potential of the machine.

Technological Advances in Architecture: Driving Modernism Forward

Although the issue of technology in architecture as a critical driving force is not new, it finds a new impetus with the advent of modernism. As the moderns seize upon the radical progression of modern technology in the form of Le Corbusier's love for the steam engine and ocean liners, and Ludwig Mies van der Rohe's belief in the potential of prefabrication and the possibilities of steel-and-glass, they seem to give architectural presence to Heidegger's notion that modern technology has transformed our relation with the world. In Heidegger's argument, earlier forms of science and technology remained within a traditional relation between man and nature. The *techné* involved may solve a problem, but it still demanded that the creator understand and adapt to laws of nature. With the advent of industrial technology, we were no longer beings living with nature, but we achieved the possibility to *demand* of nature what we desired. Therefore, our understanding of the environment was no longer that of our 'grounding' in the world, but rather of an object to be 'harvested' at will. In other words, since the advent of modern physics, we have been able to force nature to give us what we once accepted as gifts.[9] This understanding of modern technology underlies many of the questions rising in the 1960s, and has even now not yet found its equilibrium. In the 1960s, the forcefulness of modern technology was questioned, yet its transformative potential was still an important part of the discourse. Two primary texts played an important role within this aspect of the architecture discourse: Marshall McLuhan's *Understanding Media* (1964), which found a cult-following among many technophiles, and Banham's *Theory and Design in the First Machine Age* (1960), which questioned the accepted perception of the role of technology in modernist architecture.[10]

In part it is the element of force or determinism that underwrites many of the modernist tracts on the relation between technology and architecture. The Enlightenment belief in liberation through rationality underlies the belief in salvation through technology. Once again, this is an aspect of modernism that was under attack in the 1960s. The claims and complaints will sound all too familiar: technology dehumanizes; it takes away freedom of choice; it is not made to suit human form; it is cold, abstract, unfeeling, unthinking. The imagery that accompanies technology expresses precisely these perceptions, and new representations were also instrumental in attempting to find a new role for technology in architecture.

The issues revolving around the relationship of technology and architecture involve a number of different questions, such as control and dominance (man's control over nature, followed by technology's dominance over man).[11] The question of control contains within it the question of choice: freedom of choice was seen as one of the ultimate triumphs of the 1960s, but when that choice is limited at the outset by parameters of, for example, consumerism and maximum profit, the choice is merely a pseudo-freedom.[12] One of the typical arguments utilized in pro-technological manifestoes since modernism is the promise of leisure. Each machine introduced in the household or workplace promised less labour and more free time. Household devices in the 1950s were continually praised for the relief from drudgery they would offer the housewife. To some degree this is of course true: a washing machine allows a significantly shorter time to be spent washing clothes. However, the introduction of such appliances also changed household habits, and work often shifted elsewhere rather than disappearing entirely.[13] In other words, the leisure time was usurped as much as it had been created. Another question revolves around the presence of the body and the distinction between the mechanical and the organic body. As will be seen in the work of Archigram and

Technology formed a visual and functional reference for modernism: industrial structures, motorized traffic in city. Dziga Vertov, *Man with a Movie Camera* (1927)

the science-fiction imagery of the 1960s, the issue of embodiment becomes more and more powerful, especially in its resistance to full technologization – the body then becomes the locus of human 'authenticity'. This question of embodiment has become even more critical in the age of cybernetics, where disembodiment is an important mode of being and the boundaries between the human body and the technological body are increasingly indistinct.[14]

Technology thus becomes more than the physical presence of the machine in modernism – it extends to the invisible networks of electric circuitry and similar intangible elements of technological progress. In this sense, the distinction between the 'machine' and 'technology' begins to reconfigure the discourse. The modern age was seen as the age when 'mechanization takes command' and the machine became both the emblem of the new technology as well as its defining character. In the 1960s a distinction was increasingly made between the machine and mechanization on the one hand and technology in general on the other. Technology as a whole was not necessarily perceived as a failure, but the mechanization at the root of the architecture discourse was.

In the earlier fascination with mechanization 'taking command', technology was handled in the modernist manifestoes as both instrument and expression of order, rationality and efficiency.[15] In this context, imagining a 'playful' technology as Archigram did: not purely oriented towards efficiency and not entirely rational, seemed to open up new possibilities. Analogous to the situationist notion of the *dérive*, an intentionally different use of technology was explored to help undermine the pure functionality of the machine as posed by Le Corbusier. The work of Archigram in particular can be seen as exemplary for this development. Its members did not contest the importance of technology for contemporary life and for architecture, but they did contest the manner in which it was employed by the modernists, again (as the inevitable target of high modernism) exemplified by Le Corbusier's discussions of the machine.[16] Their proposals for visually 'organic' machines such as the Walking City helped reconfigure the typical understanding of what a machine should both look like and do.

Developing a Technological Sensibility: Forms and Strategies Suggested by Technology

As with the recalibration of ideas in other areas of the architecture discourse, certain keywords surface time and again throughout the 1960s, resonating throughout the critiques. Specific shifts can be discerned that revolve around a number of similar themes, such as an increased attention for the organic instead of the mechanical. This can be seen in an increase in references to biology and the environment as a whole, but also in the attention for human qualities *besides* rationality, focusing on, for example, the needs and desires of the human body rather than the intellect. Technology is often adjusted towards a 'natural' appearance rather than encouraging people to become more machine-like (more efficient and more rational, for example). Another recurring issue involves freedom of choice, which is often expressed through distinctly identifiable individual elements in contrast with modern standardization. Not only does this respond to the idea of industrial standardization, it also opens up a new shift, from an economics of production (focused on efficiency) to an economics of consumption (focused on the market). The issue of proliferating media technologies and their impact on architecture resurface not only in projects, but in the very media they are published in: this is truly the era of 'little magazines'.[17] The realm of the virtual is present not only in the early beginnings of the computer age, but also in this endless self-reflection in the media, an early hint at the simulacra that Baudrillard will later explore so thoroughly.

Many of these shifts seem to support the idea of a 'technological sensibility' as put forward by Banham. In his doctoral dissertation, which resulted in the book *Theory and Design in the First Machine Age*, he offers a critical contribution to a revision of modernist propaganda, especially in their relationship to the machine.[18] The book explicitly addresses the role of technology and the machine in architecture. He suggests that modernism employed technology in a way appropriate to an early form of technological society (what he calls the 'first machine age'), and that the work of the 1960s indicates the advent of a 'second machine age', which heralds the era of a 'technological sensibility' that offers a deeper understanding and incorporation of technology than the machine metaphor of modernism. Also, Banham makes a distinction between the rhetoric and the production of modernism, as does Alan Colquhoun in a slightly later essay on the 'Symbolic and Literal

Aspects of Technology'.[19] The machine is revaluated in terms of its functions, its presence in the discourse as a metaphor, and its visual manifestations in architectural design.

Banham and Colquhoun are quite similar in their critiques of the modernist attitude to technology, and thereby indicate at least part of what caused such diverse yet similar reactions in the 1960s.[20] Two main points come forward in their work: first, that the reception (and writing) of modernism falsely denies the symbolic function of machinery in modernist designs. Second, they both in their own way note that the so-called progressive technology espoused by the moderns was simply not so progressive.

A progressive understanding of technology was especially strong during the modern era. Technology was one of the driving forces behind modernism: the potential of the modern machine appeared limitless, and it was believed best to utilize it to the fullest. Yet at the same time, as Banham points out, the architecture of the time was still oriented towards a traditional conception of space:

> Cooking facilities went into the room that would have been called 'kitchen' even without a gas oven, washing machine into a room still conceived as a 'laundry' in the old sense, gramophone into the 'music room', vacuum cleaner to the 'broom cupboard' and so forth.

In the same paragraph, he contrasts this with Buckminster Fuller's highly technological home, which brings all the mechanical services 'together in the central core of the house, whence it distributes service – heat, light, music, cleanliness, nourishment, ventilation, to the surrounding living-space'.[21] Apparently, the rhetoric of technological progress is not as simple as it is generally applied, and as McLuhan argues, the form of technology is equally important.

The relationship between architecture and modern technology is more complex than it appears. In the simplest of terms, many of the modern masters (Le Corbusier and Gropius as perhaps the most vocal of them) firmly believed that technological progress was not only inevitable, but also desirable, since it could bring a utopian society within reach. The flaws of the industrial society were easily overlooked in favour of the powerful imagery of machine technology (silos, steamships, automobiles, factories). This fetishization of technological artefacts offered an image of progress (the machine), a representation of the all-powerful rationality of man (in his engineering capabilities), and a means to a better society (since technological progress will solve problems of everyday living). Le Corbusier in a piece on town planning writes of the 'lofty satisfaction of mathematics'.[22] CIAM also retains the belief that technology is the means to better city planning:

> To fulfill this great task it is essential to utilize the resources of modern technology ... The machine age has introduced new techniques which are one of the causes of the disorder and confusion of cities. Nevertheless it is from them that we must demand the solution of the problem.[23]

And although the importance of distinguishing technological achievement from architecture is noted by Mies van der Rohe, he does proclaim his belief that when 'technology reaches its real fulfillment, it transcends into architecture'.[24]

The machine as a means to a utopian end was present in modern manifestoes ranging from CIAM to De Stijl, especially because of the perceived correlation between the idea of the machine on the one hand and a scientific and objective foundation to design on the other. The expressive qualities of the machine were especially manifest in Le Corbusier's *Vers Une Architecture*, where the clean lines of the machine were seen to represent (or embody) the ultimately rational character of man.[25] Similar to his diatribes against the clutter of the city, on the scale of the object and the idea of modernity, Le Corbusier turned to the wonders of engineering to express his ideals of enlightenment of the common man. In Le Corbusier's utopia, to be achieved by means of technological developments in architecture, people would function in the same manner as the parts of these machines: each piece would have its place and by functioning in the most efficient way possible, the whole of society would embody the mechanical perfection he saw in steamships.

It is important to keep in mind here that technology assumed an ambiguous position in modernist manifestoes. First and foremost, it stood for this idea of objectivity and rationality (and thus a Platonic ideal). In part as a result of this fixation on objectivity, the discussion of 'beauty' as an end or a sensibility in itself, as a classical order and harmony that was dependent on the individual qualities of the artist, was largely 'outlawed' in modernist tracts. Yet at the same time, technology was also used in a symbolic manner to express the power, speed and excitement of modernity. Although hidden behind the rhetoric of objectivity, the concept of beauty was continually utilized in the argumentation on machinic perfection. Moreover, the tension between technology and architecture was continually present in modernist manifestoes. Yet the radical development of the discourse towards a full-blown mechanization of life, rather than a complex whole of interrelated developments, essentially prefigured the resistance that was to arise in the 1960s.

The basic premise of the Enlightenment revolves around the ideas of human rationality and technological capability. Both of these qualities distinguished man from the other creatures he shared the world with. Descartes' *cogito ergo sum* defined man's very existence as founded on and defined by rational thought. At the same time, the advances being made in physics, chemistry and all the related natural sciences brought the confidence that given enough rational thought, all the secrets of nature would finally be unlocked. In the advent of the industrial age, when our technology was beginning to transform the face of the earth, and also to *replace* certain natural modes (notably in travel, but also in mining and manufacturing, for example), the joint concepts of rationality and technological progress encouraged the confidence that at some point in the future the world itself could be perfected.

In the dominant modes of modernism, this confidence shifted its locus from the expression of an Enlightenment belief through rationality and technology to being essentially situated in the machine itself. Through this displacement of emphasis, the machine became not only the instrument by which human rationality was expressed to its fullest, but also the very representation of that rationality: the image of the machine achieved equal importance to its functions.

Throughout various explorations of the role of technology, from the 'first' and 'second' machine ages of Banham, to the 'literal' and 'symbolic' technologies of Colquhoun, to the distinction between 'mechanization' and 'technology' of Marshall McLuhan, there is a shared conviction that the relationship with technology has changed around the 1960s, and that it is now necessary to reconsider the conventional understanding of technology and its impact on architecture and society. Each one of these thinkers also acknowledges that the *image* of technology is as pertinent to this discussion as its typical *usage*.

This becomes evident in the distinction that Banham makes between a machine aesthetic, or an engineering sensibility, which he attributes to the moderns, and a technological sensibility, which is what he believes is beginning to manifest itself in his own time.[26] The distinction is largely founded on representation: the machine aesthetic, in his view, is an abstraction of the idea of a machine into imagery that is smooth, abstracted, devoid of ornament. These qualities are seen to represent an idea about engineering and the machine, rather than the actual machine. Hence his emphasis on the technological sensibility: to Banham, a true technological sensibility will incorporate technology rather than represent it formally. He sees it as an attitude rather than a style of design.[27] His argument reframes the modernist position on technology as an issue of form, of 'style' over 'substance', as evidenced by projects that were crucial to the development of modernism but repressed in the publications surrounding it. For example, Banham points to the expressionism of Mendelsohn and the futurists as critical to modernist architecture yet denied a proper place in its written history.[28] According to Banham, technological progress in architecture was only incorporated when it suited the style of mainstream modernism.

The work of Banham in particular explores two primary issues here: the relationship between architecture and pop, and that between architecture and technology.[29] The two tendencies follow their own trajectory at times, but are united in the work of Archigram. The imagery is all the more powerful through its references to (popular) science fiction, while the attention to technological detail represents a break with the manner of addressing technology in modernism. An earlier instance of this junction is also latent in the meetings at the London Institute for Contemporary Arts in the 1950s, which Banham was deeply involved in.[30] The 1956 exhibition 'This Is Tomorrow' in the Whitechapel Gallery in London supported Banham's conviction on the importance of pop: the use of pulp imagery was to him a step forward in the democratization of culture, as it took architecture out of the ossified discussion between high and low, culture and the masses.[31] The intersection between mass culture and technology underlies the exhibition, since the references used would not have been possible without technological developments such as the moving picture. The exhibition can be seen as a moment in the continuum between the arguments of Walter Benjamin in 1936 and those of Marshall McLuhan in 1964, both of which are founded on the effects of technological progress on the object itself.[32]

Banham has much to teach us in his meticulous examinations of architects such as Mendelsohn; it is precisely the specificity of his work that makes it so important, yet his prejudices are also legible in this specificity.[33] As already noted, however, the relationship between technology and architecture is fundamental to the discipline, and can be seen to encounter a turning point in the 1960s in two fundamental ways. First, there is a shift away from the progressivist ideal of the machine being purely instrumental and offering nothing but good, since it is up to society to utilize it as such. Second, there is a shift in the very nature of technology, from the industrial machine, which is a tangible object and has a direct impact on the physical environment, to cybernetic technology, which is both networked and invisible, thus making its impact on our environment far more difficult to trace yet potentially much more powerful.[34] At the same time, the transformation is both fundamental and only partial: while Banham offers a revision of some of the myths of modernism, his passionate love for technology also exemplified the modern myth of technology. He intimated that not the relationship with technology was to be revised, but rather the objects of technology themselves: the moderns were simply not modern enough.

In sum, the reconsiderations of the position of technology in architecture again responded to modernism: its fetishization of the machine and faith in the transformative potential of technology produced an architectural climate that was too easily simplified into the technophilia of progressive architecture or technophobia of traditional, conventional architecture.[35] In the resistance to a modernist treatment of technology, both form and use of the machine were reconsidered. Some of the potential of this revolutionary stance remained unfulfilled thanks to its continuing dependence on future technology as saviour. However, by actively questioning the relationship between architecture and the technology of the society it builds for, the 1960s opened up the possibility that a mechanical society might not offer the pure perfection of the machinery Le Corbusier admired.

An Environment Defined by Technology: Cities That Plug In, Fold Out and Walk

The Plug-In City project of 1964 by Peter Cook is one of the most well-known projects of Archigram, presenting a radical transformation of the city into a new, highly technological environment.[36] It contains a critique of city proposals such as the Ville Radieuse by Le Corbusier, where each individual is completely subsumed by his insertion into the greater (mechanical) whole of high-rise with grand vistas. Instead of a systematic grid of equalized dwellings, there is a complex and systematized infrastructure that allows highly individual dwelling pods to plug into the larger system – the communal structure and the connections are standardized, yet

Visualizing a flexible and additive structure. Peter Cook, Plug-In City (1964)

Basic infrastructure with interchangeable infill, section. Peter Cook, Plug-In City (1964)

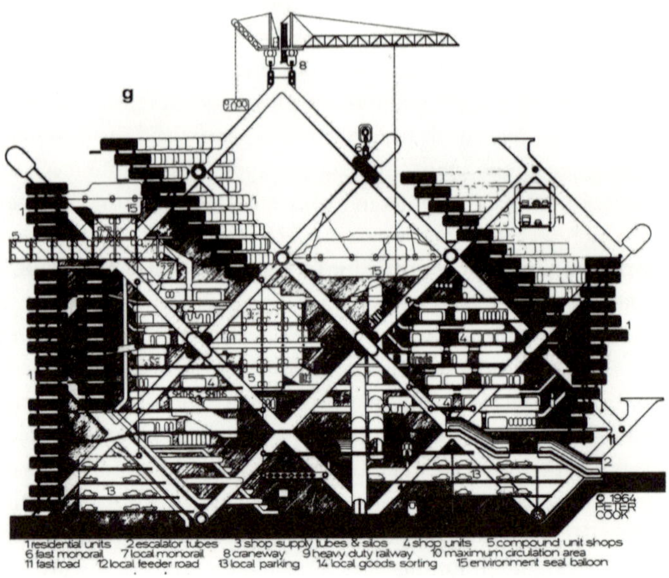

each dwelling is potentially completely different.[37] Literally, the inhabitants may 'plug in' their dwellings wherever they so desire. While the basic infrastructure is given, the rest of the city is formed and reconfigured over time. This use of infrastructure parallels the Corbusian ideal of a radiant city, where the technological infrastructure is instrumental to an ideal type of dwelling; yet it is distinct in both the flexibility of its infill, and the visual language used to express it. Gone is the language of a pure and transcendental architecture that solidly offers its occupants space, light and air. Rather, in the Plug-In City we are confronted with an architecture that is much closer to an industrial design object, offering its owner a sense of flexibility, mobility and expressive identity.

This immediately begs the question of what happens to the work of the architect: it has now been transformed (or reduced?) to the design of an (urban) infrastructure, and its infill (as an industrial design product). The notion of spatiality as an architectural intervention, as Alison and Peter Smithson propose, has thus been reduced to a simple question of efficiency: how much space does one need?[38] This is in direct contradiction to the arguments Cook makes in his own mini-manifesto *Architecture: Action and Plan*, in which he discusses the important distinction between technology and architecture, as well as the influence of technology on architecture.[39] He also notes the use of the machine as an *image* as critical to modernist work.[40] His analysis here is not as sophisticated as that of Banham or Colquhoun, yet he clearly sees and tackles part of the problem in using mechanistic imagery as a substitute for technological developments.

The questions addressed in the Plug-In City also find a resonance with their contemporaries. In the 'Metropolis' issue of *Archigram*, issue 5, the discussion of the Plug-In City is embedded in an evaluation of metropolitan projects such as those of the metabolists, Constant's New Babylon and Yona Friedman's Spatial City. These projects discuss and incorporate keywords typical of the 1960s' discourse such as growth and change, clusters, networks, connectivity, continuity and environment. The transcendental overtones of a universal machine-oriented metaphor of modernism have again made way for the importance of more human-oriented ideas of convention, change and growth. Whereas all these projects employ new technologies (or potential technologies) in order to facilitate new environments, Archigram is the most explicit in utilizing and questioning the role of technology itself in architecture. For Archigram, the Plug-In City demonstrates a technology that is used to facilitate the creation of a total environment (much as Constant hoped his New Babylon would), rather than the Corbusian notion that emulating technology would lead to a perfect environment. In other words, in response to the rationality and mechanization of the functional city, a new *form* of technology was envisioned which would initiate and encourage the development of a living, breathing 'total environment'.[41] This is the fundamental premise of the Plug-In City, which it shares with other projects by the Archigram architects as well as the work of their contemporaries: rather than holding up an image of the machine (as used by Le Corbusier in his *Vers une architecture*), they explore how technologies can enable a more human environment.

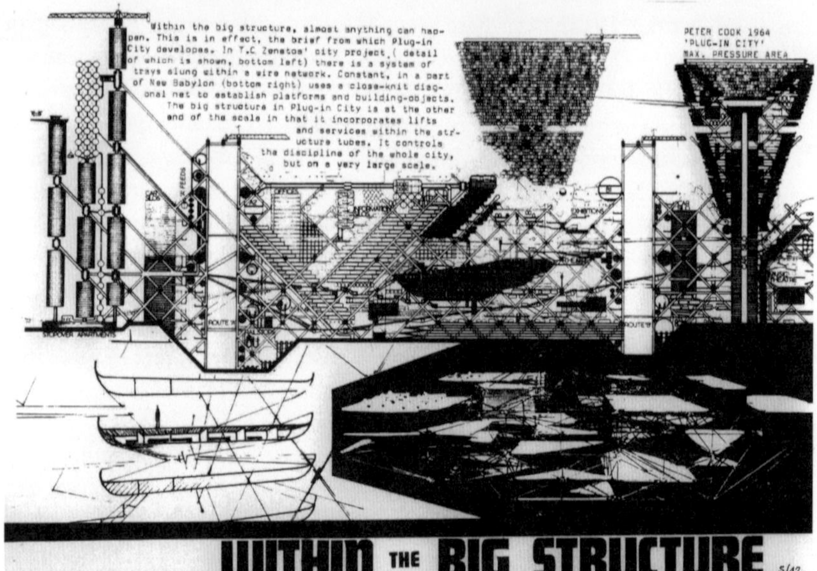

Pages from *Archigram* 5, Metropolis and Molehill: Plug-In City, Spatial City, New Babylon, Erskine, Sauvage

The idea of the 'total environment' returns in various projects of the time, including the Spatial City of Friedman, but notably in Constant's New Babylon. Begun a little earlier, in 1956, it is also presented in *Archigram* 5. Both the Plug-In City and New Babylon are designed as an infrastructure with flexible infill. However, as noted in the accompanying text, the infrastructure of New Babylon is little more than a load-bearing system of columns and beams.[42] Based on the principles of unitary urbanism, it is meant to be transformed by its inhabitants. As little as possible was meant to be defined by the architect. In the case of the Plug-In City, the infrastructure fulfilled a dual function of load-bearing system and, for example, sewage and transport (elevators). Although it maintains the same distinction between infrastructure and infill, the architecture of the infrastructure itself becomes more defined and more loaded with technology in the Plug-In City, whereas the infill becomes more flexible. Both projects believed that a future technology would be somehow enabling towards a more beneficial and total experience of the city environment. But for Constant, this technology was to be employed almost as a phantom: it was meant to make the human environment possible, not to make the technology somehow 'visible'. Peter Cook instead utilized the actual space of technological implements such as wiring and plumbing to further define the basic structure of the space, and to rid the infill of autonomous technology. In both however, as in the work of the Smithsons on the Cluster City and Golden Lane Housing, the city was in the end understood as a conglomerate form, as something that could grow, change and develop.[43] This basic notion was a response to the pure rationality and functionality of the modernist city – the 'balanced brief' of the functional city was placed against a notion of the 'total environment'.[44]

National network of plug-in cities, sections including time span of probable obsolescence. Peter Cook, Dennis Crompton, Plug-In City (1964)

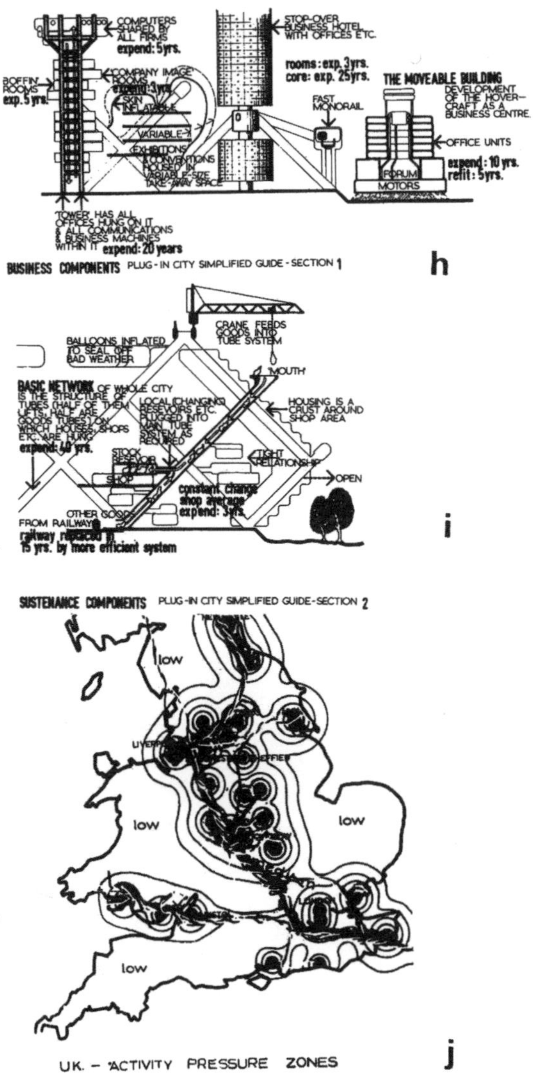

As a 'total environment', New Babylon perhaps shares more with the Walking City. Although its structure follows the scheme of the Plug-In City, its commitment to the artificial environment (extending even to the interior being cut off from the natural cycle of daylight) echoes the overwhelming sense of hermetic self-sufficiency present in Ron Herron's Walking City of 1964. All three projects evoke a sense of technology itself becoming architecture. As is pointed out by Peter Blake, this is not so strange in a time when the structures on Cape Kennedy were outgrowing most buildings:

> I took off for Cape Kennedy (and I've gone there several times since) and saw that 'walking buildings' easily the size of Seagram were, in fact, a reality; that plug-in capsules containing highly sophisticated workshops, and unpluggable at any time, were, in fact, a daily reality in the huge gantries that service the Saturn rockets; that megastructures with floors that slide up and down and sideways were not something that Harvard students did when they wanted to cop out, but were, in fact, a stunning reality in the largest building on earth – the Vehicle Assembly Building, a structure so vast that it could have something like eight Seagrams wheeled into it, and plug those Seagrams into capsules and mobile floors and all the rest.[45]

Blake also notes the analogy to the earlier visions of a new architecture in Le Corbusier's *Vers une Architecture*, which had argued that the steamship already by far surpassed the apartment building in size. The progressive steps from steamships to oil rigs and rocket-launch structures, to the megastructure of the Walking City are thus smaller than they would appear when considering these projects purely on their own, or in relation to the programmatic manifestoes of CIAM. And yet these steps are not only based on technological advances in themselves: serious issues concerning the built environment were taken into consideration, but approached from an interest in developments outside the traditional realm of architecture. The Walking City, though inspired by the very real engineering structures of Cape Kennedy, addressed the question of global shifts in labour supply and

Travelling without leaving home: entire cities that walk. Ron Herron, The Walking City (1964)

Temporary and transformative technologies. Ron Herron, Tuned Suburb (1968)

demand, and the expanding and shrinking needs of housing in the city. It was proposed as a self-sufficient living environment for the labour force that could simply travel where there was work to do.

A further step in the expansion of the technological urban environment is to be seen in the Instant City project of 1969. Evoking the interconnected elements of the Plug-In City while also incorporating the mobility of the Walking City, this project consists of a series of fold-out units comprising a 'travelling metropolis', in order to temporarily offer the urban experience to sleepy little villages. The project is dependent on primarily ephemeral technology (in the form of screens and projections) although it also colonizes a space in or alongside the town 'giving it a taste of the metropolitan dynamic – which is temporarily grafted on to the local centre'.[46] This space is filled with temporary structures, 'trailered units, pneumatic and lightweight structures and entertainments facilities, exhibitions, gantries and electric lights'.[47] After the Instant City leaves, a connection is maintained as part of a 'national hook-up' that will eventually grow into a network of communication and metropolitan events. In the five years that have passed since the development of the Plug-In City and the Walking City, the architecture has begun to give way to temporary interventions and an environment that is substantially transformed by being positioned less as a 'city' and more as a 'node' in a larger network. The physical environment is still present, albeit in the form of temporary structures, but the technological potential to create temporary cities is now beginning to define (sub) urban spaces more in relation to their surroundings and by their connection with others. This attention for the network over the city as an object in itself recalls another trajectory of earlier projects by Archigram: a series of self-contained individual environments in the form of capsules, which temporarily colonize space, leaving behind little trace of architectural permanence.

From Capsule to Cushicle: The Steady Dissipation of Architecture

The dissipation of architecture begins with the capsule, as early as the Capsule Tower by Warren Chalk (1964). The retrospective text on the Capsule Tower describes the distinct nature of the capsule: 'Conceptually the "capsule" serves to describe an approach to housing by presenting a series of very sophisticated and highly designed elements locked together within a "box" which is itself highly tailored. It is an industrial design approach.'[48] It introduces a more fleeting treatment of the life within the home: oriented towards lifestyle rather than treating housing as 'folk art'. This is an explicit departure from the discipline of architecture in favour of 'design', which will later figure so prominently in the work of Banham. It follows on the heels of issue 3 of *Archigram*, in which expendability is touted as an opportunity for architecture rather than a threat to it. In particular, the possibility of architecture to be addressed from the perspective of obsolescence changes its role from shelter to 'technique'. As it is developed in 1964, the 'capsule' becomes a dwelling type perfectly suited to the new urban environment of the Plug-In City. The capsule projects by Archigram resonate with the work of the Japanese metabolists, who are similarly experimenting with the possibility of singular enclosed capsules. The notion that an individually designed capsule could be plugged into a tower, or even into the city, refers to the consumer society in which it will play a significant role. At the same time its singular focus on the individualization of space intimates the fundamental disappearance of architecture as a solid, built environment.

Another significant aspect of the capsule (and the later bubble, as it will become manifest in the Cushicle and the Suitaloon) is its fundamental sense of accommodation. Rather than demand adaptation from its inhabitant, its formal definition is based on the mobility, needs and desires of its occupant. It stands in contrast to the dominance of the mechanical paradigm, parodied so well in Jacques Tati's film *Les Vacances de Monsieur Hulot.* The very space of the capsule evokes the sense of gadgetry that Archigram was so famous for, yet at the same time clearly implies the sense of a custom-made or mass-fabricated suit.

From the capsule to the Cushicle is still a large step. Yet it seems an inevitable trajectory, initiated by what Banham calls the 'mechanical invasion', referring to the various service elements in the home. During one of his stays in the USA, Banham is quick to understand the potential consequences:

> When your house contains such a complex of piping, flues, ducts, wires, lights, inlets, outlets, ovens, sinks, refuse disposers, hi-fi reverberators, anten-

Service packs overtaking architecture: for 'the man who has everything else'. Reyner Banham and François Dallegret, Standard-of-Living Package (1965)

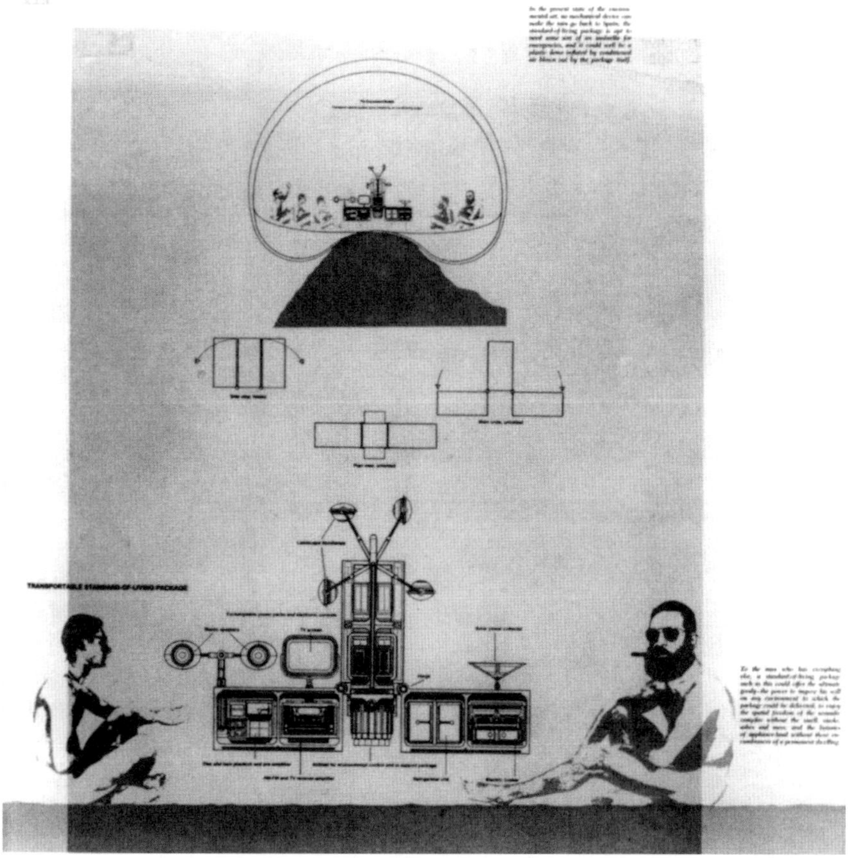

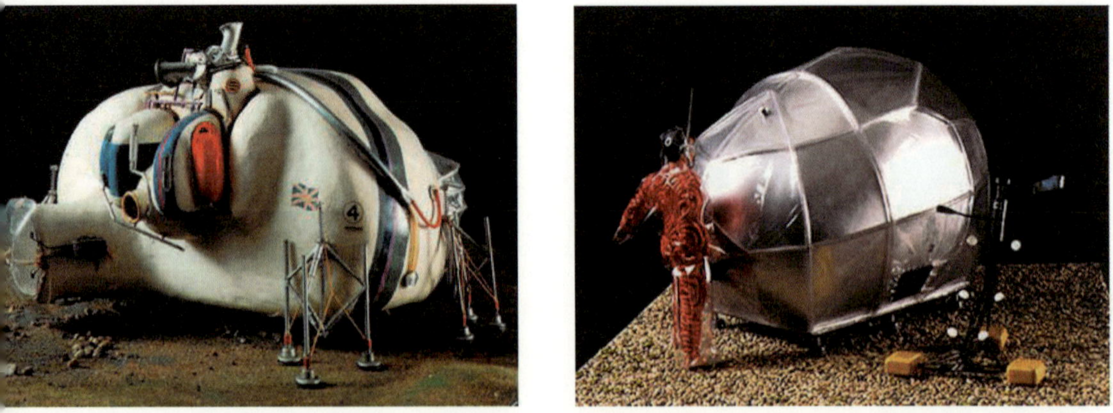

Increasingly ephemeral forms of architecture. David Greene and Mike Webb, Living Pod and Suitaloon (1965 and 1967)

> nae, conduits, freezers, heaters – when it contains so many services that the hard-ware could stand up by itself without any assistance from the house, why have a house to hold it up?[49]

While the capsule home can still be considered a contemporary replacement for the house, it is later described by Archigram as a necessary 'half-step' in the development of a radically different design object. 'The half-step living capsule can be seen as the prototype for a generation of capsules gradually evolving until the term and definition of capsule is irrelevant to the developed hybrid.'[50] In contrast, the Cushicle (and indeed most of the developments after 1966) 'must all be seen as increasingly freed from the hierarchies of parts that buildings with their traditional rules have hitherto sustained'.[51]

Mike Webb in particular moved in the direction of the individual shelter, making architecture smaller and more intimate. He produced projects that walked the fine line between technology and architecture, often combining the two to an extent that every 'existential' aspect of architecture in terms of its relation with the surrounding context and notions of stability and 'grounding' completely disappeared. The Cushicle and the Suitaloon offer the most minimal structures of technological architecture, where space is reduced to no more than clothing. The Cushicle contains two main parts that 'expand out from their unpacked state to the domestic condition'.[52] This is a shell that can expand into a minimal dwelling space including food, water, radio/TV and heating, sufficient to basic survival in any environment. These projects are an architect's interpretation of the spacesuit: a self-sufficient bubble that allows its occupant to move about freely and live anywhere. Eventually, the Cushicles might develop into a larger, more comprehensive system of 'personal enclosures', thus transforming this technological object not only into an architectural space, but also into an entire urban environment.

Traveling light: architecture reduced to clothing. David Greene, Inflatable Suit-Home (1968)

In 1966, Warren Chalk's 'housing as a consumer product' refers to the latent creativity of architecture's inhabitants, and notably comments: 'The present gulf between people, between the community and the designer may well be eventually bridged by the do-it-yourself interchangeable kit of parts.'[53] Here again, the design activity of the architect is transformed from a permanent definition of space, into a 'kit of parts' to be assembled and reassembled at will. This development will continue steadily onward over time. The kit of parts that recurs throughout texts by Archigram and the 'standard-of living package' (an idea of Buckminster Fuller's) referred to by Banham become the guiding force in truly shedding the skins of architecture. Rather than stable spaces, Archigram is now designing hybrid objects: 'Sometimes machine, sometimes architecture, sometimes animal-like growth, sometimes electrical circuitry, sometimes part of a mathematical progression and sometimes completely random.'[54]

From the capsule to the Walking City, the radically technological environment becomes an all-encompassing logic. The relation with the environment is entirely reconfigured in both directions: the total environment, with technology expanding ever outward to become a new form of architectural definition; and the capsule, with technology become increasingly prosthetic, and allowing architecture as space to disappear, replacing its role as shelter with a role in the domestication of the natural environment. This belies the enclosure of the capsular environment: in the period of the Capsule Tower, the objects may still maintain a traditional sense of the box: well-designed, smooth, stylish, but a box nevertheless. The truly radical nature of the capsular environment is, however, not about self-enclosure but about expansion. It begins to appear when there is no longer a capsule but the hybrid referred to above: part event, part space, part skin, part senses. The 'bubble' is about expansion into the environment, about domestication of that environment, and in its ultimate form, dissolving into the technological mediascape.[55]

The nomadic traveling pack.
Mike Webb, Cushicle (1966-1967)

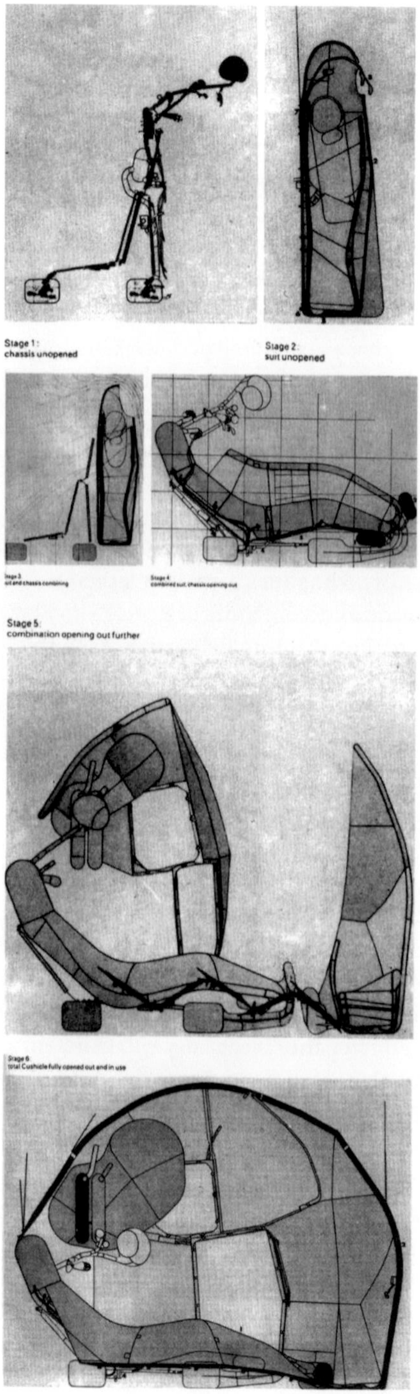

Rediscovering the Body: The Machine as Organism and Prosthetic Technology

This dissolution onto the extended technologies of new media has a counterpart in the designs of the time: there is an increasing presence of the living, biological body, both literally as a formal reference point and more embedded as a tactile, sensing apparatus within the space of architecture. Archigram puts forward projects such as the Living City of 1963, in which the city is conceived as an 'organism', while Aldo van Eyck refers to the life of a tree and its branches. The Smithsons and Constant imply a logic of growth and evolutionary change in their cities.[56] In architecture, this reference to the 'organic' is not new: it is present in the emulation of natural form in Art Nouveau, and early in the twentieth century Lewis Mumford, Frank Lloyd Wright and Hugo Häring all explicitly turned to some notion of 'organic' to describe a generative logic that must be obeyed in architectural design. They all betray an appeal to an all-encompassing logic of some abstract natural force, however, while the biomorphic references in the 1960s tend to appeal more to the specific and the individual: appealing to the asymmetry of evolution rather than its overarching logic.

A biomorphic expression of machinery was one way of reconquering technology in order to create a more human environment. Archigram's transformation of the visuality of technology both responded to the mass culture of the period, as well as to the discomfort with the increasingly mechanical surroundings of the modern city. Anthropomorphism became more important at the same time that technology became more about the substructure than its visual expression. The film *Barbarella*, for example, introduces a materiality together with its high-tech society – this is not only about the ephemeral or dystopian technology of Jean-Luc Godard's *Alphaville*, but also about fur-lined spaceships and walls with soft antennae. Here again we find an ambiguity in the projects, how-

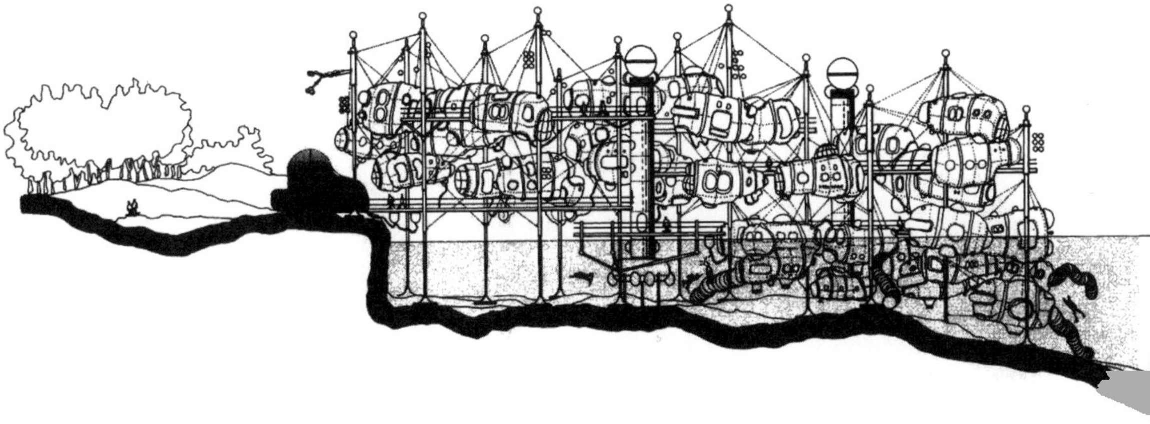

Organic capsule forms and additive structure. Ron Herron, Capsule Pier (1965)

ever. The imagery was on the one hand radically technological – the notion that cities might someday walk the globe – yet also referred continually to traits typically considered the domain of living creatures: walking, growing, transforming. In this sense the visual manipulation presented both a radical inversion of earlier perceptions of technology and a familiar context with which to judge them: these objects were biomechanical life forms that made contemporary technology seem truly lifeless. Thus the Archigram series offer us both the visualization of a new technology and at the same time a thematic questioning of the possibilities.

Works such as the Spray Plastic House (1962) by David Greene are not only conceptually interesting but express a different kind of formalism than that of modernist houses.[57] Le Corbusier tended to use engineering and technology as an argument for the reduction of ornament, the need for thinness, order and a rational appearance. The earlier capsules of Archigram tend towards organic forms and smooth surfaces, responding both to the desire for a reintroduction of biomorphic forms, as well as an increasingly sophisticated language of design. Greene and Webb in particular tended to make highly technological looking artefacts that nevertheless contained a certain organic formal expression. In the case of the Spray Plastic House, this was expressed through the non-linearity of the house itself: the dwelling is a kind of bubble, with not a right angle to be found in it. Since technological expression was often employed in a symbolic fashion, this 'organic' reformulation of the final result of technological architecture may have transformed the perception of the machine. Although Greene's 1965 project for the Living Pod is later referred to as a 'replacement home' and dismissed as 'probably a dead end', it does offer an important role for biomorphic formal references.[58] This kind of expression is found as early as 1956 in the Smithsons' House of the Future, where plastics are seen as the new concrete. Equally malleable and durable yet extremely lightweight, it helps achieve an expression of organic forms, shaped around the human body, moulded to the most comfortable ergonomic form.

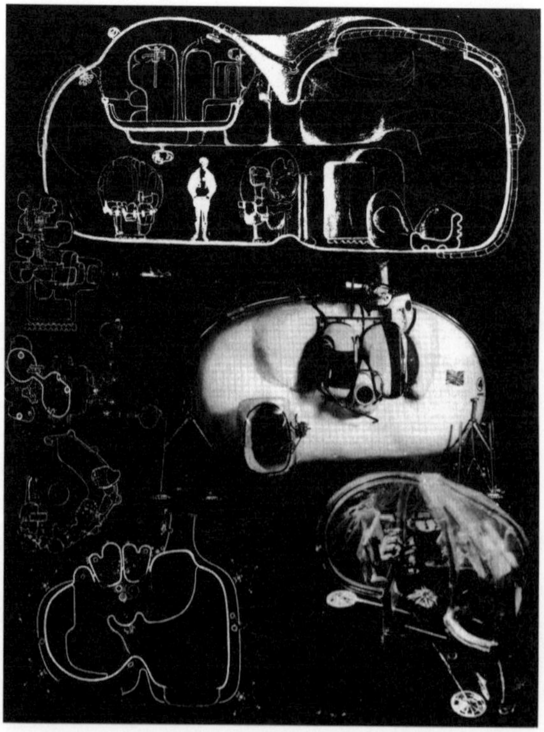

Organic form made possible through the technology of prefabrication. David Greene, Living Pod (1965)

The reintroduction of the specifically human element in a more embedded fashion is primarily present in two forms: a return to the scale of the body and the appeal to senses beyond the visual, in particular the tactile. A return to the human body was one manner of shifting the focus of technology from the primacy of the machine to the primacy of the people it was to serve. Both the Cushicle and the Suitaloon, besides reducing architecture to a very bare minimum, also bring architecture closer to the body. Rather than the social, communal aspects of architecture apparent in the megastructures, these projects bring architecture down to the scale of a piece of clothing, to that of the individual body. This hypercorporeality became one manner of reintroducing the human element into an increasingly technological and industrial society. This recalls the work of many contemporaries such as the Smithsons and Jacobs, as well as the Situationist International: the human element is crucial. The individual person, in this case exemplified by the individual human body, is what defines the new position of architecture, the departure from modernist mechanization.

On the level of the body, many of the architectural interventions are at the scale of the private space (small plug-in capsules), elemental living pods and space suits as the membrane between the individual and the outside world. In this space, architecture often begins to manifest itself as the space of a single body (and therefore the pure expression of individuality) settled within a larger infrastructure. At this scale, the machine is challenged as an expression of the intellectual progress of man, while intimate technologies give presence to senses other than vision. The tactile begins to figure in the movies of the time, as well as being introduced in the designs. The tactile experience of space, a shift from seeing to feeling, undermines the modernist hegemony of vision (which results in a disembodied representation and experience of architecture).[59]

The body becomes increasingly present in the smaller, lighter projects of Archigram. Warren Chalk's Bathamatic of 1970 is a confined technological plug-in with 'spray 'n scent' and a control panel as well as television screen to while away

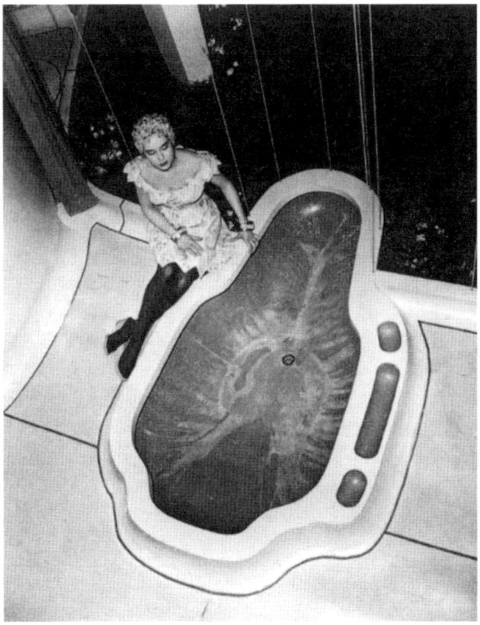

The malleable nature of new materials such as plastic. Alison and Peter Smithson, House of the Future (1957)

the time. It can hardly be a coincidence that it bears such a close resemblance to the 'orgasmatron' from the 1968 film *Barbarella*, a machine that is meant to play all the senses until one literally dies of pleasure. The 1969 Electronic Tomato was not defined in terms of a function, but rather presented as a 'groove gizmo that connects to every nerve end to give you the wildest buzz'.[60] At the scale of the body, architecture becomes a prosthetic device, blending with its user.

While the later blow-out environments have lost some of their explicitly biomorphic formal references, projects such as Webb's Suitaloon and the Environment Bubble by Banham and François Dallegret also illustrate the intimate connection between the biomorphic metaphors and these physically individualized spaces. They are no longer the industrial design objects to be plugged into the Capsule Tower, nor are they part of the proliferating technological environment of the Plug-In City. Rather, they are truly 'prosthetic' in the sense of Marshall McLuhan. They are devices for containing heat, not much different from our own skin. 'Architecture' may have disappeared as a form of shelter and defining spaces, but it is replaced by a technological design object with a prosthetic function. Architecture as a form of domesticating the environment is grafted onto the skin of its occupant, becoming part of him or her.

The Medium Is the Message: Visualizing Radical Technology

The fusion of the environment, mediating space and the user begs the question of the impact of technologies. Not only their content becomes important, but also the form they take. Prosthetic devices suggest a different relationship with the surroundings than shelters. This notion is of course essential to the work of Marshall McLuhan, who first suggested that the 'medium is the message'. The interest of Archigram's members in the visual aspect of their work suggests not only a spirit of the time – visible also in the work of the Independent Group, Venturi and Scott Brown, Archizoom and others – but also their intuition that the discourse could be transformed through other media than the traditional drawing.[61] The epithet that Banham left them with – that they were 'long on draughtsmanship and short

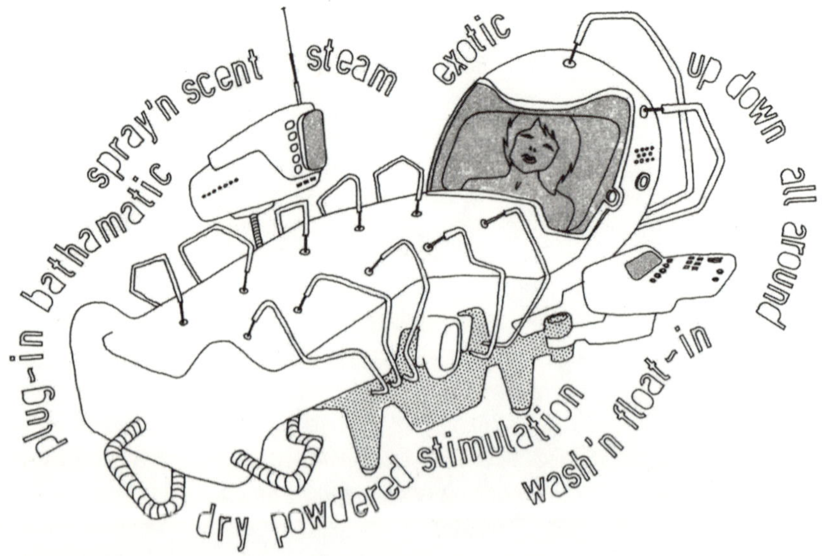

The personal dimension of architecture. Warren Chalk, Bathamatic (1970)

Woman versus machine: Barbarella conquers the orgasmatron. Roger Vadim, *Barbarella* (1968)

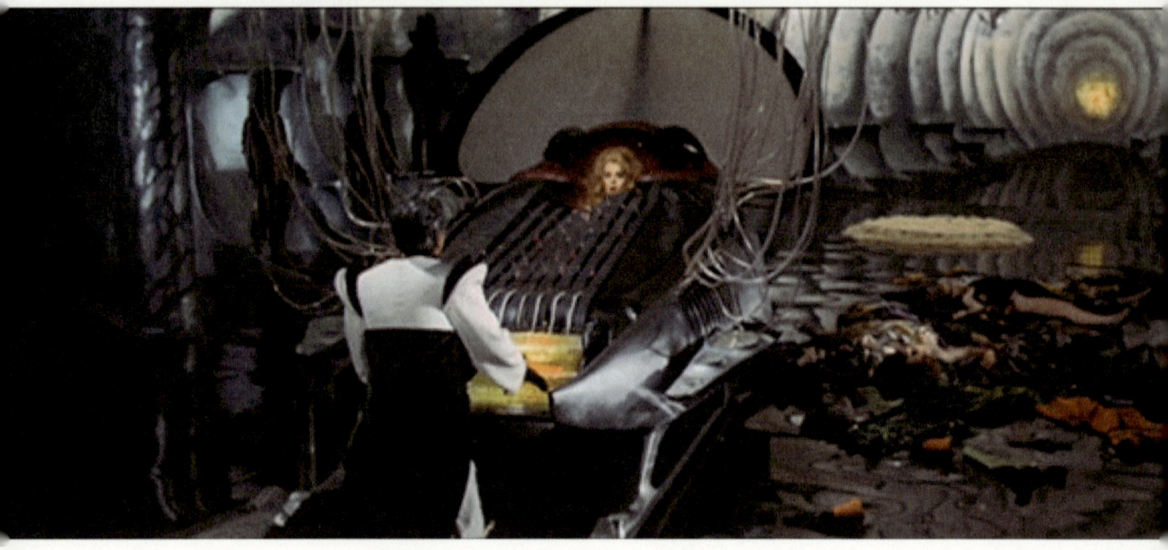

on theory' – is in fact only partially true. They were certainly long on draughtsmanship, but they can only be seen as 'short on theory' if we consider theory in the written, linear, manifesto-based fashion traditional to modern architecture. The 'theory' of the Archigram group was as associative an assemblage as the time they were dealing with – with pluralities becoming manifest in imagery and the various connected aspects of technology no longer able to fit neatly into a box. The evident clarity and simplicity of modernity, its technological progress and the ensuing paradise had been undermined by the economic efficiency of late modern building, and the urban blight was beginning to become evident in many cities built according to modernist principles.

In contrast, the issues of *Archigram* offered a platform for their collages and assemblages of a highly technological near future. Their images were closely related to the imagery of science fiction, of advertisements and billboards, all part of the visual language becoming increasingly familiar in the early 1960s. Moreover, as a new development, the explosion of colour and low-culture or 'light' images such as comic strips opened up a new world of visual expression for this reconceptualization of technology – in stark contrast to earlier images of steel latticework and smooth concrete surfaces. Instead, the public was now offered colourful bubbles of plastic housing units and inflatable dwellings. Both the platform of the 'little magazine' and its visual content resonates with other repositionings of the time: the Independent Group, as the direct precursors of Archigram in England, introduced collages of contemporary mass-culture images (in colour), in the USA Venturi and Scott Brown presented the colourful and glittering neonscapes of Las Vegas, while the Situationist International turned to the small pamphlet as a direct method of approach, not trapped within the constraints of a high or academic culture.[62]

Just as their colleagues of the Situationist International, the members of Archigram developed their ideas mainly in and through their pamphlets. The issues of *Archigram* explored various approaches to technological developments in and outside of architecture, while they were also an experiment in the visual medium itself, employing cut-out figures and do-it-yourself techniques. Each pamphlet remained primarily visual and full of architecture drawings, approaching its questions not only as an intellectual exercise but rather as a collision of design concerns, ideas and visual culture. This stands in contrast to the Situationist International, which in its visual production was continually attempting to undermine the visual sedation of the spectacle. Furthermore, it is notable that the *Archigram* issues slowly congealed more into single questions per issue. As they produced more, they began to find themes they shared. *Archigram* 3 was the first of the series that revolved around a single theme, which became the format for the rest of the series. This issue revolved around technology, obsolescence and consumerism, and what impact they might have on architecture. Other themes Archigram addressed in its pamphlets included science fiction (*Archigram* 4), the (future) city in issue 5, and early premonitions of architecture and its impact on the environment in issue 9.

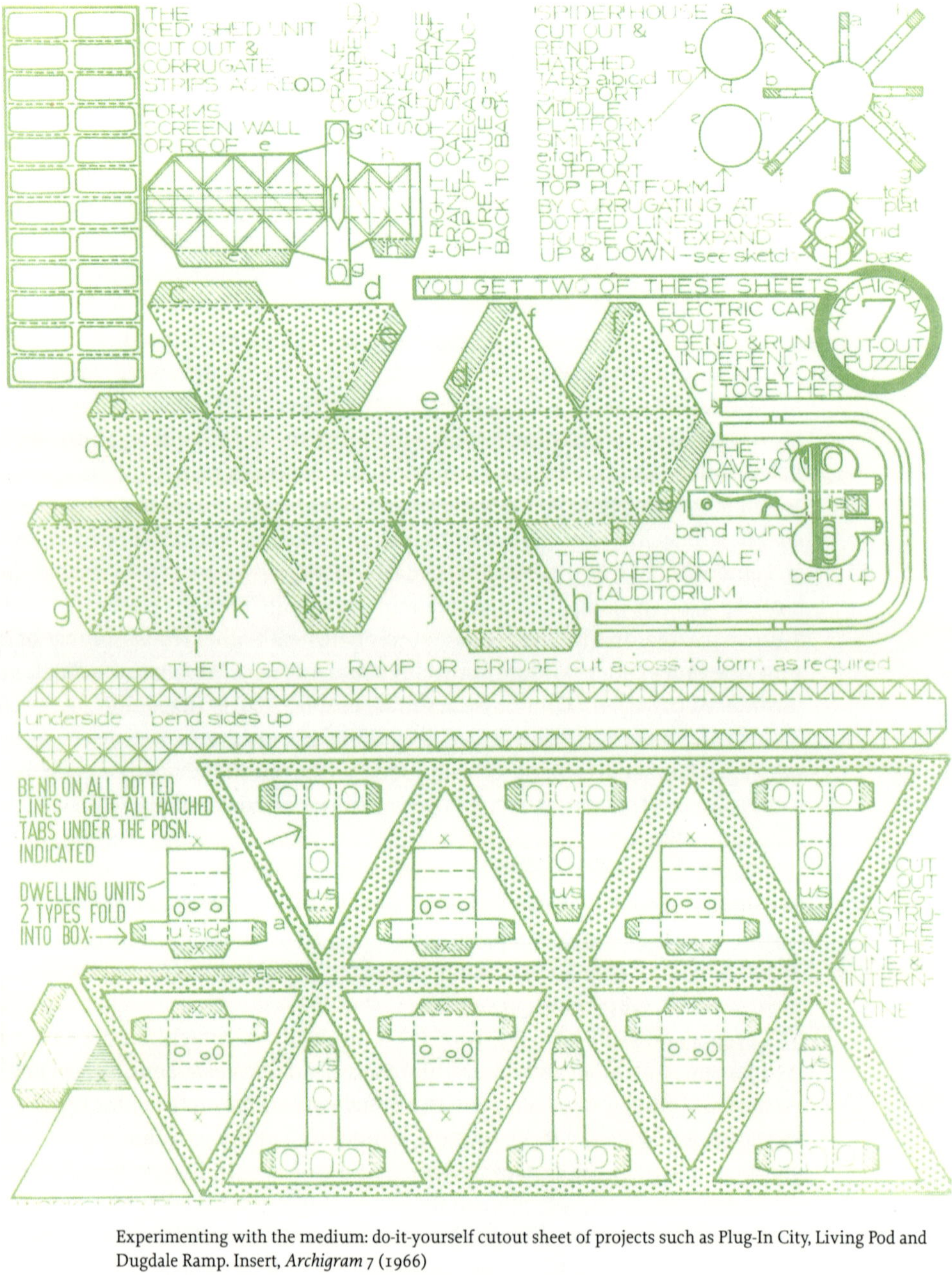

Experimenting with the medium: do-it-yourself cutout sheet of projects such as Plug-In City, Living Pod and Dugdale Ramp. Insert, *Archigram* 7 (1966)

The fact that they produced their most significant work in this form confirms the importance of this work in the revaluation of the position of technology in the architecture discourse. The distinction between early- and mid-twentieth-century treatments here is that technology may be the foundation of the culture around us, it need not necessarily be employed as an image. Where modernism was still concentrating on the iconic value of the machine, the technology of the 1960s was seeking ways to be less visible, less present. The American handling of technology was more pragmatic, it was simply put to use. Warhol understood that the technology of replication allowed an artist to remove his 'authenticity' as artist from the equation and instead become part of the machinery of reproduction. The medium of the pamphlets allowed Archigram to remain closer to technology as a primary instrument, since the speed of print and distribution by far surpasses the agonizingly slow trajectory of architecture.[63] The medium of the pamphlet also allowed a radical position similar to that taken by the Situationist International and the Las Vegas manifesto of Venturi and Scott Brown. In comparison to the construction of actual buildings, the platform of a pamphlet or a publication was a more effective means to communicate ideas. The complexity of architectural production, ranging from the expense to produce it and its dependency on a patron, to the many influences on its final appearance like urban regulations and the scores of people required in its construction, makes it more sensitive to compromise, or the adaptation of ideas to suit its preconditions. In this sense, the very medium of the pamphlet (or 'paper architecture' as it was often dubbed in the 1980s) allows a freedom of discourse and ideas. Banham argues that the 'second machine age' will require an architecture that develops at equal speed.[64] Yet the radical quality of the imagery in projects such as the Walking City also demonstrates the dichotomy between architecture as a medium defined by tradition and convention and the proposition of an architecture subsumed by technology.

Although Archigram is deeply interested in the potential of technologies, the pleasure these young architects have in their gadgets is of a different conceptual order than Le Corbusier's or Gropius' missionary zeal in proposing the model of silos or factories as a transcendent form. They worked more on the basis of 'What might this button do?' Their imagery is comparable to that of the mass cultural imagery around them of the time – the TV series *The Thunderbirds*, also an English production; the space comics they use in *Archigram* 4 (Zoom!); Robbie the Robot in *The Forbidden Planet*. This too is an essential trait of 1960s' technology: it was inundated with fun and frivolity, to offer a counterweight to the sober abstraction of modernist technology. This can be seen in Banham's passion for American cars, as well as in the Electronic Tomato, defined by little more than potential fun and excitement, while it remains unclear towards what end.

Much of the work of Archigram is comparable to this: instead of the reduction of form appealing to a perceptual construct of engineering (straight lines, no ornamentation) that in its plan and façade was often still extremely classical (the symmetry in Mies van der Rohe's work or the golden section in Le Corbusier's villas), there was an explosion of form that expressed a technology run rampant. In

Exploring new frontiers between puppeteering and science fiction: Jerry and Sylvia Anderson, Thunderbirds (1965-1966)

ZOOM! Cover of *Archigram* 4 (1964)

this case, the technology was not meant to serve a higher formal ideal, but rather to explode those formal ideals from *within.* In a visual manoeuvre similar to what was presented in *Learning from Las Vegas* or in 'This Is Tomorrow', the abstraction of modernist forms (in this case of machinery) was subverted by presenting familiar and everyday imagery.

Banham's distinction between an 'aesthetic' and a 'sensibility', or an attitude, serves a purpose. His theory was also based on the non-sanctioned aesthetic of American cars and Las Vegas neon. The Archigram group was not progressing steadily towards a preconceived aesthetic, but like its contemporaries was collecting, collaging and assembling things and materials that seemed striking in terms of their technological or architectural ramifications, or their visual qualities. Again this seems analogous to what Venturi and Scott Brown were doing with Las Vegas, or the situationists were appropriating from the culture of the street. Archigram certainly had some connections with the Independent Group (primarily through Banham), which may have encouraged the assemblage quality of everyday imagery. Archigram, however, was not turning towards the working class and sociology in the manner of the Independent Group and New Brutalism, but rather towards mass-culture items such as science-fiction films and at the same time technological breakthroughs such as cybernetics.

Comics and science fiction as space to explore architecture. 'Space probe', *Archigram* 4 (1964)

Archigram approached the question of technology explicitly, but also implicitly in the medium itself. On the one hand there was a highly direct appropriation of certain perceptions of technology, primarily from science fiction and popular science, yet at the same time there was another level of discourse that revolved around a reconceptualization of the role of technology, especially in response to the place it held within modernism. This second aspect primarily found its expression through the visual forms of mass culture in opposition to the abstracted forms of modernist references such as grain silos.

In the case of Archigram, the imagery used was intended to remove technology from its transcendent throne – to reintroduce the idea that technology was meant to serve the ideas and interests of people, rather than the other way around. In so doing, the modernist connection between rationality as the highest human trait and its manifestations through technology is questioned. Yet in their arguments, the members of Archigram also clearly retain a closely related belief in technocracy – that 'true' functionalism (which in their eyes should still be objectively attainable) will create a flexible environment perfectly adapted to the needs of its inhabitants. In other words, beyond the non-functional factors such as symbolism and representation, there is an objectively functional ideal that will hold in all cases. It remains unclear whether they see this functional ideal as something economical (as one could see the *Existenzminimum*) or as something perfectly attuned to all systems (in a more network-oriented context); it also remains unclear whether they have considered the kind of compromise often necessary when conflicting interests all need to be considered (which is perhaps a condition of paper architecture: it can remain radical because it remains unbuilt).

The work hovers between Colquhoun's symbolic and literal aspects of technology, and in doing so perhaps goes beyond Debord's fear of idyllic modernist representations of machinery. Yet a light form of critique, still visible in the disturbingly happy faces of the domestic women in Paolozzi's collages, does not seem present in the Archigram oeuvre. Thus throughout the highly provocative and visual assemblages of possible technologies, it remains somewhat spellbound by a modernist sense of promise inherent in technology itself.

Throughout its work the Situationist International, and in particular Debord, remains more sceptical of imagery. Each image encountered is easily dismissed for its complicity with the status quo, and creative expression should be something from within each individual, something essential to each human being and expressive of his or her uniqueness (and liberation from the world of the spectacle). Technology in and of itself, however is not suspect unless it is wrapped up in the same world of consumerism and spectacle. This presumes an ability to distinguish between 'good' and 'bad' uses of technology, and again presupposes that technology is simply instrumental. While the situationist critique also distinguishes the image of technology from the use of technology, it is directed more towards the untenable alienation between reality and appearance. To the situationists, technology may someday still prove the instrument of liberation, once it has freed labourers from the drudgery of work that can be done by machines. In this case, in contrast to Archigram, the fundamental presupposition is not so much a transformation of technology as of the way it is utilized. Throughout this position, technology remains an instrument, potentially neutral even, in the hands of humans. Its incorrect employment has everything to do with the narrow-sightedness of the dominant power structure.

Of the situationists, Constant is the most engaged with forms and potentials of technology. While Debord retains his critical position towards consumerism and the use of technology within that, Constant is seeking ways to envision a technology that would help create the human environment he proposes in New Babylon. Constant's writing about this environment is strangely reminiscent of McLuhan, who hopes that eventually the new technologies will become the true extensions of man. Debord's discussions of technology remain somewhat more abstract, although both seem to agree that someday man will be freed from labour thanks to technology. They underestimated the new types of labour that would arise with the introduction of the network society and its global time schedule.

Technology and the Mass Market: Obsolescence, Consumption and Choice

In the increasing affluence of the 1960s, the rise of a consumer society also begins to figure more prominently in the architecture discourse. As early as 1963, Archigram introduced the notions of expendability and the consumer as fundamental to contemporary architecture, not merely as decorative elements added to an architectural environment.[65]

> Perhaps it will not be until such things as housing, amenity-place and work-place can become recognized as consumer products that can be bought 'off the peg' – with all that this implies in terms of expendability (foremost), industrialization, up-to-date-ness, consumer choice, and basic product design – that we can begin to make an environment that is really part of a developing human culture.[66]

For Archigram, the consumer appealed to a different relation between technology and architecture, shifting from a logic of production to a logic of consumption. If the modernists represented the logic of production with their emphasis on functionality, efficiency and the machine, Archigram's fascination for disposable items, individualization and temporary enclosures perfectly suited a consumer society based on change, desire and the market.

Disposability is crucial to the proliferation of the consumer society, as is the notion of 'planned obsolescence'. The latter in particular not only allows products

The logic of obsolescence applied to architecture. *Archigram* 3, Expendability (1963)

'The pre-packaged frozen lunch is more important than Palladio'. Problem statement on expendability, *Archigram* 3 (1963)

to conform to the (temporary) needs of the market, but by limiting the lifespan of products it continually ensures the potential to form new desires. Whether that planned obsolescence is built in through the fashionability of an article, the lack of replacement parts, or its incompatibility with the latest software is irrelevant, as long as a consumable good is not built to last a lifetime. Along these lines, Archigram envisioned the relevance of architects in a society of temporary forms, no longer in conceiving a single monument to last forever, nor in designing product-lines that can be assembled as the occupant wishes. But rather as an industrial designer: to build houses and offices and other buildings that suit a very specific need, in a very specific time, to be replaced within a human generation or less. In the editorial to *Archigram* 3, a 'welcome-life span' is referred to as opposed to the traditional life span of objects, noting that the 'attitude of mind' that accompanies the consumer society should be welcomed as 'the product of a sophisticated consumer society, rather than a stagnant (and in the end, declining) society'.[67]

By introducing the consumer as the inhabitant of its architecture, Archigram crossed the line from incorporating the enlightened rationality of a (Marxist) revolution in architecture to embodying the cultural logic of late capitalism. Above all, the possibility of change transforms one of the essential roles of architecture, as the embodiment of stability and the connection to place. Its role as the placeholder, the local, and the permanent is now seen as characteristic of a 'stagnant' society. Archigram was not the first group to unhinge architecture from the soil; the modernists were there long before. The *pilotis* so popular in modern houses, the skyscrapers of the Radiant City, were all about a position freed from the earth and freed from the solidity of generations of tradition. By taking this principle to its logical extreme in the Plug-In City and the Walking City, some of the more monstrous aspects of this technological relation with the world became apparent. Within the wondrous imagery of large, insect-like walking cities there was also a shadow of dislocation, of the loss of architecture as a guarantor of existential stability.

In part, this was simply a response to conditions external to architecture: there was no denying the rise of the 'affluent society'.[68] Increasing affluence opened up a market for new objects, most commonly in smaller design objects such as household gadgetry. Nevertheless, the field of architecture was also unmistakably charged with new potential roles, focused on reinvention, distinction and sophistication of design.[69] Technology on this level opens up a culture otherwise closed. Technology is instrumental to the rise of mass culture, encouraging the democratization of a formerly elite culture. In the USA, the architecture debate focused more on this enabling character than on potential threats. The progressive potential of the machine, still part of the American dream, was thus incorporated in a consumer ideal of more things: an emulation of wealth was becoming steadily more attainable in the form of vacuum cleaners, two cars, kitchen gadgets and TVs. As the modern machines before them, these gadgets evoked dreams and desires, but now more cut to the human form, to everyday use and to individual tastes. Yet at the same time, each new gadget produced new desires and laid a new demand on

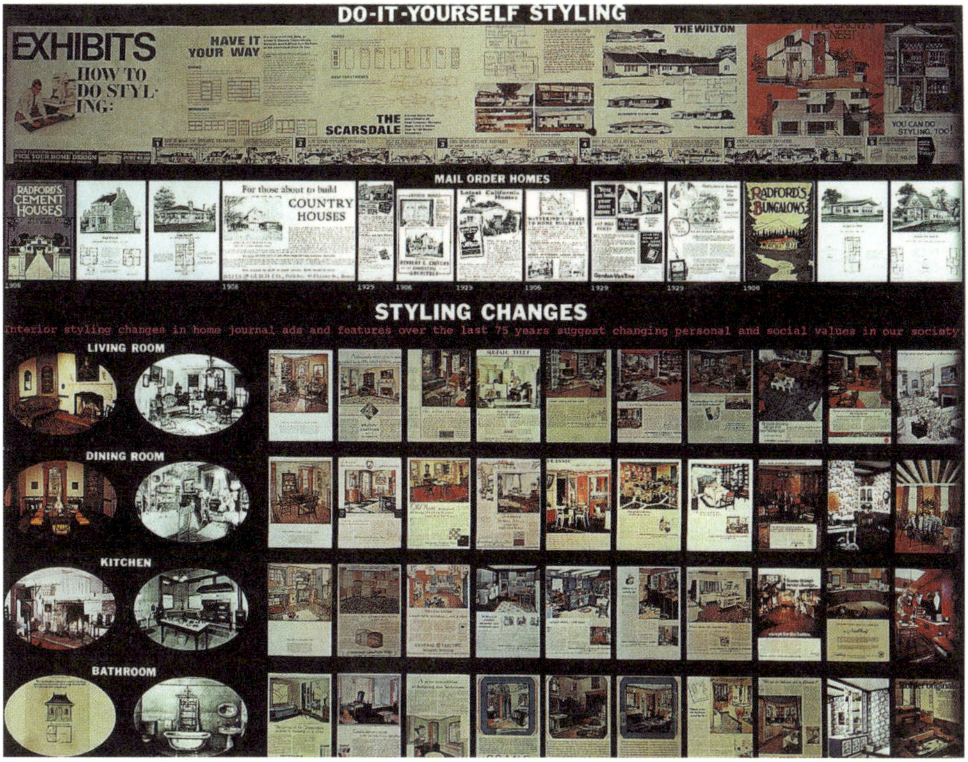

Individualization of the home by catalogue: 'have it your way' and 'mail order homes'.
Robert Venturi and Denise Scott Brown, Learning from Levittown studio (1970)

the consumer, requiring continuous renewal (the well-known consumer logic of 'keeping up with the Joneses').

The early post-war housing development of Levittown emphasizes the enabling aspect of the logic of consumption. Thanks to the new possibilities of semi-standardized technology, soldiers returning to the USA from the Second World War were able to choose from a range of (affordable) homes. In Levittown, each future occupant was given a choice between a number of standard types and extra features. This allowed a 'mass customization' of the living environment. Progress in the technology of building had now created the opportunity for people to actually have impact on their space, evoking the situationist notion that technology should not only enable, but also encourage the freedom of individual expression and action. Yet here, too, this freedom is still limited to preselected choices, clearly visible in overhead photos of the Levittown developments: an endless sea of identical homes, no less standardized than Le Corbusier's *Unité*, with seemingly no room for individuality. Yet if we zoom in on an everyday scale, as Venturi and Scott Brown did in their 'Learning from Levittown' studio, we find many expressions of individual preference: small additions, variations in lawns, gardens, front doors and the like. These small manifestations of freedom within the consumer society figure prominently in the ideas of Venturi and Scott Brown, since its inhabitants have the choice to fulfil their own desires (even if predetermined by advertising) by going to Las Vegas or emulating a colonial home with a do-it-yourself kit of parts. Archigram simply takes this logic to a more fundamental position on the liberating aspects of the consumer society: it clears the path for a realization of desires simply by reorganizing architecture practice to respond to user-based needs.

A specific exploration of the enabling aspects of technology as such is seen in the 'Control and Choice' project of 1967, representing Great Britain at the Paris Biennale of that year. Paradoxical couplings, such as control and choice, were central to the project's inception. Finding ways to leave the architectural environment free to be determined by its occupant while still representing possibilities was one of the problems Archigram was confronted with. Choice becomes an expression of individual agency, described as follows:

> The determination of your environment need no longer be left in the hands of the designer of the building: it can be turned over to you yourself. You turn the switches and choose the conditions to sustain you at that point in time. The 'building' is reduced to the role of carcass – or less.[70]

In the images produced for this project, hints of a situationist sense of action are scattered throughout the texts, containing phrases such as 'anarchy city' and 'architecture is just a game'. Implying the creation of 'situations' in this project, we are seen to be in control, because 'in this architecture time and ephemera replace bricks'.[71] Although there is an apparent freedom of choice, the actual range is still limited by 'programming' – on TV, choices are still made by network executives, while Archigram of course also offers only a limited range of choices. Its members remain conscious of the paradox that each design presents a limitation of choices, and typically note in their texts that this is one of many options. Is Archigram's verbal acknowledgement that each solution has its limitations simply the best architecture can offer?

In contrast to the Situationist International, Archigram saw no problems inherent in the combination of technology and consumerism. Whether the consumer society actually fulfils the needs of the user is not the issue: the economics of consumption is based on the availability of choice. Introducing choice also introduces the possibility of distinction: in this sense, the freedom of choice in consumer-driven capitalism appears to seamlessly integrate with the ideals of autonomy and self-realization, although the situationists would point out that this would concern no more than a pseudo-autonomy, one already predetermined by the conditions of capital and the spectacle. In contrast, Archigram tended towards the American belief in consumer freedom as a means towards self-realization. The striking similarities in the two underlying positions are, however, immediately visible in a piece by Warren Chalk in *Archigram* 3, 'Housing as a Consumer

Product'. Although the title would appear to be at odds with the anti-consumerist position of the situationists, Chalk writes that it is time to realize that 'everyone in the community has latent creative instincts', and promises a future not unlike New Babylon: 'In a technological society more people will play an active part in determining their own individual environment, in self-determining a way of life.'[72] The underlying resonance of ideas shows a certain 'spirit of the times', while the primary differences seem to reside in the presumed audience: Archigram was not producing these projects for workers alienated by their subjugation to industrial labour, but was moving more towards the realization of what could be considered a middle-class ideal. This liberation, by means of a continually progressing technology, was not from the consumer-driven spectacle, but rather from an overly mechanized and repetitious environment.

Both Archigram and the Situationist International agree that freedom (of expression, self-realization, choice, individual action) is paramount. And both somehow maintain the belief that technology will engender this freedom. Yet Archigram approaches this from the position of freedom of choice within the consumer world. This presupposes that the consumer is able to make a carefully considered choice. In other words, in Archigram's position the consumer remains an autonomous entity. To Debord, each choice made from within consumerism is already constrained by the system of control enforced by capitalism and the spectacle. Therefore, to Debord the only liberating technology is one that would be positioned outside of the system of consumerism and spectacle. The need for distinction is not contested, but where Archigram sees this as embedded in the consumer society, the Situationist International sees the consumer society as a threat to it.

The issue of choice is critical for two reasons: first, it exemplifies a distinction with modernism. The dominance of the machine aesthetic seems to echo in Henry Ford's famous comment on his T-Ford: 'They can have any color, as long as it's black.' In a sense, the notion of choice is limited in modernism: by presupposing that man is largely, if not exclusively, a rational being, the issue of choice is almost obliterated. Each situation, when rationally assessed, is presumed to have one ideal solution. Therefore, once we have unlocked the full rationality of human society, choice will no longer be an issue: everyone will 'choose' to respond in the same ideal fashion. To oppose this homogeneity, the idea of different choices as being expressive of the uniqueness of individuals helped redefine a 'humanity' in opposition to a rationalized, machine-like version of man. In this sense, choice becomes a means of manifesting the humanness of the individual in the face of an overly rationalized (and thus machine-based) society. Second, it offers the means to assert individuality. This is related to the previous point: both ideas, the rationality of modernism and the freedom of choice of the 1960s, aim towards a final goal of self-realization. In the one case, however, this is achieved through the discovery of the essential similarity of all human beings through their shared rationality. In the second, it presumes the individuality of each human being, expressed through their desires and distinctions (which is also emphasized in situationist writings).

This issue of control and choice remains complex and absolutely fundamental to the 1960s. Choice in each case implies a personal freedom that was seen as liberating from the constraints of a class society in some cases, or a deterministic mechanical society, or other forms of limitation. In the case of the Situationist International, however, this choice was about being able to free oneself from the constraints of consumerism and the spectacle. In the case of Archigram, certain aspects of consumerism were seen as constitutive of freedom of choice. These notions of freedom return in various forms, be they the freedom from place in the case of the Walking City or the Plug-In City, or the freedom to transform the individual environment in the case of New Babylon. What distinguishes New Babylon from the Plug-In City is that it does not refer to consumer freedom, but to the freedom of self-determination inherent in creating one's environment – liberty and emancipation are achieved through *production*, rather than the selection of prefabricated products of consumption. This follows the Situationist International argument that the *apparent* freedom of choice in consumerism (with a preselected range of choices and an overbearing marketing mechanism) again takes control away from the individual.

The tension between the consumer society and the 'real world' is often presented as a fundamental opposition, particularly in the work of the Situationist International. Yet it also rests on a false dichotomy, since the 'real world' encompasses the consumer society as one of its manifestations, and is also configured by the images and desires that construct the consumer economy. This complicated blending of the two, and their mutual influences are the crucial contribution of Marshall McLuhan to this debate. By understanding the interrelation between the medium and the message, and by reconceptualizing technology as an 'extension' of man, he literally reincorporates technology. He makes it part of an embodied experience, not purely an intellectual construct or a metaphor. Archigram experiments with this reincorporation in its projects and through its use of popular imagery, embedding the technology not only as explicit topic of inquiry, but also in the very media used. Yet the uncomplicated joy in the gadgets produced also echoes a modernist faith in the inherently progressive nature of technology, as well as the ability to control it.

It is in the more convoluted notations by McLuhan that we find a suggestion that the interference between a medium and its content brings unforeseen consequences that are not easily reduced to an oppositional framework.[73] The opposition between creativity and purchasing an identity is not as solid as the discourse of the 1960s often makes it appear. The work straddles the line between an anarchistic understanding of technology as enabling a (pure) human creativity, and the possibly liberating potential of a consumer-oriented form of capitalism. His belief that all forms of technology are 'extensions of man' also echoes Constant's premise that the technological environment he proposed in New Babylon is full of these 'extensions' of man into the environment. While Constant treats the technology as an instrument of engineering and architectural design, McLuhan has no qualms about incorporating consumer-oriented forms of technology in his ideas.

Instrumentality and Autonomy: Paradigms on the Role of Technology

The introduction of 'mediation' and the question of who (or what) is then in control point to the question of autonomy as an underlying issue to the treatment of technology. McLuhan's arguments offer an entry point into the question of autonomy. Is technology a mere instrument to give us more control with respect to the environment, for example? For Heidegger, prefiguring McLuhan's arguments by almost 20 years, the technologies we utilize also reconfigure our relationship with the world. The notion of autonomy underwrites both the use of technology as a mechanism of control and a discomfort with technology as a mode of domination. McLuhan's statements on technology, though focused on its liberating potential, extend to a fundamental incorporation of technology on an individual basis. This allows him to treat technology as an embodiment of a new relation with the world. 'The medium is the message' suggests that technology is not as easily separated from its inceptions or its ramifications as we might otherwise think. As 'extensions of man' technologies cannot be understood as instruments external to us, McLuhan argues. The machine can no longer be understood in a modernist sense as a symbolic expression of the rationality of man, but it is a prosthetic device, entwined with the corporeal nature of man. It is not an autonomous yet subjugated object, an instrument in the hands of enlightened scientific man, but it extends him outwards, it begins *with* him and connects him *to* the environment. In contemporary terms, technology is an interface, bridging the gap between man and environment, and between symbolic and literal. By becoming an interface, an intermediary, technology as McLuhan understands it is both 'there' and 'not there': the medium itself is now indeed the message, and the two can no longer be extricated from one another.

The medium is the message: technology as invisible instrument. Marshall McLuhan (1967)

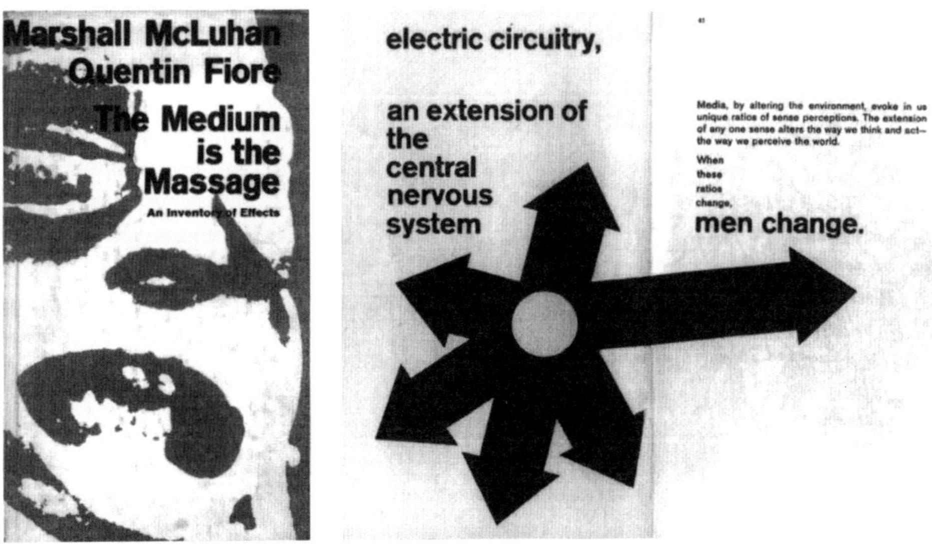

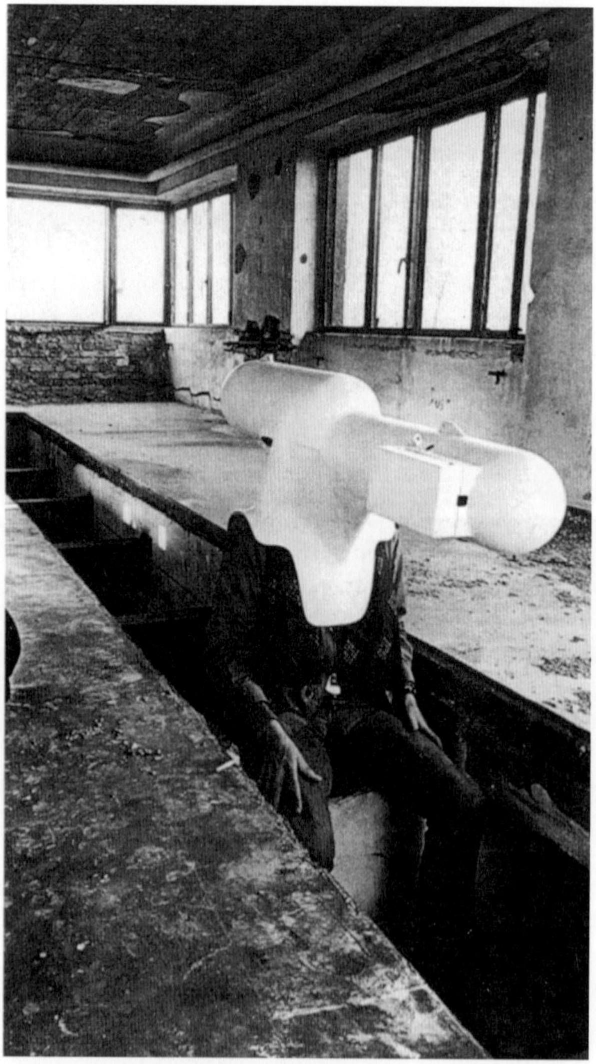

Technology as prosthetic device. Walther Pichler, *TV-Helmet* (1967)

This fundamentally embodied mediation that is present within technology leads to the paradox of the 1960s as a 'second machine age'. The presumed neutrality of technology was certainly questioned throughout the period discussed here – by Colquhoun in terms of symbolic and literal uses, by Banham in his distinction of machine ages, by Debord in his understanding of the mechanisms of the spectacle. Yet in each of these arguments, the perceived neutrality of technology did not disappear, but was simply displaced. To the modernists, the neutrality of technology was an emblem of the modern era, demonstrating the universality of human endeavour and rationality. In the discourse of the 1960s this universality was no longer tenable, nor was the presumption of a neutral technology since society was increasingly dominated by machinery. Yet in the end, neutrality remained present in the notion of instrumentality. That a machine was not 'culturally neutral' became obvious. However, it was still seen as 'morally neutral' to the extent that it could be reconfigured to suit the human needs denied by their subjugation to the image of the machine. This moral neutrality is expressed in highly technological future cities such as New Babylon and the Plug-In City, which are premised on the ability of their inhabitants to create or transform their environment with a kit of parts. The image of these cities is technological, but the idea is that the final form of the city remains undefined. This implies that the technological image they present is not something to aspire to directly, but rather a subtle means towards human freedom.

In the end, architecture more or less by definition has a relationship with technology – even the most 'low-tech' forms of building have need of connections between the different parts, and certainly the contemporary scale of building has made it increasingly dependent on technological components. Therefore architecture must find a mode of relating to or engaging with the technology that sustains it. However, the very nature of technology has changed so vastly between its origins in the Greek *technè* via the industrial era to the contemporary postindustrial or digital era that this relationship has of necessity undergone changes.

Archigram entered into an explicit dialogue with the simplified rendering of technology as good and progressive, addressing it through various smaller topics. In this sense, the work can easily be classified under the general culture of questioning the primacy of technology and rationalization following the late 1950s. At the same time, Archigram used technology in a symbolic fashion to create a powerful fantasy world, seducing the viewer with images of walking cities and nomadic villages in Martian landscapes. This aspect of its imagery made technology a given – a fundamental factor in a brave new world; only this brave new world was populated by happy individualists, not encumbered by a Big Brother watching them. It envisioned the ultimate autonomy of the individual enabled by technology, while it effaced the potential autonomy of technology itself. The visualizations contribute to this reinforcement of the instrumentality of technology, as Robert Maxwell also points out.[74] He implies that the difference between the work of Archigram and that of the technophilic modernists preceding them is minimal, yet that the detailed visualizations of technological elements allow a critic like Banham to see (or construe) a real difference. Thus it becomes important to examine this difference more closely: the formalism resulting from a conceptual treatment of the phenomenon 'technological' versus Archigram's fantasy world that is stabilized and made powerful through the use of *visual* renditions of technological elements. In other words, was the work of Archigram simply replacing the *idea* of technology with an *image* of technology? Was the relationship between architecture and technology truly transformed, as the nomadic dwellings and instant cities seem to proclaim?

Although technology is typically treated as purely instrumental, especially in the modernist era, this apparent moral and cultural neutrality (and its dependence on the ethics of the people utilizing it) begins to be questioned in the 1960s. The development is one towards ambivalence: technology is neither purely instrumental nor purely deterministic.[75] This begins to open up the idea that a pragmatic yet critical use of technology is necessary; yet especially in architecture the optimistic designs of such groups as Archigram still contain the utopian implication that technology may be freely turned towards a more human-oriented use. In the end, the 1960s' focus on technology works two ways: it is on the one hand aimed at resistance, sketching out the problems of technology, thereby also attributing it great power.[76] On the other hand it also maintains the sense of unlimited promise available in future technologies – the potential remains ever greater, despite the threats of current technology. This is what allows the Situationist International to simultaneously critique the dominance of the machine in the modern era and maintain an inherently optimistic belief that technology will someday liberate all humans from labour. This position, both critiquing and reinforcing the modernist relation with technology, is dependent on an ambivalent treatment of the transformative nature of the material technologies that surround us. Only McLuhan seems to approach an understanding that technology can be both instrumental and transformative, and that its consequences cannot be entirely foreseen, only understood in retrospect.

As noted earlier, Colquhoun and Banham both play an important role in unravelling the different manners of addressing technology in architecture, as metaphor and as instrument. Their early resistance against the modernist fetishization of the machine lays the groundwork for understanding the premises of instrumentality upon which the discourse of the 1960s continues to build. In 1962 Colquhoun explicitly takes issue with the position of technology in modernist architecture, distinguishing between the expressive aspects of technology, the 'symbolic', and the instrumental aspects, the 'literal'.[77] For him, the symbolic value of technology is more manifest in modernist architecture than its literal value: in modernism, 'the new technology was an idea rather than a fact... Our admiration of the buildings it created is due more to their success as symbolic representations than to the extent to which they solved technical problems.'[78] In other words, the idea of technology fulfils a symbolic and ideological function.[79] Modernist architecture offered a symbolic rendition of the value of technology (speed, power, rationality, order) more than it actually used the latest technologies to transform the art of building. Although his notion of the literal aspects of technology are perhaps a little closer to a truly instrumental understanding of technology than he acknowledges (thereby neglecting the inherent cultural and symbolic content of even a 'literal' application of technology), the subdivision does allow us to distinguish between an expressionist use of technology and an investigation into the technologies available to solve a specific problem.[80]

Striking is of course this distinction between the cultural meaning of technology and its instrumental use-value. Colquhoun was one of the earliest critics to incorporate this almost Heideggerian position on the ramifications of technology – he and Banham may well have been the first architecture critics to point directly to the *perception* of technology as an important factor in the modernist debate. Moreover, Colquhoun's essay offered a clear sketch of the disjunction between the perception and its actual implementation. In other words, he was one of the first to point to the difference between what the modernists said they were doing and what they actually did. Moreover, he also warned that this position was still too widespread precisely due to this lack of clarity, 'because many architects considering themselves to be the heirs of the Modern Movement fundamentally misinterpret its aims and its virtues. The science of building, the rationalization of construction and assembly, however vital in themselves, remain in the world of literal action.'[81]

Colquhoun was in London at the time these questions were being raised, and part of the circle gathered around Banham, the Independent Group and the

Architectural Association. Banham is especially important at this time in (re) defining the position of technology in relation to architectural production; the separation of the two spheres of influence is both a result of the representations of a malignant technology (in science fiction), and a constitutive part of these new symbolic depictions. The distinction sketched by Colquhoun allows a first questioning of the ideological role played by technology in the realization of a modernist utopia. Yet as is often pointed out, the realized utopia is a dystopia.[82] It is this realized utopia that was showing its teeth in the late 1950s, or even as early as 1948 in George Orwell's *1984*. The aftermath of the Second World War had left behind the distaste for what technology could achieve if unquestioned and put to purely instrumental use. Mass destruction was now not only a possibility, but had been a reality. It had become necessary to examine how benevolent the technological society Le Corbusier aspired to really was.

One of the great arguments about technology was thus on a symbolic level; and because its symbolism was denied until the early 1960s, it also became difficult to see the extent to which the existing symbolism of modernist technology was simply reinforced, since the field of debate was shifted away from the actual issues at hand. This is an important distinction, because although Banham and Colquhoun do clearly discuss the symbolic issues involved in technology, the production of the era still follows a utopian drive not unlike its modernist predecessors, but then conveyed in a different *form*. The fundamental opposition remains between an architecture drenched in the notion of technology as symbolizing progress, or a Luddite resistance to technology as maintaining the quality of human existence. Hence again the potential usefulness of a more pragmatic approach: by merely acknowledging the complexity of the relationship between technology and architecture, the discourse might circumnavigate the ossification into pure and universal presumptions such as 'technology is by definition good'. This might allow the more difficult yet crucial question of what goals a specific technology serve and how at the same time innovations may introduce unexpected results.

Banham in a different manner acknowledges the symbolic content and use of technology and rationalism. Yet he also notes that it is precisely the way the debate developed that caused functionalism to become crucial to arguments on architecture – moving the debate away from aesthetics was a better way to achieve goals than by appealing to a sense of symbolism. So here we find symbolism present yet cloaked; since it was cloaked, Banham points out that the debate was easily reduced to the notions of logic and necessity.[83]

Just like Colquhoun, Banham here clearly notes the need for acknowledging the symbolic aspect of technology. This point is a critical one to the general debate on perception of technology, since its very formalization, and moreover *finalization* in the sense of universal form, in modernist design contradicts one of its inherent principles: that of continual transformation and development.[84] Banham himself observes this inherent contradiction in the work of Le Corbusier:

> There is a curious point here: Le Corbusier had made great play with the idea of a fairly high rate of scrapping, but he seems not to have *visualized* it as part of a continuous process inherent in the technological approach, bound to continue as long as technology continues, but merely as stages in the evolution of a final type or norm, whose perfection, he, Pierre Urbain, Paul Valéry, Piet Mondriaan and many others saw as an event of the immediate future, or even the immediate past.[85]

This 'high rate of scrapping' as Banham calls it, is in direct contradiction to the idea of universal form, and presumes a need to remain continually reactive to new developments. This is indeed the ephemeral quality of modernity that Baudelaire wrote about, the *other* side of which is eternal and immutable. Also, Banham here emphasizes the importance of visualization as an autonomous and critical element in the process of investigating the relationship between technology and architecture. In other words, might we then regard visualization as clarifying that technology is both symbolic and instrumental – and if so, what impact does this have upon the architecture discourse as a whole? The arguments put forth by Banham and Colquhoun imply that the technology of the 1960s will soon fulfil and surpass the ideals merely illustrated in modernism. However, the technology shown in many forms in the 1960s still retains a similar symbolic function. Images showing the plasticity of 'organic' form, streamlining, space-exploration and computers play a similar role to the grain silos and industrial machinery shown in earlier modernist work.

Yet the discrepancy between these images and the return to traditional form is another aspect of symbolism: the symbolic quality of technology is also dependent on its ability to communicate. Colquhoun distinguishes an earlier time in which symbolism was so embedded in tradition that meaning was easily interpreted or at least derived from symbols.[86] The 1960s largely seem to have reverted only to an 'original' symbolic content of traditional forms – or at least, the preludes to post-modernism follow that trajectory. On the other hand, Venturi and Scott Brown's attention to the vernacular offered a view to symbols that were both of our time and related to mass communication. Technology itself is, however, still placed outside of the symbolic realm.

One of the main oppositions throughout the debates on technology is in essence whether technology produces effects of alienation or liberation. The results of the first machine age were considered dehumanizing due to the emphasis on standardization and mechanization and their inability to adapt: 'The paradox of mechanization is that although it is itself the cause of maximal growth and change, the principle of mechanization excludes the very possibility of growth or the understanding of change.'[87] In the 1950s, the discourse began to focus on the dominance of the machine, the lack of natural surroundings and how to reintroduce a sense of identity and individuality in this highly technological era. Ironically, the means for this transformation was often seen as in the technology itself – the quote above, from McLuhan, introduces his idea that electricity marked the beginning of instantaneity as a condition that will reconfigure the world into a global village.

Most of the propositions discussed in this chapter were highly sceptical of the way technological progress had been employed as inevitable solution, yet were still confident that technology itself was not to blame, but rather the manner in which it was utilized. This again is something we find throughout much of the production in the 1960s. The alienation of the modernist environment could be overcome by transforming its machinery into the technological wonders that would truly be suited to man. Banham believed that the problem with the modernists was not so much their ideas of technology, but rather the sad state of the technology available to them – the first machine age was characterized by promises 'never properly delivered'.[88] Plug-in homes and do-it-yourself environments were an answer within the realm of technological progress that answered the disillusion with the results of a mechanized society, if not its premises. McLuhan, believing that the electric age was different in its very nature from the mechanical age, ventured a step further, claiming that the world itself was already different: 'We actually live mythically and integrally, as it were, but we continue to think in the old, fragmented space and time patterns of the pre-electric age.'[89]

As was pointed out by Heidegger in his *Technik und die Kehre*, the notion that technology is a neutral and objective, or amoral, instrument has been destroyed by the advent of modern science.[90] In *Die Technik und die Kehre*, Heidegger persuasively argues the transformation in the relationship between people and their environment due to modern technology – for instance because we can now truly subjugate nature to our needs. However, this argumentation leads him to conclude that we need to rediscover a more 'authentic' way of living in the world (or that we have given that up forever). In a sense, he again dichotomizes the position into entirely for or entirely against modern technology.[91] What we have gained by his arguments is an insight that technology cannot be deemed an amoral or neutral instrument; it does, however, still possess an element of instrumentality. There is, as Colquhoun notes, a literal side to technology: the aspect of 'How shall we make it?' This is what can aid in analysing the opportunities of the middle ground as can be found in realism or pragmatism.[92] Just as analysing imagery in its fullest depth and breadth helps undermine the reductive quality of earlier debates, so the manifestations of (underlying) technologies may do the same.

Unseen Networks of Control: Reconstructing Autonomy in the Electronic Age

While the 'pure' instrumentality of technology was being questioned, the type (or nature?) of technology confronting society was transforming as well: from the industrial works of the modernists, there was a perceptible shift to a more organic and more integrated form of technology, through cybernetics. Also, inverting the logic of Lang's *Metropolis*, the imagery that had shown us how people were forced to adapt to enormous machines, reducing themselves to mechanical elements was now transforming into the imagery of *Fantastic Voyage* (1966), where a spaceship was reduced to microscopic size and then injected into the bloodstream of a human being. In part this may be attributed to the advent of the computer age. For example, in Godard's *Alphaville* computers have transformed human society; yet the transformation Godard shows us is the rationalized ideal of modernist technology: words describing human emotions have been eliminated from the dictionary, which is also the new 'bible' for this society. Godard's depiction of this society is critical, and remonstrates modernism for its technological idolatry. At the same time, he is also aware how thin the line is becoming between man and machine, a development presaged by Lang's portrayal of the robot in *Metropolis*.

Banham offered us the 'first machine age' in his analysis of the modern masters, positioning his own time as the second machine age and distinguishing it from the first. Yet in his final sentence he also reminds the reader that 'we may believe that the architects of the First Machine Age were wrong, but we in the Second Machine Age have no reason yet to be superior about them'.[93] By 1964 he did appear to be somewhat more confident that the work of Archigram offered a good direction for the second machine age. While the definitions for this first machine age centred on standardization, repetition and the idea of technology in terms of speed and motion, it framed all these highly modern ideas within a traditional architecture. The second machine age should at the very least acknowledge and utilize the fundamentally different formal language of technology, as manifest in, for example, American cars. Archigram, in a further justification of its own work, also appropriates Banham's idea that the 1960s are the advent of the second machine age.

Rethinking our relationship with technology is impossible without addressing popular culture, as the two have gone hand in hand since the advent of the printing press. Each technological innovation is deeply entwined with the (unexpected) uses it is put to by a broader group of people. The Internet, originally constructed as a network to link scientific and military institutions so as to more easily communicate scientific progress, is now the domain of a reconfigured virtual public. It is not limited to military secrets or obscure scientific discoveries, but has been inundated with everyday functions such as shopping and chatting.

The relationship between technology and the image has been extremely complex since the 1960s, and before that was almost inextricable as of the 1920s. Walter Benjamin points out some of the complicated connections in his 'Work of Art in the Age of Mechanical Reproduction', while Andy Warhol's work appears to embody the paradigms and paradoxes of this relationship between technology and aesthetics. McLuhan's motto 'the medium is the message' is nowhere more appropriate than here. As discussed in the previous chapter, the Independent Group worked with much of the popular imagery of its day; in its use of imagery, one could argue that an approach was followed that accepts technology as underlying condition; yet also fetishizes the gadgetry involved. The mechanics of reproduction and the technology underlying the society of the spectacle are accepted as preconditions, and the main body of work focuses on the power of the image itself. The fact that the image is omnipresent remains unquestioned. Archigram follows the other side of this technology-art equation. Its members express technology in such a visually powerful way that it becomes laden with the kind of symbolism we would traditionally expect from a 'purely' aesthetic endeavour. In other words, this is an aesthetic technology, and the medium is the message.

Jurjen Zeinstra argues that Archigram's tendency to design hyper-technological artefacts that are no more than a lightweight mobile shell for the human body reduced the very essence of architecture not to a problem of dwelling, but to a kind of zero-degree issue of clothing.[94] He prefers the Smithsons' House of the Future simply because it still sees a future for the discipline of architecture: the Smithsons are still making spaces for the future dweller, while Archigram is producing artefacts that will end up making the space around them flexible, undefined and thereby generic. What this argument dismisses, however, is the very specificity of the

Prosthetic technology and the pleasure principle: 'guaranteed to give every nerve ending the wildest buzz'. Warren Chalk and David Greene, Electronic Tomato (1969)

visualizations of technology in Archigram, the fact that it does (especially now) show itself as a polemic engaged with both prior uses of technology (in modernist architecture) and the potential when one enters the fantasy world of young boys with a passion for science fiction and future technologies. Possibly, Archigram never meant for technology to kill architecture or to make it obsolete – maybe it simply wanted to explore how far we could join in these experiments, in the pleasure of exploring new possibilities. However that may be, it is clear that Archigram displayed the same kind of undisguised and unapologetic joy as its predecessors in the possibilities of technology and media, in the various manifestations of the spectacle society.

Again, we can see the very direct attacks on earlier uses of technological idolatry, yet at the same time it is not so much destroyed as sidestepped by introducing a different form of expression. Again, this work on the one hand poses some extremely critical questions: Should we want to live in a mechanistic world? Should we want to standardize our environment? Should we want to follow only the rules of engineering, and if so, should those rules dictate our aesthetics? If we want to appeal to functionalism, should this offer a functional appearance, or simply 'be' functional? These questions approach the condition of pragmatism as suggested by Martijntje Smits, yet remain just shy of entirely subverting the dichotomy inherent in the questions.[95] In the end, technology remains both a symbol of a better world soon to come, and a neutral instrument that requires little more than some well-designed guidance to help us attain utopia. Archigram has envisioned many different potential technologies, but the gadgetry it revelled in prevents a careful assessment of how these technologies impact everyday life. What appears necessary here is a form of critique that can navigate the McLuhanesque condition of contemporary technology, a critical position that simultaneously acknowledges how strongly technology has become embedded in our world.

This position both helps understand our contemporary society and indicates some of the problems we have created by maintaining a firmly progressive stance towards the machine. The 'hybrid' understanding of technology as both medium and message is endemic to contemporary society: we can no longer isolate ourselves from technology, yet we also cannot examine it as an autonomous object (since it is part of our daily existence). This also follows from Heidegger's position that modern technology and science already determine how we understand the world, not just what we do with it (therefore we cannot step outside of this understanding). In the optimistic years of the 1960s, this was taken to indicate that we were again moving 'forward', that a new step in human evolution had arrived.[96] The scepticism towards the technology of the moderns was at the heart of a transformation in understanding technology, but the transformation concerned again its *form* rather than its fundamental 'position' in society. The belief remained that technological progress was good, as long as its potential was utilized in the right way.

The critique of Archigram was aimed at the one-dimensional use of technology in modernism and the symbolic use of technology in modernist architecture. Instead, we need to incorporate an essence of technology in architecture. This was expressed through new uses of technology that were closer to the body (scale and presence of body), through the form of technology (organic form), and through an acknowledgement of the shifting space of technology (the medium is the message and consumer society). Yet Archigram's approach remained inundated with an instrumental approach to technology. It did not address the problematic condition of autonomy, and how this was either enforced or destroyed by technology. It did not seem to grasp that the very notion of autonomy was, as Kockelkoren suggests, an 'exponent of mediation'.[97] The suggestions of McLuhan perhaps most closely approach a fundamentally revised relationship with technology, acknowledging its instrumental and autonomous character simultaneously, which can only truly be addressed through its material reality.

Autonomy and mediation cannot be conceived of separately in this day and age. They are entwined with the increasing 'unseen networks' that form our world and have an enormous impact upon our everyday existence. Thus the physical manifestations of technology are as important as their intellectual constructs, be they visual or conceptual. The physical becomes embodied in unexpected forms of technology, be they in entertainment, new media, or the digital world of the Internet. This introduces them in a different fashion than typically addressed within the architecture discourse. Although the members of Archigram had a good intuition for alternative forms of technology, and their attention to popular culture made them sensitized to unexpected uses, they maintained a belief that the answer lay within a new form of technology, and not in the complex interrelationship of architecture, technology and culture.

IV

Architecture in Its Own Image: Pop Reflections

The 'Pop Years': Opening Up the Discourse of Architecture

One of the most striking transformations in the architecture of the 1960s is the introduction of popular imagery – those colourful collages of advertisements and magazine people, the presence of bright and shiny consumer objects and the use of techniques from comic books and films. Archigram, the Smithsons, Venturi and Scott Brown, but also collaborations such as Superstudio and Haus Rucker Co. make extensive use of this newly discovered resource for their architectural expressions. Surely this tells us something about what was lacking in modernism – the cheerful images of pop culture were positioned in defiance of the abstract modern environment. Yet it also involves a general democratization of values. Rather than the *Bildungsideal* of an earlier time, the aesthetics of 'low culture' were used as a protest against the hermetic elitism of architecture and the arts. Furthermore, the affluence of the post-war years reconfigured the relationship between culture and economics.[1] The economics of consumption became entwined with mass production, starting down the road to the introduction of what would later be called the 'creative consumer'. Although these developments encompass a number of diverse ideas related to mass culture, the society of the spectacle and the problem of representation, their manifestations in the architecture of the time reveal a number of specific transformations that are still relevant to contemporary discourse. In today's field of iconography and city branding, and the continuing tensions between architecture and its media representations, the 1960s mark a turning point. The work of Robert Venturi and Denise Scott Brown can be seen as exemplary for the radical changes taking place in the field of architecture and its treatment of popular imagery.

In general in the 1960s, there is a marked increase in attention for 'the image'. This comprises a diverse set of issues such as mass-cultural imagery, the expression of the surface, the importance of symbolism and ornamentation, as well as an interest in the manifestations of an increasingly visual culture. Although this may seem an extensive range, there is a clear demarcation in the articles of the 1960s that opposes these questions to a perceived lack of visual vitality in modernism. This focuses on the importance of figuration (towards a symbolic and communicative value) and on an expressive surface (as opposed to the white walls of modernism). In the broadest sense, we might take Jencks' definition of pop as a guideline here: incorporating new influences from outside the profession (and thereby opening the field of architecture to such 'debased' influences as mass culture).[2] On the

Poster for exhibition 'This Is Tomorrow'. Richard Hamilton, *Just What Is It that Makes Today's Homes So Different, So Appealing?* (1956)

other hand, we could remain quite close to the question of imagery and ask which images allow architecture to 'reconnect' with the human factor so prominent in the 1960s. Both sides are valid and crucial to the debates in the 1960s.

The introduction of 'pop' to architecture begins as early as the mid-1950s, when an increasing correlation was perceived between the modernist rhetoric of emancipation and enlightenment, and urban blight, a sterile environment and the depressing conditions of the factory worker. As noted earlier, sociological studies of the mid-1950s begin to address these conditions on various levels, with an emphasis on city structure and the denied place of the individual. Well-known are the studies of East London by Young and Wilmott, later used by the Smithsons; and the studies of Herbert Gans in the USA, used by Venturi and Scott Brown. As in early modernism, sociology was the field in which a number of concerns in the disciplines of architecture and planning were being voiced; yet by now, a reasonably direct application of sociology seemed more fruitful to urban designers.[3] In architecture, the question was how to find a visual and spatial expression for the issues uncovered by sociologists. Moreover, there was a sense that the discipline could be transformed through these new visual expressions. The 1956 exhibition 'This Is Tomorrow' at the Whitechapel Gallery in London stands as an example for the introduction of an everyday imagery and popular references. If the city had become bleak in part due to its sterile functionalist forms, then perhaps introducing a new style of imagery based primarily on profusion would change the sense of the city. As such, mass-cultural imagery was utilized as a critique against modernism.

As an influence in architecture, 'pop' is mainly a response to two conditions of post-war culture. On the one hand it overturned the sterile and abstract visualizations of modernism by introducing a profusion of imagery culled from everywhere – magazines, movies, comics. On the other hand, it was also simply an accommodation of a society in which visual information was increasingly present. Therefore it is not surprising to find that the influence of 'pop' found its most radical form in the USA, where the general level of affluence increased quickly as of the mid-1950s, while the country had not suffered the level of destruction that Europe had in the Second World War. In terms of the architecture discourse, the importance of 'pop' as an imaging mechanism was an obvious response to the incapacity of the modernist debate to handle any kind of (mass) imagery.[4] The functionalist aspects of modernism had no place for the symbolic and often kitsch aspects of pop culture, while the abstract metaphors of the machine age were visually not conducive to the candy-coated everyday imagery of ads, comics, films and magazines. Therefore it is perhaps unsurprising that, much as 'everyday life' became a label signifying 'vitality' in the city, 'pop' came to signify a vitality in the realm of the visual. Or, in the immortal words of Venturi: 'Less is a bore.'[5]

There is also a general background to these issues, which has to do both with a reaction against abstract expressionism in art and with changing conditions of everyday life.[6] Especially in the USA, the affluent society of the post-war era was leading to increased purchasing power and beginning to fuel the economy of consumption we are familiar with today.[7] Again we find resoundingly similar critiques, against the elitism of Herbert Read and Clement Greenberg (critiques by the Independent Group and by Susan Sontag, for instance); and again, we find numerous connections between how these critiques are expressed and what they lead to – there is an overwhelming turn to everyday imagery and popular culture, as well as a consistent use of collage and assemblage techniques. American and British projects show a strong similarity in their specific references as well as their open approach to pop culture (for example Hamilton and Paolozzi in the UK; Tom Wolfe in the USA; Banham and Jencks in both the USA and the UK), while the approach of the Situationist International is distinctly ambiguous. The revolutionary capacity of imagery is implied in the definition of *détournement*, while at the same time the critique of the 'spectacle' embodies a suspicion of the capitalist power structure implicit in the visual culture the situationists see proliferating. These differences between the American and (continental) European approach to imagery contain the seeds of contemporary struggles with the relationship between culture, politics and economics in particular.[8]

Pop culture and Pop Art combined the various aspects that were important to the discourse at the time: they played with the signs of affluence and were embedded in the consumption economy. The profusion of images reflected an increasing sense of complexity, yet they were also playful and critical, albeit in a gentle fashion. And they even had mass appeal. By themselves, these transformations in imagery and visuality need not have an impact upon the architecture production of the time – they could have remained within the discourse of art. However, in the general critiques of modernism and functionalism, there was a turn to popular culture here as well, in a hope that architecture could somehow reconnect with the inhabitants it was designing for.[9] As in the discourse on the city, where individual experience was used as a way to offset the increasing mechanization of the modern city, in terms of the visual field, symbolic and kitsch elements of popular culture were utilized to transform the abstraction and lack of symbolic communication in the modernist environment. In this way, the notion of a popular or a mass culture became important as a reference for architectural expression.[10] There was a hope that the images of mass culture could revitalize a discourse apparently stuck in modernist abstraction. Therefore, instead of rigorously mechanized buildings, architects produced frivolous and colourful imagery. They gathered their sources from science fiction and comic books, preferring the glittering worlds of Las Vegas and Hollywood to the urban utopias of Le Corbusier. In the most radical manifestations, anything was fine as long as it expressed personal freedom, the creativity of the individual (any individual, not only artists), the pleasure of living in an age of consumer freedom and increased wealth, and the necessary rebellion against standardization and the repressive authority of the older generation. As is most obvious in the works of Venturi and Scott Brown, the populist imagery of the USA became a new benchmark for a different kind of visuality, one that was less demanding perhaps than its modernist predecessor.

Finding new reference points for architecture: science-fiction imagery in magazines and films

Glamour in the desert: photographs of signs in Las Vegas. Robert Venturi and Denise Scott Brown, *Learning from Las Vegas* (1972)

The newly found freedom of commercial advertising imagery. Tom Wesselmann, *Still Life #16* (1962)

This different kind of visuality was both reflected in and formed through images. In the architecture debate, the discussions of these representations were typically more about the intent of the architect than the general aesthetic, cultural and visual context. Yet it is also obvious that images are powerful in creating a collective understanding of architecture and its agenda – one that is not entirely under the control of architects. Where the modernist agenda was expressed through a purity of line and form, through empty spaces that implied the liberated, rational, new and unfettered society to come, its disturbingly inhuman aspects were exhibited in later representations of these same rational and orderly spaces, some of which did not even belong to the domain of the architecture discourse. For example, we can think of Tati's *Playtime*, where Monsieur Hulot looks out over an office space that is organized on a perfectly square grid, by modernist standards a space of perfect clarity, calling upon the most rational faculties of the occupant in its navigation. Yet our protagonist Hulot shows only the distressing disorientation that results from a space so thoroughly lacking in recognizable 'landmarks' or anomalies that can trigger a sense of uniqueness. In fact, since it is a square grid, even the directional orientation by length or width disappears, as is shown further on in the scene. As Hulot is running between the office cubicles, the camera makes a number of 90 degree rotations, completing the sense of being lost.[11]

Absolutely crucial to the developments in the 1960s is that this transformation embodies a vast democratization of aesthetic values and their significance. This also implies the increasing sophistication of the audience, which was explored by critics and writers such as Banham and Wolfe.[12] The discourse not only takes place within the hallowed halls of academia and professional practice, but also in the public arena of mass culture. This implies a two-way influence: presumably films such as those of Tati are popular because they are somehow recognizable, or resonate with feelings or ideas already present in the audience. Yet at the same time these popular films begin to create a collective perception or consciousness of modernist architecture. Moreover, the relationship between architecture and ordinary images is also represented through the familiar symbols of traditional (vernacular) spaces versus the purified abstraction of modernist space. This goes into the inherently troubled relationship with imagery. For clarity's sake, this final category should be split into two parts, one involving mass-cultural imagery, the other involving the concept of 'image' as opposed to 'reality'. In the case of mass-cultural imagery, it has by and large been considered unchallenging, derivative and unenlightened (following Adorno). In the 1960s, it was understood more along the lines of Benjamin: there is so much visual material out there, so much new information, and it can be seen as productive in other ways, or at least indicative of unexplored territories. It does not necessarily need to fit the traditional categories of artistic

A moment of overview prior to entering the disorienting grid of office cubicles. Jacques Tati, *Playtime* (1967)

quality or value, although it must certainly be studied with a critical eye. This side of the issue is what people like Venturi and Scott Brown in the USA, and Alloway in the UK were picking up as a new direction in architecture.

The second aspect, the relationship between image and reality, refers to the platonic sense of an image as a 'lesser copy' of an original (where this would be an Idea for Plato, the authentic original is now often seen as empirical reality). This scepticism, involving the distrust of what we see, has remained with us even until today, though since Baudrillard's work *Simulations* the traditional hierarchy between copy and original has at the very least been questioned. This aspect of the discourse has been somewhat misappropriated by the modernist discourse in architecture when it separates the appearance of the building from the actual building, as if the two are completely unrelated.

Since the architecture of modernism, designers and theorists have been explicitly struggling with 'the image' – what its relationship might be to architecture, whether it should be acknowledged, and if so, how. This difficulty with imagery, coupled with the explosion of imagery present in contemporary everyday life (leading some, like Martin Jay, to speak of a 'visual turn') which can be said to have fully begun in the post-war period of the late 1950s, leads to questions. What made the architecture of the 1960s turn to imagery as a tool? Why is the relationship between architecture and imagery so tenuous, if not downright hostile?[13] Why did the imagery of mass culture become so important all of a sudden? Where did this trajectory start, and can we learn from it today, in our media-saturated culture?

In these still valid questions about our society of images, or what Guy Debord called the 'society of the spectacle', and the relationship between mass-cultural imagery and architecture, the importance of the 1960s can hardly be underestimated. They offer foundational questions still relevant to post-industrial society; yet they are also grounded heavily in modernism and its rigid categories of morality and aesthetics. The issues at stake here are also grounded in the problems of contemporary theory: the transitions (or so-called revolutions) between modernism, the 1960s and postmodernism all still work within the same dialectic. And especially in the 1960s and the later postmodern architecture, the relationship between imagery and architecture is crucial. Postmodernism introduces the billboard as a valid element of architectural design and reintroduces a symbolism of architectural form that was hidden in modernism, for example. The question remains whether this relationship between imagery and architecture is part of the problem of the trajectory from modernism to postmodernism, via the 1960s; or whether it is the place it all meets in critical conflict.

Architecture from Abstraction to Profusion

In his 'gentle manifesto' *Complexity and Contradiction in Architecture*, Robert Venturi discusses the importance of inclusion and the problem of modernism's exclusion of ornament and elaborate forms. Where the clarity of modernist forms was meant as an escape from the perceived decadence of nineteenth-century eclecticism, for Venturi a similar profusion in the 1960s indicated a richness of everyday life that

Billboards demonstrate the vitality of everyday communicative imagery: Times Square, New York. Robert Venturi, *Complexity and Contradiction*, page 54 (Photograph Peter Blake)

remains unappreciated in architecture. His critique of modernism stays within the realm of architecture history, yet the commentary it delivers is similar to the criticisms directed at the modernist city by the Situationist International – modernism is too 'clean', too 'pure', too 'clear', too 'simple', and Venturi adds 'puritanically moral' (these are all adjectives from the first page of *Complexity and Contradiction in Architecture*). In its adherence to the traditions of the discipline of architecture, the book cannot be considered 'pop' in the definition of Jencks. Yet there is also a transition within the text and the images of the book; halfway through, the conclusions to the chapters increasingly refer to the everyday environment. In sequence, he notes the complexity of Times Square, the scale differences demonstrated by highways alongside buildings and he poses the question: 'Is not Main Street almost all right?'[14] This transition in the book can be identified as the beginnings of Venturi's examination of the ordinary, but still framed by the history of architecture.[15] His comments are framed by a sense of historical continuity and a consciousness of his own position within the debate. The main point of criticism continually returns to a missing sense of reality in the work of architects with their 'prim dreams of pure order'.[16] When he does address the condition of the contemporary vernacular, the environment either built without the intervention of architects, or discussed without the intervention of architecture historians, it is still to demonstrate a point about architectural form and what he perceives as lacking in the modernist discourse. The attempts of modernism to reduce architecture to its very essence had caused architects to ignore essential qualities. For Venturi, both decoration and complex form are significant to how we experience

'Typical Main street, USA': almost all right. Robert Venturi, *Complexity and Contradiction*, page 105 (Photograph Wallace Litwin)

a building. Not that Venturi was looking to reinstate a flagrant form of decoration for decoration's sake – just that in the process of removing some of the expressive aspects of architecture, there was also the loss of a certain quality of depth and multilayered experiences, of jarring contradictions followed by soothing harmony. Venturi was pleading here for a resistance against oversimplification of form, arguing that our experience of the world is equally complex and inclusive of all sorts of contradictions.

The book itself is an explicit attack on modernist principles, although Venturi is quick to state that the architecture of some high modernists has important spatial qualities not to be denied. The attack is focused largely on the dogma of reduction and simplification, and seeks counterexamples throughout architecture history to construct an alternative view of design principles.[17] The questions raised in the book, as well as the general resistance to oversimplification, reflect the period in which it was written. Reality appeared to be becoming more complex and less clear cut. Where the 1950s, especially in the USA, were still largely framed by the perfect family structure and societal niceties, as well as a great respect for etiquette, privacy and social convention, the early 1960s were already rife with the resistance against stability, the dominant modes of living, and the social revolutions that were already brewing. In referring to the tendency of architects in the first half of the twentieth century to solve only a select number of problems, Venturi formulated precisely this mid-century discomfort with tradition and clarity that led to such diverse forms of resistance to modernism in architecture (with post-modernism finally becoming the dominant one): 'He [the architect] can exclude important considerations only at the risk of separating architecture from the experience of life and the needs of society.'[18] It is this separation that is at the core of so many rebellious voices, only each has their own solution. Where Debord similarly encouraged us to experience the 'totality' of life as the first steps towards revolution, Venturi offers his 'gentle manifesto' to help architecture come closer to the experience of life. In Venturi's formulation we again see the echoes of the 'human qualities' of life, of 'real life', of 'lived space'. One of the most common critiques of modernism is thus manifested through the acceptance of the world as it is rather than designing the world as it should be.

Venturi begins his journey by looking back into architecture history for an alternate route, one that does not inevitably lead to a modernist aesthetic. He finds some material in the Gothic, some in Art Deco. Although the issue of 'ordinary' is already present in the book, it becomes ever stronger as he begins to collaborate

Aesthetics of consumer objects. Andy Warhol, *Brillo Box* (1964/1969)

Endless grid of consumption: Archizoom, No-Stop City (model, 1968)

with Scott Brown.[19] His true discovery, which lies not in the symbolism of times past, but rather in the transposition of symbolism on his own time, can be in part attributed to Scott Brown, who began taking series of photographs of the everyday environment in Europe and Africa in the late 1950s.[20] Between the two of them, it led to a study of the iconography of the everyday. This had already begun to surface in various places in the late 1950s to early 1960s: the New Brutalists had discovered the power of photographing real children playing in real streets, Andy Warhol offered Campbell soup cans and Brillo boxes to unsuspecting art gallery audiences, Alloway discussed the influence of Hollywood films and popular culture and Archizoom was presenting displays of everyday objects of consumption in an abstract gridded space. Yet the work that would eventually lead to *Learning from Las Vegas* took these various developments and melded them into a radical rethinking of the role and place of popular imagery in architecture.

Although *Complexity and Contradiction in Architecture* is still focused on traditional architectural form, and analyses it in the traditional terminology of tension and harmony, we begin to see hints of some later concerns with the visual drifting through the text at times. Addressing the difficulty in assessing architectural form, Venturi comments: 'Instead, the variety inherent in the ambiguity of visual perception must once more be acknowledged and exploited.'[21] Note here the sly insertion of 'once more', implying ever so gently that there was a time, before the modernists recalibrated our vision to seek behind the surface, that the ambiguity of visual perception was understood.[22]

The visual profusion of the 1960s thus becomes a literal manifestation of the 'messy' reality already signalled in relation to the city and everyday life. In a similar fashion, the 'messy' reality of everyday imagery reacts against the radical purism of a modernist utopian agenda. Introducing the everyday implies an acceptance of imperfection or compromise. In the French discourse, along similar lines to the American discourse, there is a tendency to speak of the 'image' of space as opposed to the 'experience' of space. Here, the image of space is a purified representation, while the experience of space incorporates contradictory and indefinable aspects of reality. The two are not only distinct, but are seen as mutually exclusive. The Situationist International is perhaps the most radical in its distinction of the two and subsequent rejection of space that is merely passively consumed, but Lefebvre, too, clearly distinguishes these two perceptions of space, which he identifies as 'conceived space' and 'lived space'. To him, conceived space is 'a visual space, a space reduced to blueprints, to mere images', while lived space is opposed to this image-bound space: 'The space of the everyday activities of users is a concrete one, which is to say, subjective.'[23] This distinction, useful as it is towards a critique of abstract modernist space, does not answer how the two may influence one another. It does not necessarily help in understanding what it is about Las Vegas that attracts so many people, since it is commercial, thereby falling under the capitalist mode of domination. In Lefebvre's view, conceived space is little more than an idealized perception of a space (little to do with everyday reality), and this has by now subjugated the real, lived experience of space. Since he is arguing against the dangers of bourgeois (capitalist) domination, his notion of conceived space is also defined by its very submission to the dominance of capitalism.

In the USA, similar ideas are proposed, and 'messy' is certainly seen as a revolutionary condition in architecture. But here the presence of this 'messiness' is typically used to normalize architecture (making it more like the everyday environment) rather than revolutionize the entire power structure (as the work of the Situationist International in France might suggest). In this sense, the selfsame 'messy reality' in the USA becomes more of a formal category, as an introduction of a popular aesthetics. This resembles the collages of the Independent Group, where the profusion of everyday imagery was in part put together out of pleasure. The problems of images and symbols are approached more pragmatically than in France, which is to be seen in the work of Gans, for example, when he argues that a 'lower culture' (dictated by the demands of the market and by the culture industry) does not produce or embody less meaning to those experiencing it. In other words, where Lefebvre might argue that Las Vegas could never become a 'lived space', Gans might suggest that its significance is equal to a more romanticized Marxist version of 'lived space' that has nothing to do with mass culture.

In this sense, the introduction of complexity has everything to do with a need to find the synthetic condition of everyday experience in the built environment.[24] Le Corbusier's manifestoes were constructed on the clarity of the engineer and on the rhetoric of (pseudo-)scientific analysis. When constructing a perfect world like that of the Ville Radieuse, there is a need for the powerful language of reduction and simplification. However, the perfect world (as we know of all utopias) is not suitable to live in. The stability of perfection is an idea, not a reality, and even if the perfect world is constructed it must contend with the fluid problems of every day.

This is to be seen in the most obvious issues of our postindustrial society: despite the early twentieth-century hopes of industrialization and later globalization producing a world with no hunger, no poverty and extensive leisure time for all the working class, none of these conditions have been realized. Creating the perfect world has to do with not only a perfect environment or technological progress, but also with human factors. This problem is what Herbert Gans calls the 'fallacy of physical determinism': the idea planners have of being able to create a perfect community by creating a perfect environment.[25] Perfection on this level, although it was attacked in terms of modernist conventions, was still present in the 1960s' manifestoes: the Situationist International hoped to find its perfect world through a combination of technology (to allow for leisure) and the unleashing of inner creativity; Archigram placed its hopes in a more 'human' form of technology; and Venturi and Scott Brown believed in a form of liberation through the acknowledgment (and sometimes emulation) of popular culture.

Nevertheless, Venturi, in line with his contemporaries, attacks this notion of the ideal: 'When circumstances defy order, order should bend or break: anomalies and uncertainties give validity to architecture.' At the same time, he is quite aware of the need for some kind of order – without a system it becomes impossible to recognize anomalies: 'Order must exist before it can be broken.'[26] However, it is the rigidity and universality of this order he is questioning; there is a pendulum movement within every chapter of the book (and nearly every sentence) to place the anomaly against the system, the unexpected against the common. And it is from this resistance to the ideal that we finally run into what he is so well-known for: the use of banal objects and imagery. He finds their importance not so much in a perceived beauty (he even refers to some of these objects as vulgar) but rather in the mere fact of their existence.

> Architects can bemoan or try to ignore them or even try to abolish them, but they will not go away. Or they will not go away for a long time, because ... these commonplace elements accommodate existing needs for variety and communication.[27]

Again, here we find a quietly embedded but extremely critical phrase: 'existing needs'. The major turns in the 1960s revolved around looking at what was in the world, at acknowledging that the ideal was sometimes a little further away than expected. Architecture (and its theory) as well as urban planning found itself re-valuating its expectations on the basis of what already existed, rather than what we hoped would come into being in the future.

In *Complexity and Contradiction in Architecture*, many preludes are made to the later work in *Learning from Las Vegas*, and at the same time many similar concerns are visible to the European critiques of modernism. Against the totalitarian condition of systematic order (where he specifically refers to Mies van der Rohe's desire for order and clarity as a reaction to the confusion of modern times), Venturi poses the question: 'Should we not resist bemoaning confusion? Should we not look for meaning in the complexities and contradictions of our times and acknowledge the limitations of systems?'[28] From here, he uses the modernist tendency to maintain a rigid adherence to order and unity to argue the necessity of acknowledging and using elements of popular culture. This is on the one hand a slightly strange transition since the idea of complexity and contradiction need not be directly linked to popular culture, especially since he argues the existence of complexity throughout architecture history. However, in the context of his diatribe against modernism, and since the all-encompassing purist aesthetic of modernism is his main point of critique, the tendency to look towards mass culture as the locus of complexity is understandable. Modernism engaged with the increased massiveness of modern society, but did not visually acknowledge the mass culture that went along with that. Moreover, as we have already seen in the previous chapter, one of the most persistent critiques of modernist rhetoric is its tendency towards the revolutionary, the heroic and its concomitant denial of existing reality. Or, more accurately, the notion that existing reality must undergo a complete transformation into the utopian ideals of a truly modern society. In response to this aspect of the modernist discourse, Venturi offers: 'The main justification for honky-tonk elements in architectural order is their very existence. They are what we have.'[29] This shares the idea that there is something to be found in mass culture – but it is surprisingly tentative about the quality of it. Venturi here goes no further than to acknowledge that these 'honky-tonk elements' are simply a fact of life – here, he does not yet propose that there is also an important aesthetic vitality within popular culture, as Alloway does, but merely concedes their accommodation of an apparently fundamental need for 'variety and communication'.[30] Two pages later, however, he does follow along the lines of Alloway's argument in stating that:

> Pop Art has demonstrated that these commonplace elements are often the main source of the occasional variety and vitality of our cities, and that it is not their banality or vulgarity as elements which make for the banality or vulgarity of the whole scene, but rather their contextual relationships of space and scale'.[31]

To Venturi, complexity is a notion to be found throughout architecture history that encompasses the visual profusion of reality as opposed to an idealized stylization that appeals to the everyday and opens up the elitist discourse, and also expresses reality in a way that any idealized discourse by definition cannot.

In all this, there is an idea that 'vitality', with its implied 'real life' (as opposed to 'aestheticized' life?) is to be found in those everyday elements (Venturi usually calls them commonplace) that architects have completely ignored in favour of their own constructions of total design. Even Vincent Scully in the introduction to *Complexity and Contradiction in Architecture* praises Venturi's 'instinct for the changes of scale in small buildings and for the unsuspected life to be found in the common artifacts of mass culture'.[32] In other words, in a complete inversion of the type of modernism espoused by Le Corbusier: ordinary equals lively, and banal equals vital.

'Honky-tonk': postcard of Las Vegas

Although the emphasis on the ordinary is still primarily implicit in *Complexity and Contradiction in Architecture*, its criticism finds resonance with other publications such as those of the Independent Group. In the American discourse, the word 'honky-tonk' appears alongside the more commonly used 'ordinary' or 'commonplace', although it also fades away eventually. The emphasis will remain on the ordinary and the everyday. As we have seen, Venturi already comments on honky-tonk in *Complexity and Contradiction in Architecture*, as does Douglas Haskell in an early piece in *Architectural Forum*.[33] To Haskell, this interest in honky-tonk is related to what Venturi will later call communication through symbols and signs. *Learning from Las Vegas* will ultimately exploit the kind of popular kitsch on the Strip that most modern architects eschew, all in the name of an interest in signs and (pop) symbols as a form of communication with 'the masses'.

Democratizing Aesthetics: From Complexity in Architecture to the Ordinary of Las Vegas

Not only does the visual profusion of the 1960s represent a specific cultural transformation, it is also closely linked to the revaluation of the ordinary. Precisely by opposing the clean lines of design with the commonplace diversity of the everyday environment, the argument is made that architects have been taught not to see the richness of the world around them. One of the works that most distinctly analyses the ordinary environment of American life begins with a studio at Yale in the fall of 1970, only two years after the studio that resulted in the book *Learning from Las Vegas*. The 1970 studio, 'Remedial Housing for Architects', is meant to explore the richness of the everyday residential environment. This is an environment that is filled with symbolic gestures that are also mass-produced objects of consumption.

In 1978, Colquhoun commented on this transformation in the work of Venturi between *Complexity and Contradiction in Architecture* and *Learning from Las Vegas*,[34] signalling that the architectural themes of complexity, ambiguity and contradiction are central to *Complexity and Contradiction in Architecture* while the themes of the ordinary and populism are implicit. These then are made explicit and central to *Learning from Las Vegas*. The book originated as a studio project given at Yale in the fall of the 1968 academic year. A few years earlier, in 1966, Scott Brown had travelled to California for a teaching position, but made various stops along the way in a general investigation of the American landscape. Her interest in the everyday is well-documented, and this trip was intended as a continuation of her interest in the context around her.[35] One of her stops was Las Vegas, and this is what started the extended fascination with this landscape of the banal, the ugly, the ordinary – ultimately leading to the publication of *Learning from Las Vegas* in 1972. Surprisingly, these beginnings of the Las Vegas project are well-documented but not often discussed. In 1960, at the time of *Complexity and Contradiction in Architecture*, Venturi and Scott Brown had just met, and had begun to discuss the importance of such issues as the everyday, and although Venturi's interest in the ordinary was already quite marked in *Complexity and Contradiction in Architecture*, the introduction of the 'actual' ordinary, or the 'commonplace' in the sense of everyday architecture, vernacular imagery and popular culture must be attributed to Scott Brown.

If Venturi was particularly attuned to the abstraction of modernism and the question of complexity in architecture, Scott Brown was more sensitive to the inherent elitism in architecture, and the need to reintroduce the ordinary. In an interview Venturi noted that his appreciation of Las Vegas and a better eye for the ordinary was largely attributable to her influence.[36] This may to some degree be attributed to her background in England. The work of Venturi Scott Brown proves to have a much stronger grounding in work produced in England in the 1950s than is usually addressed.[37] Scott Brown appears to have introduced some of the aspects of what one might call 'social realism' in architecture from the UK to the USA.[38] Starting in 1956, she had taken many photographs of the vernacular environment with Robert Scott Brown, her first husband. Later, as she started studying, working and travelling in the USA she moved more towards planning, systematically examining the everyday aspects of city and suburban life, of which the studies with Venturi on Las Vegas and Levittown were the most prominent. She studied with Herbert Gans, and was familiar with the work of J.B. Jackson, the Independent Group and various sociologists. As a student at the Architectural Association in the late 1950s, she had been exposed to New Brutalism (which also has some affinity with kitchen-sink realism), and was present at many of the lectures given at the Institute for Contemporary Arts.[39] The sociological underpinnings of New

Brutalism combined with the planning studies of Scott Brown in the USA to form the foundations of the extensive visual documentation and categorization of everyday architecture in the studies of Las Vegas and Levittown.

These beginnings are further confirmed in the extensive studio notes, largely written by Scott Brown and composed of various studio assignments.[40] In an atypical studio format for the time, *Learning from Las Vegas* was broken up into themes, each of which had an introductory problem statement and a two-phase assignment.[41] By breaking the studio up into themes, a certain expertise was created within the studio, allowing an in-depth discussion of each aspect. The assignments demonstrate her broader background, incorporating research on sociological and economic conditions as well as architectural form. Didactic principles such as beginning with an analysis of existing conditions also show her foundations in more general social research. The systematic structure of the Las Vegas studio elucidates the New Brutalist underpinnings of Scott Brown's thinking.[42] Each particular aspect of the Las Vegas context – be it aspects of urban form or decoration, lighting or economics is researched and documented. More importantly, each aspect is given equal weight: there is no hierarchy here between the elements of 'architecture' and the elements of 'buildings', or between 'aesthetic' aspects of form or contextual determinants. Moreover, the studio syllabi are packed with readings such as the Independent Group, Archigram and Tom Wolfe, offering the students an extensive range of architecture, pop culture and the ordinary, in design as well as literature. Following the principles of New Brutalism, this sense of the 'ordinary', or the closely related 'kitchen-sink realism' was employed as a critique of architectural idealizations, primarily as manifest in modernism.

The importance of the work of Venturi and Scott Brown lies in this new approach to architectural questions as well as their meticulous documentation of the visual manifestations of the vernacular. Moreover, by collecting their results in a comprehensive study, they offered the possibility to utilize their work. Places such as Las Vegas were worthy of study by their popularity alone – they were ignored by earlier architecture discourses, but even this suppression was not enough to make them disappear. If they were not going to disappear, the planners concluded, it was time the professionals at the very least learned from them where possible. This attitude is close in spirit to the social realism underlying the work of the New Brutalists. Yet we could argue that it is precisely because Scott Brown had been trained in both these ideas that her influence extended further – she neither gave up the principles of social realism she learned in the UK, nor did she ignore the encouragement of her planning teachers to go look at what was popular and make them understand why. And perhaps it is because she studied under Gans, who was thoroughly convinced that visual understanding had no place in a sociological study, that she worked so hard to prove him wrong. Or maybe she simply saw the small gap in his thinking when he inverted the modernist idea of a society transformed through design into a denial of any possibility of influence through visual means.

The strategies of employing the image and the concept of the ordinary to address what modernism left out is similar to how individuality became an instrument of reform in the city. The underlying parallels between various groups come from an acceptance, and indeed an embracing of an increasingly visual mass culture. Yet there are also marked contrasts between different thinkers and designers in the 1960s. The Independent Group utilized pop imagery as a visually cheerful yet critically investigative alternative to modernist design, yet combined that with more gritty images of English social realism. Archigram stylized its technological fantasies in an appeal to the freedom of consumer choice. Venturi and Scott Brown perceived a fundamental richness in the symbolism of the ordinary environment, while the Situationist International transformed these symbols in order to resist the commercialization of everyday life. Throughout all these investigations of pop imagery, the discourse and practice of architecture was being shifted away from the monumental and heroic nature of its designs through the use of everyday images. In England this began as early as 1952 with lectures at the Institute for Contemporary Arts in London by Banham, and revolved around the Independent Group. The imagery appropriated by the Independent Group was largely American in origin and was based on advertising and glamour, while the principle of discovering the ordinary, looking at the everyday, largely derived from sociological studies such as that of Young and Wilmott on East London.[43] The excitement in architecture about the everyday was grounded in this duality: the grittiness on the one hand of social realism, of studies on what actually happened in the city areas architects only discussed in plan; and the energetic frivolity on the other hand of commercial and Hollywood imagery, which had become part of the everyday environment that was not designed by architects. The commonplace in the USA (as epitomized by Las Vegas) was in a sense already more spectacular, already oriented towards a realm of fantasy. This distinction is quite important: generally, the American treatment of the 'ordinary environment' was marked more by the conditions of the commercial, oriented towards mass consumption, while the European mainland tended to be focused on the labouring class and the conditions of production.

Venturi and Scott Brown trace the importance of the ordinary back to the Middle Ages, but distinguish it from the everyday and the ordinary as it was construed in relation to industrialization and the subsequent modernization of architectural form. Modern architecture was concerned with housing the masses of the industrial city. The larger rural centres or cities with medieval origins were simply not equipped in terms of infrastructure to handle the population explosion that accompanied industrial growth. Most of the drive towards the modernization of dwellings derived from this need to offer decent housing to unprecedented numbers of people. In other words, mass housing as an architectural problem became as relevant as earlier design problems of monumentality and the extraordinary. The culture of the everyday becomes important through a combination of the massiveness of the modern project and the denial of an everyday imagery. Machine imagery as a basis for mass housing contradicted the need for the personal yet collective manifestations of an already existent culture. The condition of mass architecture as it grew from the 1920s onward necessitated a close examination of the everyday, since this is the basic condition of the mass experience – it is ordinary, it is the norm.[44] Yet the sheer scale of this 'ordinary' since the explosion of the urban population also translated into the monumentality of physical mass combined with a rigorous and inflexible total design. The modernist understanding of the everyday went through a transformation from the need to address the massiveness of industrial society to a desire to edify the general populace, to shape it into the perfect expression of 'modern man'.

The introduction of the ordinary and everyday into the discourse and practice of architecture served as an escape from demanding technocratic designs such as the Plan Voisin or the *Existenzminimum* dwelling. It is important here to note the distinction in the uses of 'the ordinary'; although modern architects were extremely conscious of the everyday in their approach to mass housing, they saw it as their task to make the ordinary better through their designs. Moreover, this was not merely a design project, but a social engineering project. In the 1960s, a strong resistance grew against the all-encompassing nature of this social engineering

American culture enters the gallery: exhibition 'This Is Tomorrow' (Whitechapel Gallery, 1956)

project. The importance of individual freedom was pitted against the notion that there was a single ideal way to live. To express this, the presence of the ordinary was used as a disruption of modernist perfection – it introduced the dust on the windowsill and the broken garage door – in other words, it introduced actual 'signs of life' into idealized designs.

On the most basic level, these visual and spatial expressions began with people – the ones never present in Le Corbusier's drawings; the beginnings of pop were all about popular culture, or the culture of the people that modernism forgot. Some of the earliest work showing these premises is that of the Independent Group, especially of Paolozzi, Hamilton and the Smithsons, all of whom were struggling with issues of mass culture and advertising. Yet they were also thrilled with the vibrant energy they found in American imagery from magazines and movies. The beginnings of these influences of pop in architecture can be seen in the exhibition 'This Is Tomorrow' in 1956, held at the Whitechapel Gallery in London, where visitors were confronted with a large cardboard constellation of American popular imagery such as Robbie the Robot (from the film *Forbidden Planet*) and Marilyn Monroe. The desired effect was attained, because as Brian Wallis relates, this was not a typical art gallery exhibition for the well-educated only. This was interesting to all sorts of people – working-class children were wandering in just 'to hang out by the jukebox, critics loosened their aesthetic criteria and many viewers explored the exhibition no further than this whimsical installation by the door'.[45] This was a successful use of pop imagery to break through the alienation produced by much modernist work: 'The funhouse installation challenged the exclusivity of the dominant ways of regarding art, and opened an avenue for a more democratic analysis of art and cultural criticism.'[46] We could speculate that its success lay precisely in the ambiguous position taken by the installation's creators: they were not only artists creating something with these images, they were also simply consumers.[47] Again, democratization was an important premise in the 1960s, extending to aesthetic transformation as well.

In the various manifestations of 'ordinary', there is a slight but important distinction in vocabulary: while Venturi (and later Scott Brown) tend to use the words 'ordinary' and 'commonplace' in their praises of popular culture, the Situationist International and Lefebvre tend more towards the use of 'everyday' (*quotidienne*). The Independent Group and the Smithsons again use 'ordinary'.[48] The word *quotidienne* has within it a sense of repetitive action, of habits accrued over time (by repeating them every day). This sense does distinguish it from the commonplace or the ordinary, which could be seen on an almost ahistorical aesthetic level. In the choice of words alone, a difference is expressed between an activist sense of spatial appropriation and the formalist analysis of aesthetic elements.

Similar theoretical positions on the everyday can be found on both sides of the Atlantic, in the USA with Jane Jacobs and in France with Henri Lefebvre, both discussed in relation to their writings on the city. Jacobs' writing was already 'ordinary' in its directness and tone. She was trained as a journalist rather than educated as a planner or sociologist, which can be seen in how comfortably clear and everyday her language is. Her writing approached the notion of the ordinary from her own experience, from daily observations of her direct environment rather than from a higher level of abstraction that she then adjusted her observations to. Her 'sidewalk observations' introduced a new kind of seeing, based on the examination of the qualities of the everyday, rather than what should be edited or transformed. The importance given to empirical sociological research, looking at what was already there, transformed the understanding of the city.

For Lefebvre, the ordinary was still a revolutionary force, but the importance of the ordinary was less its revolutionary capacity than its ability to help us see the flaws in the way architects approached their designs. Lefebvre introduced the idea of 'lived space' to indicate the distinction between the intentions of a designer and the result of the space once it became part of the everyday spatial experience of a community. He comes close to Gans's problem with physical determinism: Lefebvre agrees that a design cannot have the immediate and simplified result that designers tend to think it will. Yet Lefebvre allows for the possibility that there is a mutual influence between space as it is designed and space as it is used or lived in. Similarly, Venturi and Scott Brown proposed that the ordinary was the very locus of vitality and organic progress. They extended this notion of the everyday into an evolutionary force. Just as Lefebvre integrates time and development in his analysis of architecture, refusing the pure formal and unchanging interpretation of modernist form, Venturi and Scott Brown argue that one of the most influential aspects of the everyday is its openness to change, its adaptability to changing situations.

There are also a few crucial distinctions between American and British pop. The American version shows a stronger affinity with the commercial environment throughout different practices: Warhol used his background as a commercial illustrator within the art world, Tom Wolfe examined the neon signs of Las Vegas and Doug Haskell discussed the interesting points of 'honky-tonk'. The focus in the UK was often on the ordinary environment (as to be seen in the art of 'kitchen-sink realism'). However, in the architecture discourse this was very strongly filtered through American magazines, films and other visual production. Alloway's only complaint about Piccadilly Circus was that its lights were inferior to the American versions he had seen on a recent visit to the USA.[49] Examples from the USA were seen as exemplary for the vibrant, non-designed, new and spectacular environment. In contrast to what the Situationist International stood for, the commercial character of the American environment was often seen as an asset rather than a problem; especially Hamilton of the Independent Group wrote about the power of commercial imagery and heralded the affluence of his time.

The work of the Independent Group was not a complete rejection of modernist principles, but rather a search for a more appropriate expression of its time, as Alison Smithson argues in 'But Today We Collect Ads'.[50] Here, she argues that Le Corbusier, for example, used popular art as well, but that the fundamental transformation in her time is to be found in advertising, since it begins to compete with fine art in terms of the quality of its images. The grand distinction between modernism and the 1960s thus becomes more a matter of the sources themselves:

while Le Corbusier's references still required an intervention, to the Smithsons contemporary advertising consisted of imagery that equalled the fine arts in their finesse. The imagery shown at the 1956 exhibition was unlike anything shown before: it was cheerful, vibrant, colourful and deeply embedded in the commercial sphere. It largely came from the USA, where the post-war increase in wealth had extended the capitalist system of selling products to selling commodities that were beginning to express a certain individuality, thus undermining the principle of standardization.

There is a distinctive difference between this utilization of the ordinary and the work of the Situationist International. Although they all involve a specific critique of modernism, and all accept the increasing visuality of everyday life, the situationists still expect the 'ordinariness' of the worker in all its authenticity to be able to transform the everyday reality of the spectacle. This stands in contrast to the Independent Group's idea of increasing aesthetic sophistication and democratization through pop imagery. The Situationist International hoped that the ordinariness of the worker's life meant that he was somehow less alienated from his own being as a human in the world, that he could somehow overthrow his own alienation, caused by the technocratic elite. There is an ambiguity in the relationship between alienation and the everyday as posited by the situationists, following the work of Lefebvre in his *Critique of Everyday Life*.[51] In this sense, 'authenticity' was an underpinning of their mode of addressing imagery. Perhaps it should not come as a surprise that their work typically returned to a text-based intervention as a transformation of the imagery they encountered. In their aim of a critical transformation of everyday life, they saw the role of ordinary imagery as the 'found material' in need of being engaged in order to encourage a new consciousness.[52] Moreover, there was the presumption that theirs was the only way to fulfil this transformation: 'They [the situationists] claim that the creative activities initiated by them over the whole range of everyday life are the one and only basis for a new definition of the revolutionary ideal in our time.'[53] As close as this is to the modernist project by virtue of its totality, there is a difference insofar as Guy Debord saw the 'common man' as the agent of this transformation. The alienation in everyday life was to be overthrown by the worker; he must delve beyond the narcotic aspects of the spectacle and understand how his own alienation was caused by the mechanisms of capital, and sustained by the imagery of advertising.[54]

In a sense, maybe there is a radicality in the American situation that is based on the fundamental condition of democracy. Even though it has arguably become an oligarchy based on money, the implicit belief that each and every person is equal eliminates the Marxist need for enlightened intellectuals to lead the way. Perhaps there is less fear for the 'blindness' or 'stupidity' of the masses in the work of Gans, Venturi and Scott Brown, and Jacobs. Perhaps they are more pragmatic or maybe even utilitarian. In contrast, how different is Debord's premise of revolution from Loos's claim that he is speaking to truly modern men? True, Debord is addressing workers and students rather than an enlightened bourgeoisie or modern engineers; yet he still addresses them as 'enlightened' beings, instrumental to a total revolution. Perhaps this is what was most shocking about the Las Vegas studio: its unapologetic celebration of not only an ordinary environment, but an environment of which its aesthetics were derived from and a celebration of commercial interests: of capital. These campy, kitschy photographs of 'low culture', of a site that the masses travelled to, were not merely an example of 'Main Street', but also showed a careful study of the mechanisms of economics, manifest in the spectacular signage of the Strip. The notion that architects might learn from these images, which became possible when the visual began to be placed on equal footing with the linguistic, overturned the traditional relation between architecture and the everyday environment.

This ambivalent position with respect to Las Vegas is perhaps best seen in Scott Brown's treatment of the architect as interpreter of the client's wishes, which Colquhoun is critical of as it is not consistent with contemporary societal conditions.[55] It is however simply a symptom of the central position of populism in *Learning from Las Vegas*. Although this is a valid point of criticism, I believe it is more interesting to examine the exclusivity of her position. In a reminder of the radical position taken by the Situationist International, where art is destined only to instigate the revolution and then disappear as the totality of art and life becomes fact, here Scott Brown makes an equally radical suggestion that there is no personal subjectivity to architecture, but only the best possible interpretation of the client's wishes. To oppose the heroic character of the modern architect with an exact opposite – the architect as the mere instrument of client and society – seems once again to deny the complexity of a reality in favour of a conceptual model. In this inversion, the frame of reference remains the same: either the architect is fully resistant or fully affirmative. Neither explores the more complicated possibilities of critique that is partially complicit with the existing power structures.

Testing the Boundaries of High Art: From Modernism to Pop

Dick Hebdige identifies four themes in pop, each of which to some degree has to do with the shifting and blurring lines between 'high art' and 'low art'. These encompass: a critical function (creating an awareness of the complicity between structures of domination and aesthetic judgement), a strategy of definition (to structure the indeterminate line between 'high' and 'low' culture, 'art' and 'non-art'), a power struggle (between the 'high culture' of Europe and the mass-oriented culture of the USA), and a discourse on new (and ephemeral) culture such as fashion and consumption.[56] Note that he thus follows the common equation of the European aesthetic tradition with 'high' and the American tradition with 'low' art. This is critical in its relation to modernism, for it is on that cusp between art and popular culture, especially that area of popular culture 'tainted' by commerce, that pop found its radical nature – and American culture is usually the generator of these distinctions in the European discourse, as is to be found in the work of Adorno and Benjamin. Throughout modern art and architecture, the idea that art was by definition incompatible with commerce has remained strong, even despite such efforts as those by Duchamp to introduce a different perspective within the realm of high art. In some critiques there have also been some notable exceptions, such as in that of Walter Benjamin, who remained fascinated by what popular culture and the aesthetics of commerce could offer to society in cultural terms.[57]

The history of popular imagery is linked to modernism and the avant-garde, both through the technology necessary to create a 'mass culture' in the first place, and through the inherently troubled relationship between 'high' and 'low' art.[58] The very terms 'Pop Art' and 'pop culture' derive from 'popular' – implying that this art and this culture are something belonging to the larger group of people out there, the masses. Its very popularity precludes it from becoming high art.[59] The historical avant-garde has always retained a difficult relationship with pop culture, or imagery from mass culture; the premise of the avant-garde was to look ahead, to predict future developments and especially to lead the way for the rest of the world.[60] The avant-garde could therefore not afford to be involved with mass culture: mass appeal would mean it was no longer radical. Yet at the same time some of the most radical work of the avant-garde was generated from objects of industrialization, ready-mades and objects of mass consumption (Marcel Duchamp, Warhol, Max Ernst, Dada, surrealism). This tension, the use of mass imagery to create radically avant-garde work, crystallized into a repression of the same imagery in the work of the modernists. In a definition similar to the avant-garde, Le Corbusier positions art as a discipline for the prescient.[61] But he diverges from the avant-garde position when he removes all references to visual mass culture in favour of his own visualization of the perfect city.

The historical avant-garde used mass culture and politicized it; in other words, it utilized mass culture as a mirror to society: not just to acknowledge reality as it was, but rather to shock people into transformative action. This is the tradition the Situationist International followed in its demand for revolution instigated by art. Modernism, on the other hand, considered the imagery of mass culture as part of the problem: analogous to the bourgeois interior that produced too much clutter

Détournement: making the unexpected operational as critique. *Internationale Situationniste* 11 (1967), page 33

to be able to see the space. To the modernists, merely holding up a mirror was not going to work – it was necessary to offer the image of a perfect world, because only then would people realize what they 'actually' wanted.

Unlike earlier radical movements, the pop sensibility was not about traditional iconoclasm; on the contrary, it was using these mass culture images to rip a hole in the abstraction of modernism.[62] Much is to be said for this subversive use of imagery. Benjamin argued that shock value was an important aspect of art in the metropolis, since shock was the only way to actually still move an increasingly blasé audience. For Debord, this idea of shock was inherent in the situationist principle of *détournement*: by juxtaposing inconsistent (or oppositional) images, the resulting image would shock the spectator into an active revolution. To even create this shock, it was necessary to combine the familiar images of mass culture into something absolutely new – the estrangement resulting from this familiar-but-new juxtaposition would be stronger than a predetermined and idealized image.[63] Yet Venturi, following similar lines of estrangement as a technique, does not attribute a politically revolutionary quality to it. In his view, the inventiveness of ordinary culture as exemplified in the American environment has formal qualities that may be revolutionary on an individual level (reception) or in the discipline (design strategies), but not towards society as a whole.

The omnipresence of imagery, and the corresponding increase in visual awareness since the 1960s, has sometimes presented a problem for the discipline of architecture. The discipline of art operates under different conditions than architecture, and although the avant-garde strategies of high modernist architecture were clearly related to 1920s avant-garde strategies in art, the agendas were not the same. Le Corbusier noted that our understanding of housing had hardly changed in the twentieth century, despite the fundamental changes throughout the world under the influence of increased industrialization.[64] There is something still unresolved in our understanding of the role of architecture in the late industrial society. Much of this is due to a perceived incompatibility between the representation of space and its 'objective' spatial qualities. Thus it is in the translation from image to architecture, or in the precise relationship between the two, that the difficulties in handling a pop sensibility begin to appear. Generally speaking, there is a different timeframe between images and buildings. This results in a problem of the expendability of time-specific imagery in non-expendable buildings, or the transitory condition of ephemeral images that lose their value when they lose their context.

This return to representation and a certain aesthetic pleasure, an indulgence even in imagery that is not edifying in a traditional manner, is critical to the struggle against the dominant visuality of modernism. Rather than seeing each image, surface or symbol as necessarily representing a loftier idea, something beyond what is directly perceived, there is a revaluation of appearances, the idea that perhaps there is a value to the surface as well. This remains a very tricky area of critique even today, because significance and meaning are seen as the domain of art, while the commercial is seen as a debased form of that. However, we could also argue that the tastes of the public are not necessarily 'wrong'. Or that whether or not a work is commercial is not in fact related to its artistic value.[65] Moreover, in this debate there is always the question of who determines artistic value – the artists, the public, the critics? Moreover, as Venturi and Scott Brown argue in their work, the significance of symbolism is a complex construction, not something that can be ripped out of its cultural context. Lefebvre's arguments run along similar lines, though the manifestations of blatant capitalism to him remain a troublesome area of power structures sugar-coated by diversions.

Within this, Venturi and Scott Brown fulfil a specific function in translating these concerns most directly into architecture. Within the Independent Group for example, which was engaged with the opportunities presented by popular imagery, only the Smithsons were architects. All the others, such as Paolozzi, Banham, Hamilton and Henderson were historians and artists. Even the work of the Smithsons shows a tension between the architecture and the ordinary life within it. In an interview, Scott Brown went so far as to suggest they gave up on trying to find a place for the banal. Smithson himself, however, even as late as 2002, discussed their work as a container for everyday qualities.[66] Venturi and Scott Brown are perhaps the most consistent in seeking an architectural translation for these ideas, but the question is whether it is successful not as rhetoric or as image, but as architectural form. And if not, is that because of a problem with the imagery, the architecture or the connection between the two? The architecture discourse consists of buildings and their representations, in words and images, but often the intention or the images of the architects take precedence over other perceptions, such as those of the users. This is one of the main points of resistance in the 1960s, but often it remains more at the level of rhetoric than actual consideration.

Two crucial aspects of this development from modernism to pop derive from a reconsideration of the place and autonomy of individual people, both in presence in and reception of imagery. On the one hand there is the simple pleasure in a profusion of symbolic, frivolous, cheerful imagery to counter the weight and importance of modernist images intended to edify and enlighten. In the functionalist world of Le Corbusier, even leisure time was intended to improve the common man; Las Vegas as presented by Venturi and Scott Brown was an analysis of what kind of leisure time and symbolisms simply attracted people, rather than determining what they should be doing. On the other hand, there is an increasing presence of 'normal' people in images, of everyday references – the grand shift from the heroic to the ordinary, as is reiterated time and again in *Learning from Las Vegas*, and as is visible from the work of the Independent Group on. Thus the demanding and austere world of the heroic common man of the 1920s and '30s is transformed into a celebration of the shiny happy world of new materials (plastic) and colourful surroundings, of increasing affluence that would allow everyone to realize their dreams to some level. Moreover, this democratization also allowed the everyday to become extraordinary, to the extent that consumption became a way of making dreams of leisure and affluence attainable for the masses.

Economics of Affluence and the Culture of Consumption

Around the middle of the 1950s, the general level of affluence was causing the consumer economy to grow rapidly, and the television was becoming a standard household item.[67] As a cultural condition, this marks the greatest distinction between the Anglo-Saxon discourse and the neo-Marxist discourse of continental Europe. In this general culture of affluence the rise of advertising became unavoidable in the everyday. The explosion of advertising, billboards and imagery heightened the contrast between the aesthetics of the everyday and of the mass-produced image on the one hand, and the demanding aesthetics of purity and 'Modern Man' on the other (as was later expressed most pointedly in the work of Andy Warhol). The images the Independent Group was using suited this general development, since they were no longer part of the 'high art' tradition that required some level of education to recognize and/or understand, but were being culled from everywhere:

Today we collect ads: advertisements for household goods as new cultural reference for architects

Eduardo Paolozzi,
It's a Psychological Fact Pleasure Helps your Disposition
(1948)

magazines, films, photographs, comic books – in short, everything that had until now fallen outside the categories of 'art' as such.[68]

In this way, the Independent Group, like American Pop Art, opened the way for an acceptance of commercial imagery in the realms of a more enclosed practice of architecture.[69] Patricia Phillips, for example, argues that the most radical aspect of 'pop' architecture is its openness to sources from outside the discipline, thus liberating it from the constraints of historical referencing and continuity. It transformed the premises of architectural design by recalibrating what was considered acceptable inspiration.[70] Originally, the type of imagery now used for commercial purposes (using collage techniques, seriality and mechanical reproduction) was the sole domain of the avant-garde. Although it often appropriated images from the realm of mass culture, it remained 'high art' to the extent that it was not involved with such 'base' sides of culture as commercial endeavour, but was geared towards experimentation with the new forms of technology available. By midcentury the techniques were co-opted by the culture industry and Hollywood, bringing these experimental images into the mass-cultural domain and engendering Adorno and Horkheimer's critique of the culture industry, as well as illustrating Walter Benjamin's slightly more optimistic essays on technology and culture.

An interesting distinction within the Independent Group is to be found between Richard Hamilton's definition of pop and the Smithsons' position in 'But Today We Collect Ads'. Where Hamilton uses the type of wording and phrasing that resonates with the typical perception of Pop Art, naming things such as glamour, gimmicks and big business;[71] the Smithsons in their article refer quite directly to Le Corbusier, thus affirming his value to their work, but they simply use different references:

> Gropius wrote a book on grain silos,
> Le Corbusier one on aeroplanes,
> And Charlotte Perriand brought a new
> object to the office every morning;
> But today we collect ads.[72]

In that sense, it appears that Hamilton distanced himself from modernist tenets in shifting the focus towards gimmicks and glamour, and above all the commercial, while the Smithsons tried to modify the modernism they started from, to accommodate post-war transformations in society. Moreover, Hamilton's references arise more from the American world of advertising and film, while the Smithsons refer solely to the European tradition of modernism in the piece above. Their sense of being revolutionary or responding to the specific conditions of their own time thus remains ensconced within architecture history, while Hamilton's social conscience seems directed more outwards to mass culture.

In contrast, the Situationist International was prepared to use the imagery of pop culture, but only with the intent of undermining the spectacle. In particular, the culture of commodification was suspect, as one of the most well-known theses of Debord's manifesto notes on the relation between capital and imagery: 'The spectacle is capital accumulated to the point where it becomes image.'[73] The only way to transform this problematic and incestuous relationship between the mode of production and the appearances it causes and that simultaneously sustain it was through the creative activities referred to above by Bernstein. In other words, everyday life had become tainted through commerce and the spectacle, through the mechanisms of capitalism which involved passive consumption over active creation. Yet at the same time, Debord did not shy away from employing these mechanisms to subvert the existing social order – even as late as 1967, he still proclaimed the virtues of *détournement*, where the very images of capitalism, albeit with an intervention (usually in the form of textual additions), were used to shock people into an awareness of their own alienation.[74] The crucial elements of *détournement* are still relevant today, such as the recognisability of its elements and the form of 'shock' that results from an unconventional use. Yet above all, a détourned image

LA DOMINATION DU SPECTACLE SUR LA VIE

'I love my camera because I love life', published with caption 'The domination of life by the spectacle'. *Internationale Situationniste* 11 (1967)

needs to open our eyes to the mangling jaws of the spectacle, by incorporating a message of general societal critique, as illustrated in the situationists' neo-Marxist commentaries inserted in comics and advertising images. In this sense, Debord might have argued that today, even *détournement* is no longer possible, as all its results are immediately consumed by the spectacle, becoming an image of rebellion rather than an actual rebellion. The Situationist International drew an equation between capital, its extensive use of commercial imagery, and the endless proliferation of the spectacle as a form of (nearly voluntary) oppression.

In contrast, the members of Archigram sketched out the potential liberation of the consumer through the mechanisms of capitalism. Their work appealed more to the potential (visual) sophistication of the consumer as argued by Banham. The more extensive styling through mass-culture imagery employed by them transformed the 'ordinary' scenes of the Independent Group into a celebration of the potential of a consumption-oriented architecture. Their main interest was in the use and potential of a more 'humanized' technology, but the styling of their images is illustrative of how mass culture began to be seen as important to the 'normal' experience of architecture. Again, this imagery of (an everyday) mass culture was seen as a potential point of liberation. However, their choices in imagery were also quite specific: they collapsed different scales of imagery from product packaging to architecture (people packaging); they turned quite explicitly to the imagery

Simple comic imagery with unexpected conversation: *détournement* of comic strip. *Internationale Situationniste* 12 (1969), page 38

of science fiction as a source of inspiration that combined the 'everyday' (insofar as it showed the images people were watching) with the fantastic (thus offering something more interesting). Furthermore, in their focus on future worlds, they used everyday items to reconfigure our expectations of architecture. In their installations, the Archigram architects presented everyday objects as an integral part of city life (in contrast to Le Corbusier's manipulated cityscapes). In a drawing for the British embassy (1964), they incorporated not only people, as the Smithsons did, but included their views – undermining the god's-eye view typical of Le Corbusier's drawings. In their use of detail, colour and the visual culture of advertisements, they related to the increased visuality of everyday culture. Moreover, by presenting their schemes as they did, they made a connection between the ordinary and the fantastic that is typical of an advertising culture – linking dreams and fantasies to products, or making the ordinary extraordinary.

In the end though, the basic strategy for this critique on modernism was the use of what had remained beneath the surface before – where Le Corbusier engaged his imagery to move towards a purified version of modernity, one free of the clutter he loathed in New York streets, the Independent Group introduced an aesthetic of overwhelming numbers of everyday and commercial images, to reflect the everyday environment people were living in. Although the differences between the work of Hamilton and the Smithsons are clear, their choice of critical instruments is the same, and reflects a similar sensibility later to be found in *Learning from Las Vegas*, with its radical emphasis on billboards and signage as (the only) meaningful elements in the architecture of the time.

Communication and Figuration: From Buildings to Signs and Symbols

With the publication of *Learning from Las Vegas*, Venturi and Scott Brown's analysis of the everyday visual environment took on the radical form that not only shocked the architecture world at the time, but later earned them the labels 'pop architects' and postmodernists. In *Learning from Las Vegas*, Venturi and Scott Brown make a plea for truly looking at the existing environment.[75] They note that 'orthodox

Modern architecture is progressive, if not revolutionary, utopian, and puristic; it is dissatisfied with existing conditions ... Architects have preferred to change the existing environment rather than enhance what is there.'[76] To Venturi and Scott Brown, however, the purity of the drawing and the design – where the architect can still determine who will be presented as inhabiting it – will always meet reality, which will never be as neatly arranged as the diagram for it.[77] They felt a need to incorporate the visible and sometimes messy reality that was absent from the modernist vision of cities that bred orderly inhabitants; this need arose by necessity from what had been repressed. In the case of Venturi and Scott Brown, as well as the Independent Group and the Situationist International, it was expressed through a turn to ordinary people and ordinary images, an investigation of what insights those images might have to offer to existing aesthetic principles.[78] Again, it is important to note how intertwined these reactions are with modernist work – the turn to an everyday imagery was to reintroduce precisely the messy aspects of an everyday that Le Corbusier had attempted to banish in his designs.[79] This attitude recalls Jane Jacobs' distinction between seeing the environment 'as it is' or 'as it ought to be'. This also explains why there is a perceived need to address the ordinary: it offers a strategy or a means to incorporate the vitality missing in the environments proposed by Le Corbusier. The problem, as we shall see later, is that simply incorporating a notion of 'the ordinary' as a design strategy eventually leads to an equally idealized perception of 'honky-tonk' as an environment, by which it eventually becomes stripped of the vitality it seemed to offer in the late 1950s and early 1960s.

Colquhoun also notes the latent presence of the decorated shed in *Complexity and Contradiction in Architecture* 'since it had established the merely indirect connection between the appearance of a building and its substance and had drawn attention to the arbitrary nature of the architectural sign'.[80] This eventually leads to the more dramatic position in *Learning from Las Vegas* that the symbolic content of the sign should be given full attention in architecture, and that the 'substance' or spatial content behind it is in essence irrelevant, or at least less relevant. As Colquhoun points out, the very strength of Venturi's attack on a form that expresses its content led to the idea that a turn to surface, symbol and sign was the only viable alternative. Again, this forms a radicalization of the discourse that reinforces the problems it is trying to address. The polemic and the general theory overtake the everyday reality of specific applications. By focusing so pointedly on the qualities of the sign, Venturi here denies the possibility that substance and sign may interact, and that sometimes, the form might express a content. As such, he simply reiterates the problematic modernist dichotomy: while in the early twentieth century ornament was a crime, following Venturi's argument here, ornament becomes central, and everything else is irrelevant. This reveals a problem within the argument itself: If the role of symbols is communication, but the 'substance' as such has nothing to communicate – why bother? The focus on communication and figuration for its own sake separates sign from substance as much as its predecessors.

> The implications of the notion of the decorated shed are therefore far-reaching. They lead to the assertion that architectural meaning has become irretrievably separated from its substance. Architects are impotent in the face of a society whose values have made this split inevitable. It is not by the vision of an alternative architecture that these values can be criticized, but only by the manipulation of its surface appearance, and then only by means of an equivocal irony, in which these values are alternately condoned and 'exposed'.[81]

This correlates with the position of the Situationist International, which also signalled that sign and substance were separated as one of the fundamental problems of the society of the spectacle. The situationists, however, saw it as the task of the artistic avant-garde to reintegrate them, while Venturi and Scott Brown accept this condition as fact and see it as their task to accommodate an imperfect situation. In a sense, this returns to the question of whether or not critique is possible in a visual world. To Debord, the conditions of the spectacle preclude the possibility of critique. For Venturi and Scott Brown, the question revolves more around the interventions that reveal the fabric of cultural traditions that have remained unacknowledged in the modernist architecture discourse.

The extra introduction to the second edition of *Learning from Las Vegas* notes that *Complexity and Contradiction in Architecture* could be considered a treatise on 'form' and *Learning from Las Vegas* a treatise on 'symbolism'. This distinction reveals the interest in the communicative qualities residing in iconography and collective imagery, which comes to the forefront more in *Learning from Las Vegas* and the later studio on Levittown. Colquhoun frames this question in terms of 'form' and 'figure', where 'figure' is that type of expressive image that has fundamental culturally embedded connotations. It is this type of 'figure' that Venturi is trying to reinstate, to reconnect architecture to the people who use it every day. While modernism operated under the idea that there were universally comprehensible forms, the retaliations in the 1960s revolved around a revaluation of visual convention. The idea that tradition offered embedded meanings that were worth examining rather than erasing was a way to help architectural form reconnect with its occupants.

While *Complexity and Contradiction in Architecture* discussed the tradition of form within architectural convention, the increasing presence of the mass media and a new visual language of consumption allowed the shift towards the more iconographic orientation of *Learning from Las Vegas*. In other words, visual convention (as a language in itself) became an equally valid point of study towards the understanding of architectural meaning. The line of questioning from architectural complexity to the kitsch of Las Vegas challenged the modernist supposition that surfaces are by definition tainted or misleading. This discussion is based on a false dichotomy, presupposing that surfaces and substances can be separated and have no mutual influence. However, the work of Venturi and Scott Brown also encouraged the favouring of surface over substance, reinforcing this opposition.

Critique: Linguistic or Visual? Pop Images and Modern Vision

The fundamental question underlying these various explorations of pop imagery revolves around the status of 'critique'. Is a critical mode of imagery and cultural production conceivable? And if so, can this be understood within the visual realm, or only as a linguistic construction? The situationist position on *détournement* embodies an ambiguous position, insofar as it typically relies on a linguistic understanding of critique, yet employs the visual realm as its arena.

Abstraction and overview – the architect's hand as all-powerful.
Le Corbusier, Ville Radieuse (1935)

Perspective of individual viewpoint. Alison and Peter Smithson, Golden Lane Housing (1952)

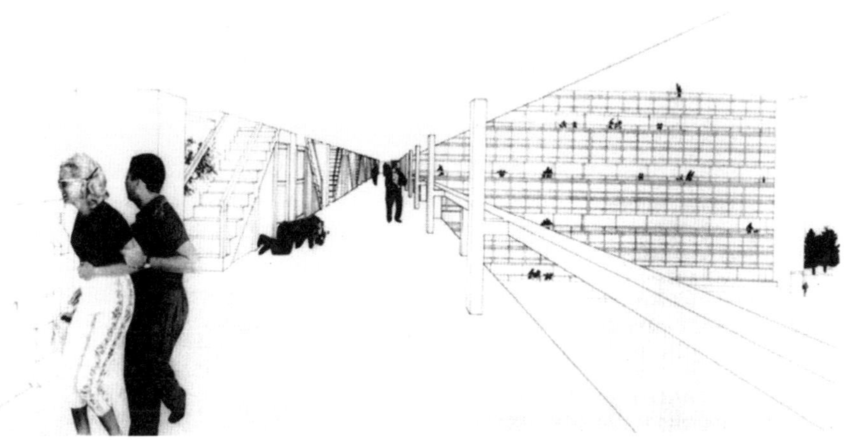

One of the most striking examples of the British use of pop imagery to transform at least the perception of their buildings is an eye-height perspective view of the 1952 Golden Lane Housing project by the Smithsons. The perspective is placed so that we are looking along the 'elevated street' of an apartment building, and its 'streetness' is expressed not through the lines themselves, but through the people collaged into it. Where Le Corbusier in his work on city proposals, from the Ville Contemporaine to the Ville Radieuse, made extensive use of the bird's-eye view, and reduced human presence to the drawings of cars in his city, the Smithsons introduced photographs of actual people into their drawing.

In this classic image for the Golden Lane Housing project, we see not so much the façades as the person on the walkway leaning down over a small child, as ordinary as a scene on any local street. At the same time, we notice a couple sneaking off into the left margins of the image, as if they've got much better plans that we're not a part of. A second glance shows us that the couple is no ordinary couple – they are (or seem to be) Marilyn Monroe and Joe Dimaggio, giving our perception of Golden Lane both a hint of glamour and an immediate connection to the everyday presence of Hollywood and the media. Although today this drawing may seem quaint, this kind of intervention in an otherwise traditional architecture was radical at the time – the very idea of introducing actual images of actual people into these pristine drawings was unheard of. As with all formal innovations, it has become part of a common visual language. Using actual people, or at least magazine photos, collaged into drawings is now so typical in architecture images that it seems almost banal from today's perspective. Le Corbusier's people either left behind an aesthetically arranged hint of their presence or were drawn up to suit the Modulor-construction based on the golden section, or were safely tucked away in their cars on the boulevards of the Ville Radieuse. When humans are present in Le Corbusier's drawings, their details are reduced, they are stripped down to as pure an essence as the architecture around them: arms, legs, torso, head. But no hair colour, no eyes, no specificity. Nothing even resembling the specificity of a movie star unabashedly inserted into a housing project in England.

What then is the actual intent and impact of this kind of imagery? First, the images made by the Smithsons express their need to engage in a dialogue with Le Corbusier. This type of direct response to the paradigms of high modernism was common by the early 1960s, but in its earliest manifestations also clarified what the problems with modernism were. First, there is the shift in the perspective of the drawing itself: moving from the bird's-eye (or god's-eye) view to eye-level concedes that perhaps the architect is not all-knowing. It allows the viewer to engage with the space proposed, to see the presence of the windows and doors, rather than admire the formal perfection of a composition of volumes, all arranged by a trained architect. Furthermore, the eye-level perspective allows for the presence of 'actual life' in the presentation of a project. A bird's-eye view can never hope to offer more than the abstracted composition of everyday elements. An eye-level view might confront us with the offending presence of a person standing in our way. Besides this shift in perspective, there is the transformation in drawing technique:

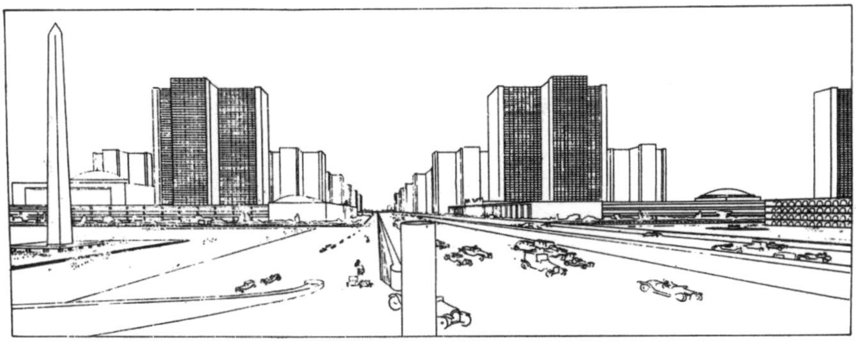

Building blocks and motorways. Le Corbusier, Ville Contemporaine (1922)

Overlaying drawing and existing photographs. Alison and Peter Smithson, Golden Lane Housing (1952)

the introduction of photo-collages. Addressing Le Corbusier in their own way, the Smithsons introduce the actual site, not the site as it will become. The Smithsons present another drawing for the Golden Lane project with a photograph of the existing site not only inserted into the drawing, but even interrupting the clarity of their own lines along one side of the drawing. This image of the existing site intrudes on the architectural 'perfection' of a project conceived in detail. Also, as mentioned before, the use of photographs allows a sense of everyday reality, or at least of unfiltered reality, in that the people now inserted are no longer delineated by the architect's aesthetic decision. Moreover, these 'extraordinary' additions of images from magazines offer the profusion of the visual culture of everyday life, but also include various associations or the desire for identification (such as the dream of a glamorous Hollywood life). This too is an important function of symbolism. In relation to architecture it bears on Levittown and the transformation of standardized houses as documented by Venturi and Scott Brown.[82] Scott Brown argues that their own documentation of suburban manifestations of these ideals is more directly aligned to the everyday, while the work of the Independent Group still demonstrates an overly aesthetic education, in its desire to 'educate' or enlighten the masses.[83]

In contrast, the situationists maintained a primarily linguistic model of critique. Until 1962, the role of art and visual communication figured more prominently in the work of the Situationist International. Debord made two films, and made the famous psychogeographic maps of Paris together with Asger Jorn as well as the *Mémoires*, which illustrate his interest in the visual aspects of his ideas at the time.[84] By 1961, both Jorn and Constant had left, possibly reinforcing Debord's belief in the need for a conceptual revolution before an aesthetic one. In his view, it was pointless to invent forms for a human being that did not yet exist. The intimate relation between capitalism and its reiterations in the spectacle played an increasingly central role. According to Debord we may use the images of capitalism, but only if we subvert them by inserting social critique. The critique itself is text-based: it rests on a linguistic conceptual construction. Is this any less demanding than the encouragement to buy a product? The categorical dismissal of consumption in Debord's work is problematic, since it reduces a general need for symbolic identification to only an individual creative expression, while 'passive consumption' also arguably fulfils this same need. The general tension between the linguistic discourses of sociology and philosophy and the visual realm is apparent in the work of both Gans and Debord. Does this tension in fact confirm that the visual can only represent or reflect concepts, and never create them or investigate them autonomously? This goes to the heart of the tension between the linguistic and the visual turn. Our understanding of critique is so fundamentally linguistic that notwithstanding the efforts of a few thinkers such as Banham, McLuhan and Rushkoff, we still find it difficult to conceive of a critical sensibility that might be incorporated in the visual.

Yet even as Debord moved away from what he saw as the futile artistic endeavours of his former colleagues, he clung to his notion of *détournement* as one of the few visual strategies of subversion. So again we see an ambiguity here: although Debord believes that art and theory must somehow become one total praxis leading to the dissolution of 'Art' as a separate activity, there are a few visual strategies that appear to be attributed a power of autonomy. Maybe *détournement* remained potent because to him it manipulated the language utilized by capitalism itself. This is even more plausible in light of later theorists who argue that these internal manipulations are far more dangerous than a full-frontal attack. In an earlier paper I called this kind of critical manoeuvre 'embedded' to distinguish it from the Frankfurter Schule critique.[85] The traditional Marxist critique is intended to rip a hole in the 'false consciousness' of our world, allowing us to become integrated into a totality of perfected praxis. 'Embedded critique', on the other hand, takes the strategy of *détournement* to its logical conclusion, blending seamlessly with the language and structure of the world it lives in. It hides in the manifestations of mass culture, in logos, in children's cartoons. Its effectiveness is directly related to its ability to blur boundaries, to blend in, thus bypassing traditional censorship in television, for example.

As to the so-called radical nature of Debord's total praxis: a manifesto from De Stijl in 1922 already mentions: 'An end to the division between art and life.'[86] This rhetoric is also to be found in a commentary by Van Doesburg, recapitulating the unity of art and life.[87] Only in this case the form of unity is embodied in technology and the machine, whereas the unity Debord is proposing is based on desire, the unconscious and the refusal to work (or to become part of the productivity that underlies the capitalist system). The difference in expression is clear, but the question remains whether these two manifestations of revolutionary principles are as distinct as Debord might wish.

The Anglo-Saxon discourse treats commercial and pop imagery with a less outspoken dismissal of capitalism. Much of this work explores the liberating potential they perceive in (primarily American) mass culture. The Independent Group used a plethora of images culled from American magazines, television shows and films, and Alison Smithson has mentioned her pleasure in poring over advertisements in American women's magazines while stuck in the depressing environment of post-war Europe. Moreover, luxury goods and their accompanying imagery, promising a better life thanks to various new commodities, were attractive representations of prosperity, something we might all aspire to now that we were gaining such freedom of consumer choice. Beyond the visual resonance between the images used, there is a constant exchange between the English and American discourses. Scott Brown's background suggests this influence in the studies of Las Vegas. Few architects were studying phenomena such as Las Vegas – while in the UK people like Alloway, Banham and the Smithsons were deeply engaged with the manifestations of mass culture, few American architects beyond Venturi, Scott Brown and Charles Moore were discussing these phenomena. Perhaps the Beaux-Arts tradition was still too strong to allow this radical shift? An interesting argument in this context is that of Andreas Huyssen, who argues that in a sense, Pop Art was inevitably American, but did not gain a 'critical value' (in the sense of the Frankfurter Schule) until it had crossed the Atlantic again, back to Europe. It was only then that a more extensive intellectual reflection was possible on what the work of Andy Warhol really meant.[88]

This would imply that the work of Warhol was radical in a way that no European work could have been, and that this was in part due to its unreflective nature – in other words, that it lived on the surface of things, and took those surfaces for its subject. Second, that there is something to be discovered 'beneath' or

Collaged elements including billboards, textures, eye-level view.
Robert Venturi, Football Hall of Fame (1967)

'beyond' this surface, and that the tools of a European brand of intellectualism are necessary to achieve this. In contrast, Venturi and Scott Brown noted about Las Vegas that they did not know whether it was good or bad – they simply suspended their judgement to examine it. Third, that the notion of critical (or rather 'critique' in the sense of the Frankfurter Schule) is necessarily connected to text, to analytic reflection through words on images (in other words, that Warhol's work had no critical value until it was analysed). Where these first two presumptions may seem either trivial, or wrong, or reasonable, depending on the point of view taken, the third is worth investigating further because it has a direct bearing on what we see happening around us today.

The work of the Situationist International functions as a counterfoil here to the English 'pop architecture' movement. In the journal *Internationale Situationniste*, American imagery was typically used to deconstruct the capitalist system and prove its flaws. Here too though, we see the use of imagery not only as a communicative device but very much as a form of critique – only the critique was often placed in the form of text around the image.[89] On this level, the Situationist International approaches a critical use of the image itself in *détournement* but is still dependent on text and theory to achieve this. The communicative aspects of the image are similar to what Venturi and Scott Brown suggest, but intended to communicate a call to action rather than a social convention. The parallels between the New Brutalists, Team 10, Venturi and Moore were elucidated by Denise Scott Brown as early as 1967.[90] These are reiterated in a later essay in which she discusses what she learned from New Brutalism and English social realism and how she was able to transform and apply this knowledge to the American context.[91]

Here again, the distinctions between the American, English and French contexts become clear. The UK-USA connection was experimenting with 'community life as it is, and not as it should be' (to paraphrase Jane Jacobs), as can be seen in the extensive use of *objets trouvés* and *images trouvées* – like the picture of Joe Dimaggio pasted in the Golden Lane drawing, or the documentary panels produced in the Las Vegas and Levittown studios at Yale.[92] This experimentation with imagery (purely on the surface of things) flies in the face of the Marxist-based theories of the Frankfurter Schule and the later ones of the Situationist International, on false consciousness and alienation. The Situationist International forms an interesting 'middle' position in its belief that the 'everyday' is critical (and thus studies it extensively, just like Venturi and Scott Brown and the Independent Group), yet it also presumes that this everyday is not the goal of its study, but rather an instrument to destroy the false consciousness produced by capitalism and modern means of production. In this sense, the Situationist International treats the everyday much as the Enlightenment treated science and rationality: as the means by which people could transcend their (earlier) limitations. The critique the situationists had on 'Art' was that it denied everyday life – and their hope was to create a society where art could be abolished entirely, since it would be subsumed under the creativity of everyday life. Yet their understanding of this creativity of everyday life paralleled the characteristics often attributed to art – as a 'lifting of the veil' between our misperception of a 'true' (transcendent) reality. The Anglo-Saxon discourse formed an attempt to rethink this frame of reference, questioning the traditional understanding of critical 'agency' within cultural production.[93] Alloway, for example, sees an essential quality in the mass media. To him, the conventions of mass culture are equally as complex as those of high art, and its products are legible on many levels from simple to complex.[94] This aspect is what Banham will primarily focus on as he spends more time in the USA, similar to Tom Wolfe, who immerses himself in the popular culture of customized cars in Los Angeles. Precisely the appeal to the sophistication of the audience is what can be seen as the quality of the American environment and its influence.

Surface or Substance, Object or Representation

Both sides of the debate: the separation between surface and substance on the one hand and the impotence of architects in the face of society miss some essential points. First, no matter how separated sign and substance are, it is by appropriation of a space and by living in it that it acquires a conventional meaning – the lived space of Lefebvre constitutes new understandings of spaces because of the process of living. Moreover, attributing and appropriating meaning to and through images or appearances is a fundamental human process. Gans shows that the largest distinction between popular and high culture is not so much about the aesthetic or non-aesthetic, but about types of aesthetic experience (largely based on education). Sociologically, there is little distinction between aspiring to a great romance along the lines of a Harlequin novel or rather following Wuthering Heights – the processes of identification with characters and ascribing meaning are similar. In this sense, one could argue that regardless of the interventions of the architect, some meaning will be ascribed, and not necessarily the intended meaning. Is this a societal flaw or a discrepancy between architects' perceptions and the world they live in? Second, the architect can hardly be considered impotent if he gets his commission to design. True, the process is full of compromises (between architect, client, contractor, technology, budget), yet in the end of it there will still be a building, be it ugly or beautiful, and this building will be used, taken up into the fabric of daily existence. It may flout convention or annoy its occupants (and what proves power more than causing daily annoyance?), but it will have an impact.

The critical reassessment of vision and the associative qualities of what I would choose to call an 'image culture' is valuable now, in a time when audiences are becoming visually ever more sophisticated. This is not to say that we should concentrate solely on the visual aspect of architecture, but that we should at least discuss the visual as one importantly constitutive aspect of architecture. It is this importance of the visual, so strongly present in the work of Venturi and Scott Brown, that needs reconsideration.

As Venturi and Scott Brown discovered quite early on, film and television productions are interesting media for this study, especially the commercial ones, because they are the ones that have the most wide-ranging influence.[95] Especially some of the contemporary productions illustrate a certain avant-garde 'technique' introduced into a commercial product.[96] This melding of avant-garde and commerce shows a certain shift currently discernible in terms of 'blurring' ideological lines; both pragmatism and aestheticism are present, and the question is to what extent they function as the (either historical or neo-) avant-garde would have them. In the 1960s we can see only the beginnings of these developments, but it is precisely the work done by Venturi and Scott Brown and their various contemporaries in art and architecture that illustrate their grounding in a questioning of the modernist ethic and aesthetic.

Where often movement and speed are seen as constitutive of the modern experience, and thus of modern vision, the 1960s and work such as *Learning from Las Vegas* pre-empt some other notions related less to vision and more to a total experience. In a conceptual sense, the work begins to touch on what the associative and networked, or communal qualities of the contemporary image are – how vision itself has become part of a larger whole incorporating advertising, projection, montage, thus forming a new *Erlebnis*, which would include not only an image but also an attitude and a form of communication that transcends mere representation.

Using 'vision' and 'image' as two critically related yet separate notions can be helpful in examining what the status of the project of modernity is today – can we see it as a critical stance, embodied in the visual? Or can we say that the cognitive transformations in cultural production (architecture as the case in point) have sufficiently reconditioned contemporary experience to necessitate a different method of analysis? If so, might the image itself become capable of a critical gesture in this different (post-industrial) mode of being?

In the notion of vision as both natural and universal there is clearly an implication of transcendence: that somehow, what the eyes can see goes beyond all boundaries of context, class, language and anything else that necessitates 'translation' of meaning. Although this too was questioned with the introduction of structuralism, the dominant understanding of the visual remained as a 'true reflection', unmediated, of reality.[97] Since the 1960s, the condition of this image-based 'spectacle' has prompted a reconsideration of the autonomy of images, combined with their capability of communication. This idea of an 'image culture' or a 'visual turn' presupposes that the visual is no longer either transcendent or the direct reflection of an objective reality, but rather accords to the visual an ambiguous status of both communication and mediation, as well as inherent and autonomous qualities that are unique to the visual. These qualities include fluidity and a network of associations, yet still retain a certain level of 'legibility' of imagery (related to its communicative nature).[98] In this sense, the dominant scopic regime of modernism has been under attack since the 1960s: it is precisely the 'easy legibility' of pop imagery that allows this 'image culture' to arise, undermining the enlightened and intellectual understanding of vision that pierces the facile nature of the surface. Yet this image culture simultaneously hides much more beneath its surface than could ever be acknowledged under the regime of modernism.[99]

Martin Jay discusses how there is certainly an element of the universal in vision – he mentions silent film as an example of how images transcend cultural boundaries.[100] Yet what we find in the early twentieth-century uses of 'vision' in texts like those of Le Corbusier is the implication that 'to see' is to see beyond the mere surface articulation. In the introduction to 'Eyes which Do Not See' he notes, in the true spirit of modernity, that we have entered a new era which requires a new aesthetic – and that we are as yet unable to see it.[101] To him, our vision is still constricted by what we are accustomed to, by the imagery of nineteenth-century eclecticism, and by earlier 'styles' in architecture. To Le Corbusier, 'vision' is more about seeing the 'true' or 'intended' order of things, or even perhaps the 'natural' order of things, as it is defined by Jay in his article.[102]

Perhaps this is also what was so fundamentally shocking about a book such as *Learning from Las Vegas*: here were a pair of architects who were not encouraging us

Billboard trumps view, image from 'Signs of Life' exhibition (1976)

Billboard acclaims building, image from *Learning from Las Vegas* (1972)

to look past the billboards and signs and clutter of commercial imagery, but rather to look directly at them, and to appreciate them for what they were: an expression of the vitality of the everyday environment.

We must also keep in mind here, though, that one of the driving forces behind Le Corbusier's manifesto has remained exactly the same for Venturi: to apprehend and to clarify the aesthetics and the spirit of an age. Again in the introduction to 'Eyes which Do Not See', he offers a definition of style which to some degree may still hold today, but certainly encompasses the true basis of modernity: 'Style is a unity of principle animating all the work of an epoch, the result of a state of mind which has its own special character.'[103] Modernity itself is a flexible thing; it is precisely about transitions and being able to incorporate the new. This idea of style is no less applicable to Robert Venturi than it was to Le Corbusier – the state of mind had simply changed, thus requiring a revaluation of the basic principles under which architecture was being designed. The internal conflict in the writings of Le Corbusier was that he was aware of the ephemerality of the modern age, yet was convinced that his architectural principles were immutable and eternal.

Jay refers to Norman Bryson's notion that images have both a discursive and a figural aspect. The figural is where notions such as composition, harmony and beauty are typically situated, the discursive is where meaning and symbolism are located. Furthermore, in the way these two aspects have developed, the figural is

Sources and references of commercial and individual styling (Remedial Housing for Architects studio, Yale, 1970)

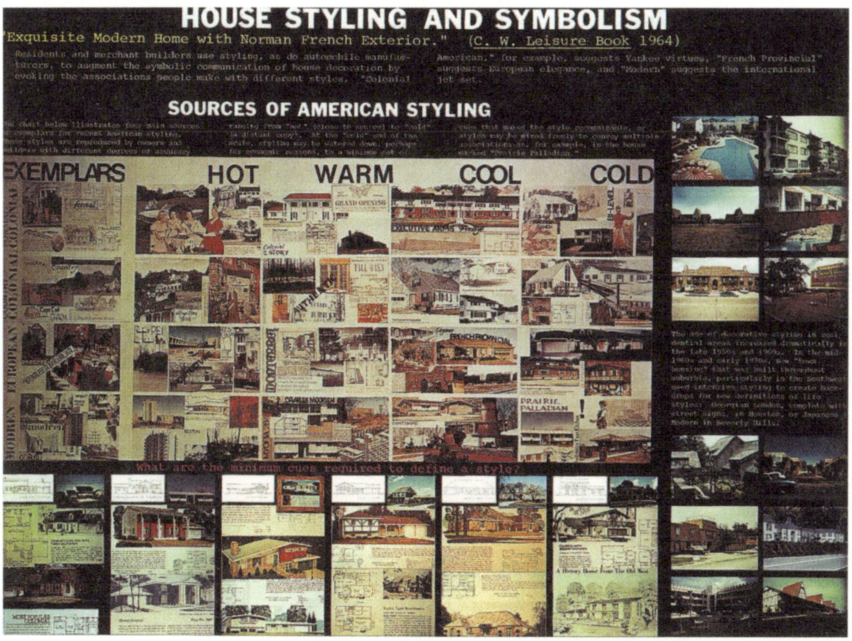

typically set in the realm of the absolute, and the discursive in the domain of the relative.[104] Having gone a full trajectory from seeing the image as only figural, and needing to imbue it with meaning, to seeing the image as only discursive, and having no grounds on which to judge its aesthetic merit, we are currently in a struggle to begin to see both sides of it simultaneously. Jay is working towards this in his article, and it is also to be seen in art reviews, architecture conferences and various writings of recent years: the notion of beauty is becoming important again, yet it does not necessarily 'remove' meaning or preclude it simply by 'being beautiful', nor is there the idea that beauty is entirely universal in the way Le Corbusier would have us believe – yet there is an agreement that it is a critical aspect, not to be entirely denied in the way we have seen it treated in the purely 'banal'.

Returning to the two aspects discursive and figural, there is a continual shifting between these poles: for already in our two key figures here, Venturi and Le Corbusier, the two sides are used as a reductivist polemic, yet then reintroduced to quietly reconfigure their significance.

To begin with Le Corbusier: his suggestions (or demands) are continually on a plane of aesthetic intent. He uses the figural notions of harmony (of geometry and plan) to offer a perfected environment. This fits perfectly within the idea of a purely figural image, denying any contextual conditions (which would be an indication of the discursive) and guiding us towards the transcendental image of pure figuration. Moreover, it fits perfectly with the Enlightenment notion that the image is an unmediated representation of reality, is a 'natural' way of expressing something. Yet, despite all this clean, ostensibly amoral, projection, he conflates aesthetics with ethics. It is not merely beauty he is seeking, but the enlightenment and perfection of man, to be achieved through this universal notion of beauty. The conflation is where a slippery slope begins. He discusses architecture, engineering and the love of machines as having a moral aspect to them, because they are about clarity and order.[105] Furthermore, the domains of art and architecture are to be left to those who are ahead of their time, who can see past the petty issues of every day. Perhaps it is only through the conflation of modern beauty with morality, but these principles of enlightenment, taken together with his use of images of contemporary technology (the steamboat, the car, the airplane), show a discursive use of the imagery that is precisely about the cult of modern technology. Moreover, if we think back to his definition of style as the expression of an epoch and the result of a state of mind, he does have a certain discursive notion of the image.

Venturi, on the other hand, pushed for a specifically discursive understanding of imagery: the idea that the experts' view of art (or in this specific case, the dominant ideology of a clean modernist aesthetic) was not the only appropriate one. He intentionally entered a realm that spoke of the relative values of one thing against another, and their embeddedness in a culture. Later, in collaboration with Scott Brown, he would also begin to talk of signs, which brings the work extremely close to the semantic games played a little later in postmodern architecture. His references to the historical value of certain styles and his understanding of continuity in the history of architecture and its images all plant him firmly in the realm

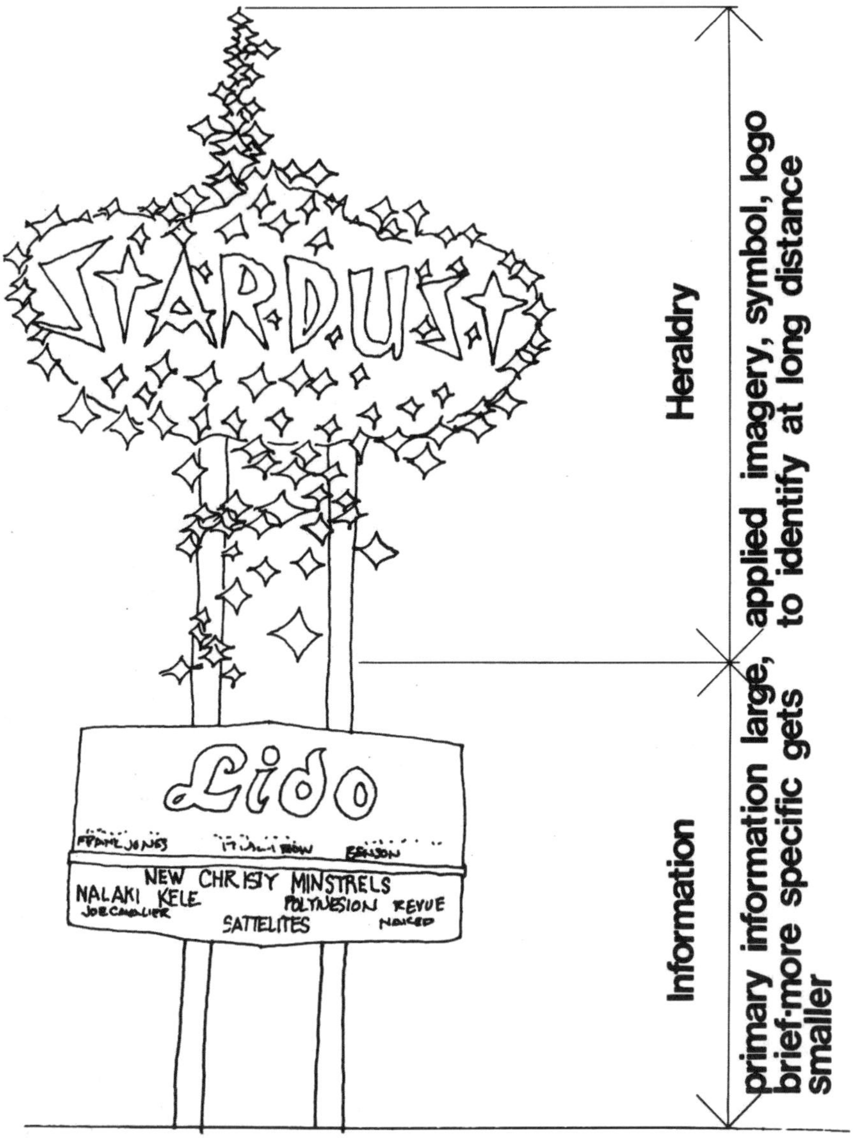

68. Physiognomy of a typical casino sign

Communicative mechanism of the billboard, image from *Learning from Las Vegas* (1972)

of the discursive – needing to understand the image in its very context. On the other hand, what Venturi does is to place, for example, ornament (in *Complexity and Contradiction*) on a figural level. He discusses notions of harmony and tension in the typical fashion of architecture history, which denies the possibility of other translations. Moreover, his analysis of these conditions of architecture are focused largely on a purely formal level; it is not until later in *Complexity and Contradiction in Architecture* (after Scott Brown entered his life) that he begins to really engage with the condition of the everyday in a more analytic, sociological manner.

> One way that this issue was addressed prior to the visual turn was to distinguish between words as conventional signs and images as their natural counterparts. . . . Whereas words were taken to be arbitrary signifiers without any necessary relation to what they signified, images were understood to be tied by natural forces to what they resembled, iconic analogues of their objects.[106]

Modernism both deconstructed and utilized the notion of the iconic analogue; its deconstruction is clearest in the work of Cubism and Abstract Expressionism, with no clearly recognizable iconic analogues. Yet the notion of a universal and transcendent form is arguably related to the idea of not so much an iconic analogue, but perhaps a conceptual analogue. The implication in modernism was still that, given the appropriate form, the conceptual understanding would be absolutely independent of culture. Postmodernism on the other hand utilized the iconic analogue very literally in its employment of nearly direct renditions of traditional architectural figures (such as the pediment and the arch). Yet this form of iconic analogue was intended precisely to subvert the 'naturalness' of modernist vision, and reintroduce the discursive and communicative aspects of the visual. These distinctions go to the heart of contemporary discourse. Although it would be hard to argue that the imagery of our spectacle society is somehow 'natural', its signs and signifiers do still constitute a structure of communication, to some degree contextual but under the forces of globalization also incorporating a certain universal legibility.

There are subtle yet important distinctions to keep in mind here: the eye as innocent or objective; vision as piercing a surface, opposed to the image as pure surface; ocularcentrism and ocular ontologies in contrast to a more embodied vision; the perceived naturalness (and thus an implicit neutrality) of seeing.

The need for mass-cultural references and an incorporation of everyday images was a response to the demanding abstraction and purity of modernism. The imagery was sometimes used as an explicit attack, in other cases as sheer pleasure. But central to the idea was first a resistance to what had gone before, and a rearticulation through the artefacts of daily life. Eventually this democratization of art and architecture led to the use of 'beauty is in the eye of the beholder' as a universal tenet – that it was not up to the architect or the artist to determine what was beautiful. And it is in this universality, in the complete dismissal of the autonomous qualities of images that danger also lies:

> Visual culture, in other words, has come perilously close to being turned into a branch office of the cultural studies conglomerate, in which ocularcentrism is trumped by logocentrism and the autonomy of visual experience is denounced as an outdated ideology of high modernist art.[107]

Many have thought, which is in a sense a modernist tradition, that the image is man's downfall. This is expressed in different ways: in high modernism, such as that of Le Corbusier, Mies van der Rohe and Loos, the imagery associated with 'the masses', with 'popular arts', with 'kitsch' is seen as detracting from the possibility to truly see harmony and geometry, and rise to the perfection of a platonic aesthetic. These are the manifestoes that follow the lines of Plato's cave theory, where we lowly beings see nothing but the meagre reflections of the real world and have no sense of what a true circle is because we are trapped in a cave and blindfolded to true vision. The philosopher is the one who can escape the cave and subsequently make others see. In many passages of *Vers une Architecture* as well as *Urbanisme*, Le Corbusier uses precisely this type of rhetoric to prove that the engineer-architect (instead of the philosopher) is ready to enlighten mankind.

The connection between this kind of rhetoric and that of Guy Debord, for example, is precisely this notion of enlightenment. Debord begins from within Marxist thought and uses the theory of capitalist production and alienation to prove that the images around us in the 1960s, specifically the commodified images of advertising, TV and movies, are nothing but an opiate, serving to cloud our vision of the authentic world. Again, here we have the orator who is prepared to bring us out into the real world, and images again are the source of our trouble: they cloud our vision through their pleasantries and simplistic reduction. It is on this level that the work of Venturi and Scott Brown is interesting and can be seen as (on the cusp of) moving beyond modernism: it proposes that the image in itself is not the wrongdoer, and that it in fact holds the power to communicate, to subvert and to open other avenues of possibility. Thus the image becomes revalued as a tool of communication, not only obfuscation. From here, it is but a small step towards understanding the image as possibly being critical rather than only representational.

This work, as a prelude to postmodernism, incorporates both attitudes towards the visual: it offers a resistance to the ocular ontology of modernism, yet still has a traditional understanding of aesthetics embedded in it. Even in its resistance, it still expresses a utopian drive, allowing its very resistance to finally become dogmatic. The Independent Group exhibition 'This Is Tomorrow' shows the ambiguity of the 1960s in its vitality and pleasure in imagery. The artists' reception of images as both consumers and artists shows a transition between high modernism and pop culture, using their imagery in part as ideology critique, yet also for sheer pleasure, for the enjoyment of something new and full of energy. In postmodernity, the issue of cultural relativism 'challenged the pretension of any one language or code to serve as the metalanguage or metacode for the species as a whole'.[108] This is precisely the kind of response we are discussing as resistance to or rearticulation of modernism. Yet the 1960s also demonstrated that 'much of the power of images, we might conjecture, comes precisely from their ability to resist being entirely subsumed under the protocol of specific cultures'.[109] Here again we see the distinctions between Colquhoun's figure and form, or Jay's discursive and figural, or even Barthes' idea of representation and figuration, becoming productive not despite the blurring of distinctions but because of it.[110]

The increasingly visual nature of the world has been blamed for problems such as superficiality and shallowness – this betrays the underlying notion that big ideas, proper relations with things, and so forth can only be had through words. Yet it is worth briefly noting that each major shift in media has encouraged this kind of rhetoric: from Plato's complaint (through the dialogues of Socrates) that people would no longer train their intellectual faculties once writing had become a common good (since memory would no longer be necessary if things were recorded), to the early complaints of shallowness in the lives of the children growing up immersed in an advertising culture; and such comments as Debord's complaining that authentic life was no longer possible in the culture of capitalism. On the other hand, there are critics such as Walter Benjamin, who tentatively signal coming developments, in a mixture of wariness and curiosity.

One way or the other, it is clear that the imagery of the twentieth century and mass culture in general (such as paperback books but also propaganda posters) have a complex relationship with each other, and with the later developments of Pop Art. One of the fundamental conditions of this relation is the hierarchy between the intellectuals or the avant-garde and the masses. The masses are an early twentieth-century concept, related to such works as Canetti's *Crowds and Power*, to mass industrialization and the workers in industry as part of a factory assembly line. These masses of the assembly line, interchangeable and eminently replaceable, are alienated from the products of their own work according to Marx. This alienation was then mollified by extensive consumption – again directed at 'the masses'. This is the line of thought that prompted work like *The Society of the Spectacle*. However, today's systems of production and consumption have become too sophisticated to talk of 'the masses' any longer. In contemporary culture, it has become more useful to speak of niches and target groups rather than 'the masses'.[111]

Banham's work on surface decoration and expendability indicates a beginning to this rearticulation, though still in the vocabulary of architecture history. Alongside this internal deconstruction of the most widely accepted principles of modernism, an 'external' deconstruction through the introduction of the imagery of mass culture was undertaken by other members of the Independent Group, notably Paolozzi, Hamilton and to some degree the Smithsons (especially Alison, with her interest in advertising images). The Independent Group intended this commercial aesthetic as a democratization of architecture and art; and as a reintroduction of a certain vitality in the slumbering remains of high modernism.

It was the vitality of these popular images and their disregard for the accepted categories of aesthetics and art criticism that drew the members of the Independent Group to them in the first place. And, like in earlier avant-garde movements (such as Dada), it was just outside of their own discipline that they found this vitality: these images were *objets trouvés*, simple manifestations of everyday culture without the intervention of architects and artists.[112]

There is definitely a pleasure of discovery in the collages of Paolozzi as opposed to, say, the more demanding experience of the sublime sought after by the Abstract Expressionists.[113] The Paolozzi work is all about a different kind of viewing – the pleasure of recognition (well-known artefacts relating to the home, technology, childhood), the enjoyment of discovery (in the extensive universe of collage, so full of things), the reframing of everyday objects, thus making them seem more valuable. The collage here works as a framing device involving jarring combinations, odd juxtapositions; it incorporates the element of shock as in Dada.

Form and its relation to meaning can perhaps be a little more easily determined on the basis of popular opinion. For significance is generally given in context, not inherently. Although again here we should refer back to Martin Jay's piece, and understand that visual meaning or significance is more universal than linguistic. In this sense, the visual turn is arguably a natural development in the context of globalization. In the confrontation with a larger number of cultures and languages, visual communication, at least on a basic level, may be the more logical path.

Here then the trickiness of the aesthetics debate becomes apparent: are images meant to convey an experience of the sublime, or of aesthetic reflection based on conventions learned through extensive education? Or are they meant to communicate meaning? To offer symbols for a society to hang its traditions on? This debate has gone back and forth throughout the twentieth century, all in the name of the 'proper' aesthetic approach. This is what made pop radical: it was not about legitimacy but about experiment, not about conventional aesthetics but about crossing traditional boundaries. And at the time it was on the rise, what better place for it to seek its images than the USA.

V

A Brave New World: Is Resistance Futile?

The Legacy of the 1960s

The 1960s remain a legendary era, constituting a moment that even now captures the cultural imagination and reminds us of the need for political engagement. At the time, architecture played a role as both enemy and saviour. On the one hand, modernist architecture was seen not only to represent a totalitarian environment of abstraction, but also to have bred many societal ills.[1] On the other hand, the faith in architecture's potential to liberate and emancipate its residents was still strong, resulting in many utopian proposals. The proliferation of utopian schemes intimating a world of equality, affluence and pleasure continues to be one of the strongest legacies of this period. While the different themes, manifestoes and projects discussed in this book are not the sole defining moments of the *années pop*, they certainly delineate some of the most radical gestures in architecture, which continue to influence the discourse today. Each group addresses a concern that transcends the 'purely' architectural to include fundamental societal transformations, while attempting to rethink the influence of architecture in forming society. In this sense, each group exemplifies a specific attitude that grew within the architecture discourse over the course of the 1960s, within which we could also position such diverse architects as Hans Hollein and Haus Rucker Co, Groupe Utopie, Archizoom and Superstudio, but also Raimund Abraham and Buckminster Fuller (a favourite of Banham and Archigram). This discourse constitutes a vast diversity of gestures, all tied together through both a critical view of earlier positions and an undiminished belief in progress through architecture, with an infectious optimism. The formats tend to be more inclusive (with the democratic aesthetic of both Venturi and Scott Brown and Archigram as prominent examples), populist (oriented towards the 'worker' through the situationists and the 'everyday' in the Anglo-Saxon discourse), and pushing the potential boundaries of technology (New Babylon and Archigram).

In each of the major themes of the 1960s that continue to resonate today, resurfacing in contemporary articles, these radical critiques focus on crucial issues that formed a direct attack on modernism. They used gaps in the modernist discourse to demonstrate its shortcomings as an environment for a vital and changing society. In brief, these terms encompass the following shifts. In relation to the city, a shift is to be seen from the universal to the individual: a shift from universal and collective tenets in city planning to a primacy of the individual, and the personal experience of city space. The discussion of the city is framed no longer by universally valid tenets of functionalism, but by the specificity of human interaction. In relation to the image, a transformation takes place from abstraction to figuration. Instead of streamlined and standardized (again universal) forms, the relation with imagery is now based on symbolic meaning and communication with an everyday audience. Rather than an 'essential' meaning that should be deduced from a non-ornamented abstract form, the role and significance of appearance has now become prime. In the realm of technology, the main shift is from mechanization to a technological 'sensibility' that incorporates the benefits of a consumer-oriented flexibility. Rather than view technology as something machinic and lifeless, technology becomes visualized more as a prosthetic device, as an extension of man himself.

At the same time, many of these issues were not merely a reaction, but also derived from a changing sensibility – new ideas that had arisen in diverse arenas and responded to a changing situation in the world. The 1960s form the transition from the modern to the postmodern.[2] And yet the 1960s cannot be positioned as a pure rupture, certainly not in architecture. By addressing the problems of modernity and the responses to a changing era as a 'tactics of resistance', the radical transformations were too easily stylized. This resistance became part and parcel of an attitude, by no means limited to architecture. It helped break through the dominance of uncontested hierarchies and authoritarian control, yet in time resistance became a goal in itself, forgetting what it was originally aimed at.

This framework of critique, embodied in resistance, marks the preconceptions that continue to underlie the contemporary debate. What on the one hand can be seen as a cheerful reminiscence on days gone by that nevertheless maintains a sense of optimism, hopes and ideals and possibly even naïveté in the best sense (an innocence towards the potential failure inherent in any undertaking), can on the other be construed as a suffocating framework that separates the believers from the non-believers. The very notion of a radical critique, the very effort put into the all-encompassing critique, prefigures its failure. For when a model collides so intensely with reality, it is doomed. The belief in a radical critique was configured by a faith in the personal perception of reality, in which the critic has an understanding that transcends that of the ordinary person, a role often attributed to the artist since the advent of the avant-garde. The 'tactics of resistance' by definition places architecture in opposition – to reality, to established conventions, to existing power structures. It is this tactics of resistance that remains one of the strongest legacies of the 1960s – the justification of the artist is determined not by the quality of his work but by his ability to resist. This is a nihilistic definition of the discipline of architecture, which denies its productive character. It also deeply limits the 'agency' of cultural production, denying it the complexity of its own traditions and its relation with reality.[3]

The specific critiques continue to hold useful insights, such as the cultural meaning attached to symbolic form. The role of the street as a place of communication that contributes to the cohesion of the community can still be helpful to urban planning in large cities. Rethinking technology from the perspective of ergonomics continues to inform the design fields, and aids in fine-tuning an environment in which many technologies are necessary to its functioning. The resonance in these critiques, no matter where they come from and which specific topic they are addressing, sketch out a larger cultural significance. Ideas and attitudes are shared and even resound throughout the words that express the appeal of a kinder, gentler architecture (Venturi's 'gentle' manifesto): new attitudes are expressed through the attention for change, flexibility and 'growth', but also in profusion, everyday imagery and the disavowal of abstraction. Individualization and personalization take precedence over standardization, and human qualities are given priority over the demands of the industrial society. Architecture was meant to shift from an idealized blueprint to a reactive, transformative environment, be it in the form of New Babylon, the Plug-In City or the already tested ground of Levittown.

However, by continuing to adhere to the reflex of resistance, and by elevating the cultural moment of the 1960s beyond the 'typical' historical process to an ideal that we have somehow failed, we lose sight of both what was gained and what was lost. The 1960s brought us an era of affluence that helped make life easier, more comfortable.[4] It also introduced a significant level of individual freedom, which was not gained without a struggle. The time offered a sense of empowerment to the disenfranchised, even if reality lagged somewhat behind. At the same time, this focus on the individual was achieved at the cost of the stability of a traditional sense of community. This resulted not only in cutting the self-reliant individual loose from the bonds of a stifling community, but also left many dangling without recourse to the safety net of a group bound by a sense of responsibility to the group as a whole. Moreover, by understanding resistance as a fundamental trait of accepted cultural production, the discourse of the 1960s reinforces the modernist project more than it undermines it. While the 1960s dissolved the eternal function of architecture into one of change and transformation, it also completed the logic of the Modern Movement by raising the issue of change to a universal law. The communal function of architecture is dissolved into individual significance: symbols are more about personal expression than about cultural meaning. Yet at the same time the modern form of this new architecture is reconfigured by looking at the everyday environment. Each time, the sense of a universal spirit of the time is reinforced, again affirming the modern project. What this does not acknowledge is that some issues are simply at odds. The fundamental incompatibility of individual freedom and communal coherence can only be resolved in compromise or struggle, and this must be done again and again. It cannot be resolved once and for all, even in an adaptable environment. Needs and desires change, traditions change and priorities change as well. Reducing these continual recalibrations to a simplified model of resistance to the existing until utopia has been achieved denies the active contribution that results from making small changes within the fabric of existing reality.

In this sense, the critique of consumption that is embedded in these projects and manifestoes also intimates the spectrum of the societal question of affluence that is still (if not increasingly) relevant to architecture today. The societal conditions of architectural practice in the second half of the twentieth century are circumscribed by the spectrum of affluence from late capitalism to the welfare state. The shifting boundaries between a focus on individual and communal effort are part of this field, and architecture is necessarily positioned within as a discipline that is determined by cultural and economic conditions, by artistic invention and general tradition. The critique of consumption must necessarily examine the question of needs and desires. In particular, it was the configuration of desires by a market aimed at profit that disturbed Guy Debord so deeply (and continues to pose questions for us today). Yet one could also wonder whether giving form to implicit desires is not one of the strengths of architecture: a sense of community in a strained urban neighbourhood, a representation of possible futures where reality continues to revolve around unrealized potentials. Ideals can be embedded in smaller transformations. At the same time, architecture is a difficult field to do this in. It cannot be circumscribed by the ads used to market goods. It is part of a cultural fabric that is by necessity complex, incorporating dreams, identities and realities. Sometimes the most practical solutions may lead to unforeseen societal benefits, at others the most well-meant idealistic projects fail due to external factors.

The Revolution and Its Ripple Effects

Neither New Babylon nor the Cushicle became fully real, and yet our world was largely dreamed up and formed in the 1960s. Many of the ideas launched in the 1960s still resonate today. The situationist distrust of the spectacle continues to ring throughout various Internet sites, while the contemporary interest in 'lifestyles' is reminiscent of the different Levittown expressions of individuality. Many consequences of the transformations are different from what was imagined, which is perhaps the root cause of the ensuing disillusionment. The 'enlightening' potential of popular and mass culture, desired in the 1960s, had ramifications that remained unforeseen (the creative individuals that were foreseen in the near future now allow themselves to be enclosed in Golden Cages, stranded on Survivor Island and observed by Big Brother). The nomadic personalized technology has done less to individuate us than it has to expand our private sphere into public space, through iPods that are audible to others and the most intimate conversations on mobile phones. The emancipation of the individual tends at times towards antisocial behaviour (rather than the happy communities projected by the progressives of the 1960s). In architecture, projections of an adaptable environment facilitated through technologies are perhaps not as spectacular as envisioned at the time, but they are being developed in various ways. The tendency to revel in everyday symbolic gestures that was taken to extremes in postmodernism have now returned in the form of 'extreme home makeovers', complete with pirate beds and drive-in movie theatres, all courtesy of the advertisers and the spectacular design team. Is this failure or unforeseen success, or perhaps both? New Babylon's artificial environment was intended to continually recalibrate the relation between individual and environment, triggering a fundamental internal (authentic) creativity. As an architectural space, this is most directly emulated in contemporary casinos, where the loss of orientation in time and space serves a vastly different purpose than awakening personal creativity.

Nevertheless, it would not be fair to say that the 1960s were nothing more than a fulfilment of the modern project, or that architecture has become merely subservient to the inexorable progress of history. In the process of rethinking the form and function of architecture, a number of important criticisms were levelled at modernism, especially in terms of how it was put into practice. A strong sense of idealism enabled many architects to imagine an exciting new environment full of creative forms that would liberate its occupants (which echoed earlier modernist ideals, but with a different focus – man rather than machine, individual rather than the masses). At the same time, the high stakes of these ideals also made it exceedingly difficult to settle for incremental change, and even to take note of the changes taking place that did not fit their model of radical transformation. The failure of New Babylon and the Plug-In City to come into being and transform society prefigured the cynical disillusionment of the 1970s and a subsequent retreat into formalism.

In other words, one of the key issues here lies in the nature of transformation, its relation to the radical gesture, and the role of resistance as the underlying precondition for progress. The realization of the architectural project is to some extent complicit with existing power structures. This runs directly counter to the idea that resistance is necessary in order to transform society and its environment. By framing this problem in such a definitive manner, the spectrum between complicity and resistance becomes uninhabitable. One must accept being part of the existing societal fabric, and then deny all possible societal transformation, or one must attempt to change society, and therefore remain outside of it. In this sense, the retreat into the formalism of the 1970s seems inevitable. If the choice is between utopia and total failure, then architecture is doomed from the start. And even today, the presumptions on the need for resistance in order to qualify as intellectually valid architecture still remain part of the inner workings of the discourse. The practical import of architecture remains disavowed unless it somehow expresses resistance. In the end, the radical tactics of resistance redirected attention to the external forces that determined architecture rather than to those within.

The ripple effects of this revolution have been so extensive because its underlying presumptions have become so deeply incorporated. On the one hand, when the building is conflated with the ideals that form it, its interpretation becomes dependent on its intention – where clusters immediately denote 'community', or soft materials imply 'humane' forms. On the other hand, this also entails a shift from a focus on the building as an object to societal conditions and constraints. The combination of these two makes formal gestures suspect (as part of an establishment, and removed from the 'noble savage'), and allows the concretized form of social gestures to be well-received regardless of architectural merit. It describes a field delineated by (societal) critique and (architectural) revolution, dismissing the trajectories of architectural form that become incorporated as cultural symbols regardless of their societal intent, for example.

Each specific theme offers a number of unresolved issues that still resonate through the debates today, primarily since the self-proclaimed revolutionaries did little beyond inverting the earlier proclamations of modernism. Underneath it all, the presumptions that formed the sense of dislocation in modernity have remained. In this process of radical critique, one revolution replaced another and yet . . . the fundamental issues were reinforced rather than resolved. Each critique pointed to a singular issue that defined the central problem of modernism and remedied it in inversion. Each time, it concerned a crucial gap in the approach of architecture, whether that concerned the human presence in the city or a diversity of imagery. Each time, of course, it concerned the dominant modes of modernism, ignoring the various alternative voices. Nevertheless, despite the reductive reception, each of these themes addresses an issue that is as important today as it was 40 years ago. The city, once the site of modernity, continues to be a place of tension where the interests of the individual collide with those of the collective. Whether we shape our cities in grids or as branching trees does not change this problem.

How we address it in architecture might however benefit from a rethinking of the position and means of architecture. Each critique offers useful suggestions, such as the fundamental need for a sense of community, especially in the face of increasingly urban habitats. Yet these suggestions need to be taken up within a flexible framework that acknowledges societal recalibrations of architectural needs.[5] The continual reweaving of our ideas about urban conglomerations, dwelling, symbolic buildings and everyday habitats with the realities of economics, technological developments, societal transformation and cultural tradition require that we remain not only vigilant in the critical sense, but also sensitive to the small beauties we can easily overlook while chasing perfect clouds.[6]

In the end, the need for critical theory answered to a reshuffling of accepted hierarchies and accepted truths. There was a general turn to questions of external conditions and how they formed us, which also marked architecture. These questions allowed an overturning of the inevitability of spatial determinism so present in modernism. Instead of conforming mindlessly to one's environment, the environment could help us explore our own personal desires. Nevertheless, it is this redirection to underlying conditions that incorporates a new form of fatalism. The spatial determinism underlying modernism remains present in the projects of the 1960s despite the differing formal expression. Although New Babylon may seem to empower architecture by giving it a new role in realizing the potential of its inhabitants, it ultimately again denies architecture a different form of agency that does not directly mirror the critique that feeds it. Utopia is total and mapped out, or it fails completely.

The manifestoes of the 1960s were so intent on critiquing modernism that they failed to see the gaps in their own production. By approaching architecture as a revolutionary tool, and by envisioning the effects of architecture in such a radical fashion, they affirmed the spatial determinism of their predecessors. This involved a negation of the more complex interactions that cannot be contained within critical theory as applied to architecture. The underlying presumption positions architecture as either radical or affirmative: it is either a product of avant-garde critical theory, where its revolutionary form derives from its critical gesture, or it is complicit with the established forces of society and capital, where its form reinforces existing and oppressive societal patterns. Both Archigram and Venturi and Scott Brown tried to rethink this framework through a form of emancipation that could be encouraged by popular and consumer culture. Yet at the core, they maintained a series of oppositions that continued to affirm the foundations of the modernists. Critical theory and its tools (and in particular their conflation with architecture) have contributed to the imperfections of a discourse based on ideal models, denying the transformations architecture can engender in and through material reality.

Rethinking the Role of Architecture

This goes to the heart of the argument on the failure of critique by Bruno Latour, where he comments that the main problem with contemporary science is its negation of the many facets of reality: it may be able to specify the wavelengths of a sunset, but it cannot qualify the light.[7] Contemporary critique has placed itself in an all-powerful position, perhaps more so even than the architects who believed that their buildings might change the world. Latour demonstrates the god's-eye view that the critic has given himself. First, critique has given us the mechanisms to deconstruct the essential qualities of things in the world, until we have come to believe that all things are equal, imbued only with the qualities we project onto them. Yet if we then feel empowered, as if we may perhaps make conscious, self-guided choices, the critic reins us straight back in, arguing that we are controlled by unseen forces of psychology, sociology and culture. There is simply no way to win. Only the critic has magically placed himself outside of the circle of influence, somehow enlightened enough to see this mechanism at work. It is the displacement of object and agent that makes the critical process appear to work. Ironically, it appeals to the same form of intellectual authority the critic dismisses by referring to the hidden forces that determine our own perceptions.

Latour identifies certain problems with the very structure of critique in cultural studies that derive from the type of analyses I have discussed in the architecture discourse of the 1960s. He also immediately warns against a facile appropriation of earlier arguments such as those used by situationism or Archigram to address contemporary problems. Although the resonance in their questions may be striking, a critical eye is always necessary. The failure of an earlier solution 'does not mean … that we were wrong, but simply that history changes quickly and that there is no greater intellectual crime than to address with the equipment of an older period the challenges of the present one'.[8]

Another reason to turn to Latour for suggestions on a different approach to architecture is his emphasis on realism. As a critic, he distances himself from purely theoretical observations that remove themselves from the world at hand. He posits:

> The question was never to get *away* from facts but *closer* to them, not fighting empiricism but, on the contrary, renewing empiricism. What I am going to argue is that the critical mind, if it is to renew itself and be relevant again, is to be found in the cultivation of a *stubbornly realist attitude* – to speak like William James – but a realism dealing with what I will call *matters of concern*, not *matters of fact*. The mistake we made, the mistake I made, was to believe that there was no efficient way to criticize matters of fact except by moving *away* from them and directing one's attention *toward* the conditions that made them possible. But this meant accepting much too uncritically what matters of fact were.[9]

The idea Latour posits here of a 'stubbornly realist attitude' encompasses a realism that goes beyond the traditional understanding of empirical realism. Latour is referring primarily to the sciences, defined by an empirical realism that was eventually reduced to *only* measurable and quantifiable entities. His desire to move beyond this to a 'stubborn realism' is about taking other factors into account as well (not instead of, but in addition to measurable traits), such as social influences or (conventional) meaning. I use the phrase 'critical realism' here to maintain the sense of careful observation and reflection implied by the word 'critical'. As an extension of his argument, 'matters of concern' entail seeing the object as more than a merely quantifiable entity, or a 'matter of fact'.[10] The real itself is so rich that a misplaced emphasis on its formative conditions obscures the objects at hand. By engaging purely with a (suspiciously) critical attitude, the possibility of examining the architectural object as it presents itself becomes increasingly difficult, while that is precisely where its strengths are. On the other hand, if a critical attitude has slowly become embedded within our culture (fed by a reflex of self-reflection that has become part of the culture at large), then that may mean that we can engage the object itself without returning to a naïve belief that one architectural intervention may change the world as we know it.

This strong sense of what I am calling a 'critical realism', concerned with both the observation of reality and the critical view of what constitutes that reality, seems precisely where architecture discourse will find a productive strategy, by both acknowledging the reality of the world it is building in, yet remaining aware of how it is constituted. Moreover, Latour's distinction between matters of concern and matters of fact is a beautifully precise formulation of one of the problems of the discourse: that somehow matters of fact have been either radically affirmed in an objective scientific tradition, without the opportunity for questioning their context, or radically negated in architecture theories like deconstructivism, where every 'fact' was constituted *only* by its context, and thereby lost its own status in reality.

By no means does Latour trivialize the historical importance of critique in revealing the subtle forces of societal preconceptions that not only form reality but also represent it as objective. In their early uses, as Latour argues, these tools were necessary in order to reveal additional aspects of the 'objective' reality we thought we understood in the first half of the twentieth-century. And yet, there has been a marked shift between these early days of critique, when it helped reveal the discriminatory tendencies that were affirmed by a specific representation of history, and now, when the same tools of critique are used to undermine accepted scientific facts such as global warming. For Latour, the only way forward is to take a step away from the many invisible forces we see as determining our reality, and a step closer to the tangible facts of material reality in the broadest sense, including sensations and perceptions alongside quantifiable scientific models. According to Antonio Negri, this ambiguity was already embedded within the struggle of the 1960s:

> In the end, when we think about it, May 1968 was not about exalting confrontations and struggle; that's still its 'modern' aspect. Nineteen sixty-eight was something else completely – the pleasure of discovering a new humanity, a deep joy in ourselves and around us, of realizing that elements of expression, imagination, and life can exist together. We went from utopia to a nonutopian concretization of the real. What we were doing, what we wanted to do, and what we had started doing contained a novel risk, a new world.[11]

The fact that this 'novel risk' was to eventually become a solidified dogma that still defines the benchmark of critical engagement should not deter us from both appreciating its optimism and its intentions, and rethinking the forms they took. It is in this tug-of-war between the very real sense of transformation and progress on the one hand, and the turn to new dogmas of emancipation on the other that we can see the everyday reality sketched out. The sense of transformation is now no longer to be found through the same means, yet it continues to be set as an example, regardless of its commensurability with current conditions.

So if we accept that the 1960s had much to offer us (just quickly glancing over recent publications on the time should suffice to impress on us the vast production of the 1960s in architecture, as well as its cheerful vitality), let us also accept that it set preconditions that have proven difficult to shed. As noted, one of the key issues here lies in the (modern) attribution of a revolutionary role to architecture that does not so much incorporate societal issues as mirror them, allowing the specifically architectural questions to be relegated to the background. Although we may have a sense that the revolution 'failed', it only failed insofar as the visions of an idealized playful society triggered by inventive architecture failed to materialize. On a small scale, many of our spaces today were configured by the ideas of the 1960s. Contemporary casinos share a suspiciously large number of characteristics with New Babylon, while contemporary advertising seems to have learned its lessons very well from situationist *détournement*. The pop-culture sense of individualized technologies has become an everyday reality with sparkling cell phones. They may not be as groovy as a tomato, but they certainly connect everyone to their own private networks, no matter where they physically are. The significance attributed to the everyday environment in *Learning from Las Vegas* has drowned in its own spectacle, having lost the edgy sense of a critical revision of elite aesthetics.

Since the 1960s, the architecture debate has marked a trajectory between the extremes of spatial determinism and formal autonomy. Underlying this pendulum movement is the role attributed to architecture. Its 'critical' and revolutionary role places it at opposite ends of the complex (and muddy) reality it must build for. While the debates of the 1960s posed some crucial questions, architects constructed answers by opposing their predecessors. The discipline of architecture itself may hold the key to escaping this pendulum. The idealism embedded in architectural projects finds a way into the reality of the built environment, which is infinitely more complex than a 'situationist city' had promised to be. The delineation of architecture in terms of critique, revolution and the tactics of resistance has not only encouraged this oppositional discourse, but may very well have formed it in the first place. Positioning architecture as a revolutionary activity negates its complicity and embeddedness within (traditional) culture. Positioning architecture as critique does not do justice to the imagination and hard work that go into conceiving a building. Architecture is embedded and responsive to external conditions, and yet it is also an autonomous activity, determined by its own traditions and rules. The framing of the architecture of the twentieth century as a battleground where critique precedes the revolution (to be fulfilled by and through architecture) rests on a foundation of avant-garde thinking and the critical theory of the Frankfurter Schule.[12] How it has been incorporated in architecture has resulted in the visionary schemes for imminent worlds, both beautiful and terrifying. The specific issue at heart here is, however, the shift in focus from the tools and history of architecture to those of critical theory. The failure of critique, or the demise of critique, as addressed by Latour, is directed at the contemporary use of critique as 'old tools for a contemporary age': suitable and indeed necessary at a specific moment in time, but by now outdated and possibly doing more damage than good.

Projective Architecture: Beyond Critique?

In architecture, this very question of the failure of critique has found a (relatively heated) ground for debate in the question of 'projective' architecture. Although this debate has remained primarily within the confines of academia, its proposition that architecture is a field of 'projective' practice as opposed to 'critical' practice closely parallels the misgivings Latour voices about the current efficacy of critique. This debate, although in a somewhat conflated manner, reveals some of the stalemates that the legacy of the 1960s has confronted architecture with.

Current ideas on the failure of the critical, and a desire to formulate a more productive variant of this in the form of the projective, are an almost direct extension of the failed ambitions of the 1960s' resistance to established discourse. In the 1960s, the 'critical' function of architecture became fundamental. The 'critical' extended to self-criticism (in reassessing the merits and especially the flaws of high modernism), and to societal critique (in proposing alternatives for dwelling and for the architectural environment that were intended to reconfigure ideas of community and the position of the individual). A critical attitude was deemed a necessary characteristic of progressive architecture, which would transform both the practice itself and the consciousness of its inhabitants.

The central position of the critical attitude no doubt also contributed to the institutionalization of architecture theory in the wake of the 1960s. The role of theory in architecture has changed over the last 50 years. Where it was once closely related to practice, it slowly disengaged itself to perform critical analyses of the various factors that comprised the formative conditions of architecture, including societal conditions, power relations and the influence of economics. In the 1960s this type of analysis was oriented towards a better future, but this idealism was slowly replaced by an increasingly autonomous theory of architecture that revealed the shortcomings of its predecessors. While the nihilistic analyses of the 1970s and '80s revealed the failure of the 1960s in the most painful light; and while they also contributed to a highly conscious mode of architectural practice (such as an awareness of underlying presumptions on gender), they also left a gaping hole where the orientation towards a better future once had been. The pure analysis (to the point of destruction) of underlying societal meanings in architecture neglects the importance of aesthetics and of architectural meaning.

In recent years, many publications have testified to the need to once again reconsider a positive, active role for theory. In 2005, Manuel Gausa put forward the idea of 'operative optimism' as one of the directions architecture could take, incorporating both an ideal and a pragmatic approach to realizing small projects as testimonies to better forms of building.[13] Similarly, positive approaches to a new role for theory resonate throughout various sources of the architecture debate, from architects' writings to philosophical and cultural studies texts. Bruno Latour's rigorously critical position on critique turns to the notion of 'matters of concern' as a new direction, which he defines as all those matters that are more than 'mere' facts. The central article in the debate on architecture as a 'projective' practice by Robert Somol and Sarah Whiting suggests that it is precisely in offering alternatives that architects can do more than merely deconstruct the world. They note that the main problem with the critical architectural project is that architecture is 'inevitably and centrally occupied by its status as representation and its simultaneous commentary on that condition'.[14] They propose an alternative, 'projective' architecture that includes its critical gestures within the expertise of the architect, which extends not only to the qualities of the object, but also to its sensibility, 'such as effect, ambiance and atmosphere'. In an overview of some of these rising voices beginning to question the validity of critique, George Baird explicitly addresses the current position of 'criticality' in relation to the field of architecture, suggesting also that this is the moment that a renegotiation of the position of theory within architecture is inevitable.[15] He even relates this to a distinction between the European and American practices of theory and architecture. He notes that criticality in its traditional form is under attack, and that critics such as Michael Speaks, Robert Somol and Sarah Whiting are all trying to formulate something other than the (by now traditional) resistance against conditions of commodity and spectacle. This would lead to the formulation of a new programme for architecture practice (called 'projective' by Whiting and Somol) that leaves behind the Marxist or leftist notion of criticality.

Part of the problem with critique as such is that we have not yet entirely adjusted to new forms of information and knowledge, and critique appeals to a more structured and hierarchical organization of knowledge.[16] The sociologist Scott Lash points out that in contemporary society, part of the problem is that the 'speed and ephemerality of information leaves almost no time for reflection'.[17] It is clear that this is considered one of the problems we are facing now: the impossibility to reconsider or reflect on anything due to the sheer speed of contemporary developments. Perhaps it is time to reconsider the relationship between critique and reflection. Maybe it is less about slow, careful 'disinterested' reflection on a single object or concept, and more about a slippery form of reflection based on pattern recognition and comparison, on discovering and examining what I call resonances in order to reflect on a more strategic (as opposed to essential) level. We might call this 'cumulative reflection', since it is based on an accumulation of objects or concepts. It requires patterns and series rather than single objects. This resonates closely with the writing of Michael Speaks on 'design intelligence' where he suggests that the twenty-first century needs to address the generation of knowledge under a new paradigm. His turn to 'intelligence' is based partly on prototypes – the accumulation of many different solutions to a particular problem, depending on shifting parameters – and partly on the notion that the information society requires a different (non-hierarchical) structuring of knowledge.[18] In relation to architecture, Sarah Whiting calls this a 'slipping in and out' of critical modes of thinking, while I have used the phrase 'embedded critique' to describe this as a general strategy.[19] Whatever the label may be, it undermines the notion of a fixed essence, but still demands definition and specificity. Related to this is Lash's observation that information 'makes no claims to universality but is contained in the immediacy of the particular'.[20] This also recalls one of the aspects of the failure of 1960s' utopias: by extending individual revolution to a universal condition, the specificity of the particular was lost.[21]

Most important in the renegotiation of critique is perhaps a subtle comment by Sarah Whiting that indicates just how crucial the intermingling of practice and theory has become in the contemporary debate. To her, utilizing architectural expertise is crucial:

> Architects must engage, lead, catalyze – *act*, rather than *react*. Our expertise lies in defining forms, spaces, and materialities; we should not be afraid of the results and subjectivities (read: *biases*) that such definition implies. Unlike other disciplines in the liberal arts, architecture's relationship to critical theory is not entirely concentric. Rather than bemoan this fact or conclude that theory has no bearing on architecture – two options that guarantee architecture's intellectual suicide – architects interested in the progressive project have no choice but to take advantage of our ability to slip in and out of critical theory's rule.[22]

The call to action is unmistakable here, and tends perhaps even to the modernist and 1960s' manifestoes; yet the idealism is tempered by Whiting's awareness of the limitations of the field. There are biases inherent in the forms and materialities of architecture – she simultaneously acknowledges this and reminds us that that need not lead to impotence. Her emphasis of architectural expertise reins theory back into a relationship with the actual production of architecture, and her willingness to accept that something must be *defined* or made specific to have an impact allows a more active engagement with the world than a permanent position of resistance. Resistance itself implies negation (and is often conflated with negation). In the 1960s this may have been utilized towards something, but once it becomes dogma, resistance as a goal is nothing. It does not serve a purpose other than to counter any existing structure, regardless of its flaws and merits.

These suggestions and many others like them share a belief in looking forward without the modernist tabula rasa, and in critique without the permanently antithetical stance of deconstruction. Each of these propositions is difficult for its shades of meaning, and dangerous for its potential to become the next dogma. The need for words of description is inevitable, but the labels again risk becoming the next big hype. Therefore, when I suggest such notions as realism, pragmatism, embedded critique, I hope their meaning and intent remain the primary focus rather than the words as a simple catch-phrase. A few publications have suggested that 'pragmatic idealism' is most appropriate to our time: it acknowledges reality while maintaining a vision of how it may be improved. Although the idea has begun to also mean a simple, non-committal form of idealism, it still captures something essential in its contradiction. This seeming contradiction can also be extended to presenting history with a more vital role: by understanding history as an essential part of our present, as part of the very fabric of our society, it may become more than either a selection of (meaningless) historical forms, or an inescapable weight determining our actions.

What is also apparent in almost all of these discussions is the difficulty of positioning critique within the society of the spectacle. Conditions of consumer culture and the omnipresence of the media return in each analysis, and the relevance of critique in this relatively new conglomeration of market forces and public relations is not in question, but the intent of traditional critique is: the radical revolution of overthrowing an entire system seems untenable, yet a critical eye remains paramount. It is within these conditions that an assessment of the 1960s' forms of critique seems to the point (if not downright necessary). In following the Frankfurter Schule and Marxism's ideas on critical theory, 'critical' has become identified with resistance and negation, while what I am suggesting here is less about resistance and more about critique from within. If public space has become too entangled with corporate interests, it is more useful to design a public space that transcends these interests than it is to not design anything at all, or than it might be to merely point out that something is complicit. Architecture, when built, is by its very nature entangled with commercial interests, or the interests of the client (which are not always the interests of the general public). After all, what good is a building to a client that 'critically' discourages people from even entering? However, architecture must have something more to offer than mere compliance if it is to remain valuable, be it a 'comfortable' environment or a 'critical' one.

There is still a role for theory as a coherent structure of ideas, as reflection on architecture and the conditions that form it.[23] Yet theory today has become conflated with a degraded sense of 'critique'. At its best and most productive, critique unravels presuppositions and helps us become aware of alternate possibilities. When engaged in as a reflex, however, critique becomes little more than a conspiracy theory that prevents us from seeing the thing itself, allowing us only to examine our presuppositions.

These topics still hold an important place in the contemporary debate. Still especially relevant are the tension between the individual and the collective and the role of a distinction between appearance and essence in the media era. It is the sheer radicality of the discourse throughout the 1960s that troubles me, whether it is radical resistance or radical affirmation (in relation to modernism or consumer culture, for example).[24] This has led me to propose a few terms for reconsidering architecture discourse (as practice and theory both) – realism, pragmatism and contamination.[25] Each of these terms is already loaded, yet they are the most appropriate to the model I am proposing here. The crux of this is the theory/praxis conjunction and the shortcomings of a radical position in its clarity and purity. The role of the critical underlies many of these concerns.

We could also question whether part of the so-called impasse or crisis of contemporary architecture lies not so much in architecture but more in two things: the simplistic rendering of the power of words and images and their relationship, and the professionalization of the discourse in the twentieth century. Especially the latter has presented some problems in the relationship with imagery, since each image was taken to signify an infinite expanse of problematic assumptions, most sociopolitical. Yet the significance of aesthetics and the image itself was demoted to a lowly spot in the hierarchy of meaning. This allowed an extensive analysis of meaning without ever needing to enter the difficult arena of the power of imagery, unless that image was somehow dominant in a dangerous fashion. Yet the poetry inherent in the aesthetic experience was set aside in favour of the social construction of meaning. The complexity of the relationship has increased – images are now not only settled within a specific cultural context, but also in a global setting. Yet the common complaint is that the richness of an earlier aesthetics has disappeared. This could indicate that contemporary imagery is lacking in imagination or aesthetics, or it could indicate that the vocabulary we have is not (yet) prepared to address it.

Along the same lines of traditional critique, the city itself can be deemed in crisis. However, the vocabulary used to address the city is often still defined by the distinctions between the rural (collective) and the metropolitan (individual). Instead, by examining the manifestations of an urban form of *Gemeinschaft*, a new set of definitions could be found to address the place of the individual within a collective without destroying his or her individuality. This redefinition of community might also involve the visual symbolism of contemporary everyday life as support for social conventions. We might even see in this a return to the communicative nature of visual understanding of the (pre-)nineteenth century. This turn towards images as communicable (as opposed to consumable) could then fulfil a counter-function to the total loss of public space. Above all, the mutual interaction between an individual and the collective should remain at the forefront of any discussions. Here again, the importance of a level of realism becomes clear: each individual has a right to self-realization through individuation, but contrary to what was claimed in the 1960s' manifestoes, each individual also has a responsibility within the collective which is not necessarily served by individual emancipation.

Technology too may find new forms of criticism from within. Although the quintessential expression of modernity has been through technological metaphors of speed and the machinic, the reassessment of technology as a metaphor in the 1960s has also opened up a different view. Yet a pure negation based on an apocalyptic view also denies the very real progress that has been offered through technologies. The introduction of the Internet in China, despite attempts by the government to regulate and police it, has helped the exchange of information.

What is striking about the various articles proposing new forms of knowledge or new interpretations of contemporary architecture is that they all to some extent incorporate a sense of making – whether it is in the references to 'acting' instead of 'reacting' or the importance of prescriptive theories, whether it is reflected in the drawings or in the building process – which seems fundamental to escaping the circles of critique. Making offers a step outside the mechanisms of critique, or of picking apart reality, because it positions something new. Yet the embedded knowledge that comes from informed making allows the critical eye to work with alternative possibilities. The debate on the projective finds concrete proposals in relation to the specific themes we have encountered throughout. The work of Zaera-Polo, for instance, again questions the role of the image.[26] By putting aside his own preconceptions about representation and authenticity – not unlike Venturi – he finds a new place for simple everyday images that communicate with a larger public. He attempts to explore a multiple role of imagery that incorporates both high and low cultures, and that ranges from formal association as communicative gesture, to design technique, helping to generate a design.

Michael Speaks offers a suggestion towards 'design intelligence' that places the creation of many prototypes at the centre of a new form of knowledge generation. These articles contain specific ideas that prefigure the work of Richard Sennett on the 'craftsman' (which he uses in the broadest sense, to include Linux programmers as well as medieval goldsmiths).[27]

Fabricating a Fresh Start

Sennett, not at all engaged with this issue of critique as such, launches a headlong attack on the Marxist principles that operate on the basis of critique in his book *The Craftsman.* Arguing that the quality of an object or a performance is more or less accessible to any layperson, he posits that 'the craftsman' contributes more fundamentally to culture than is traditionally acknowledged. Since the rise of the artist in opposition to the craftsman, intellectual endeavour has taken precedence over material reality, even though it is the physical engagement with a craft that can develop a work of art further, that can increase the quality. Not all is settled merely by talent, but also by experience and practice.[28] Both Latour and Sennett point to the shortcomings of a model that is a purely intellectual construct, and that neglects the tangible wealth of information that can come either from a sensitized experience of reality (Latour) or the physical trajectory of making (Sennett).

Sennett suggests that precisely in the work of the 'craftsman' we can find that the work of the hands as well as of the intellect combine to allow a sense of reflection and making inform one another.[29] He explores a broad scope of activities that require physical mastery of technique and not solely intellectual reflection, from traditional goldsmiths and sculptors to lab technicians and computer programmers. In the second part of the book he focuses more precisely on what this 'mastery of the hand' means when it reaches a level that it becomes a subconscious activity, incorporated in reflective explorations. Through the three fields of music, cooking and glassblowing, he specifies his argument on craft as an activity that goes beyond mere replication of traditional (artistic and cultural) standards. These activities stand as examples of crafts, or perhaps disciplines, that cannot abide by talent and thinking alone: they all require doing. And not only do they all require doing, but they also require reflection on the results, as well as a critical ear, palate or eye. This list of disciplines that combine reflection and making could easily be extended, and indeed architecture returns throughout the book in examples of the mutual influence of thinking and making.

What makes this particularly interesting is that it might help us redirect the 'critical/projective' debate. We are now no longer speaking of intellectual models but of concrete problems, which bridge the divide between sociopolitical conditions and the work of design and execution. In Sennett's argument, quality does become a determining factor, which is not only recognizable by a small group of people specially trained, but rather extends outward to the general public.[30] Simply put: any layperson can to some degree distinguish between a beginning piano player and a talented, advanced one. The further the musical education, the more specifically the distinction can be made: why someone is better, on the basis of which techniques and qualities, or how improvements might be made. Yet the baseline is more or less in agreement. This is in direct contradiction to the debates of recent years that suggest that discrimination is solely based on social preconceptions or acquired tastes, or that the uneducated viewer is in fact better equipped than the educated one. In Latour's diagram, quality is nothing more than an expression of invisible societal mechanisms.

What is interesting here is that Sennett's argument offers us a direction for the contemporary debate in architecture, by no longer sealing tight the inevitable opposition between social impact and architectural quality. Critique has not disappeared in favour of a pure formalism, but is rather embedded within the very object of architecture. This requires not less, but more architectural definition.

Whiting was early to note the importance of the material reality of architecture: 'Our expertise lies in defining forms, spaces, and materialities; we should not be afraid of the results and subjectivities (read: *biases*) that such definition implies.'[31]

The point is to transcend the unsolvable oppositions that have informed too many critics, and to escape the fenced-in discourse of academic architecture. The legibility of the building need not conform only to populist notions, but rather should transcend the temporary quality of the discourse. Its spaces must be well-organized and not reduced to a mere model of the programmatic demands. Manuel Gausa hints at it in his idea of operative optimism, which requires the proposition of new designs and new buildings in order to engage with society.[32] *Arch+* spoke of the production of 'presence', relating the notion of the projective to Sloterdijk's 'spheres' as a fundamental (and essentially shared) form of experience based in the realm of sensibility and aesthetics.[33] Whether framed in terms of a 'pragmatic idealism' or a focus on 'affective' qualities in architecture, critics and theorists are still struggling to find a vocabulary to suit the architectural production that appears to cross over the boundaries of either political engagement or aesthetic perfection, mainly because they seem unable to escape the critical framework they have confined themselves to. The implicit or tacit knowledge incorporated in the craftsman through many years of practice and reflection that appeals to what 'works' can help here. The craft is, after all, not defined merely by its means – by the experience embodied in practicing techniques – but above all is also determined by its ends. The notion of what 'works' implies the question: works towards what?[34] These questions are increasingly important, for in the meantime, architects continue to build, exploring their ideas within the material forms of their discipline. Some have simply given up on the kind of 'theory' that redirects all discussion of the building to the networks of power that underlie it. Some continue to cloak themselves in provocative statements that direct attention away from the architectural aspects of the design.

New Directions: From 'Critical Agency' to Expertise

How can we possibly turn this position towards a more productive discussion? First, it seems worthwhile to turn to the fundamental agreements within the discourse. By and large, architects seem to agree that they cannot solve societal problems with their buildings (a better home will not relieve the misery of unemployment or poverty). At the same time, most would also seem to agree that entirely ignoring the societal preconditions or the demands for which they build is also fruitless (designing an expansive villa when asked for low-cost social housing would seem to miss the point). Nevertheless, the relation between societal intervention and architectural form is infinitely more complicated than the spatial determinism of either the modernists or the architects of the 1960s would have imagined.

Perhaps first we need to acknowledge the responsibility architecture has. Instead of the notions of autonomy so present in the work of Peter Eisenman (one of the primary targets of the 'projective' debate), which allow him to remain fully enclosed in a self-referential design, Manfredo Tafuri suggests that architecture is by its very nature complicit. What Tafuri does not do is suggest that architecture should therefore abrogate its position within society. Its complicity can become a tool to perform small gestures, to perhaps even offer solace in the urban fabric that is so imbued with tensions. Architecture cannot be seen outside of its societal role, yet we do need to acknowledge the limits of architecture: the 1960s' utopian projects placed so much emphasis on the transformative power of architecture that they almost inevitably led to the cynicism of current theorists. Acknowledging the limits of architecture's agency does not, however, imply the complete denial of its relation to the social and cultural fabric. Precisely by redirecting our attention to the expertise embodied within the discipline, we may create space for a new form of agency to arise, one in which architects may read the newspaper and engage with their sociocultural framework, but do so first and foremost as architects, not as sociologists, economists, or philosophers.

In the end, although it is crucial to remain aware of both the societal preconditions and the field within which architecture works, its way forward may be precisely in what was left behind in the 1960s. As the identification of the gaps in modernism resulted in a rethinking of the role of architecture, now the gaps in the 1960s' critiques may help us reconsider what architecture can contribute today. This is to be found within the discipline itself, in the extended history that encompasses both the critical position of the architect in the 1960s, including the qualities that sustained experience and practice encompass. Learning from the complexity of the building process is a different skill with which to see, study and position current questions in a larger (historical) framework. Theory and practice need one another. The theorist is nowhere without the inventions of a practicing architect, responding to the demands of client and material, urban regulations and building tradition. The practitioner needs the support of the theorist/critic who can take a step back and identify issues that resonate throughout the building world, transcending the specific problems of one building in one place with one client.

A brief glance at the magazine *A10*, with its broad base of local reporters, shows the richness of various formal vocabularies, a diversity of approaches, sensitivity to context and an often undogmatic approach to large societal issues, incorporating critique within the very presence of architecture. Precisely this diversity and light-hearted yet serious production belies the heavy-handed radical nature of established architecture. This is the kind of work Gausa is referring to when he writes of an 'open logic' or an 'operative optimism'. These are the heirs to the postmodern, who are working hard to make their environment better in a sometimes humble, sometimes playful manner, at times with the utmost restraint. This group of architects is also the direct heir to the 'pop' generation in the sense that they are not afraid to combine traditional architecture with experiments in new materials, or even references to various other forms of production.

It is theory, in this case, that lags behind. It is the task of theory and criticism to be open to these diverse developments, to look carefully at this work without the preconceived notions that were built on political conviction, but rather to take a deep breath and dive into the specificity of the work, to take culture into account while understand that most of this work is simultaneously embedded in a global sensibility. It is the task of research to carefully work through the societal problems at hand and aid in addressing them through the craft of those in the profession. This demands a combination of sustained attention for the craft of architecture with a longer horizon of attention for pressing research questions.[35] Architects operating professionally remain dependent on the presence of clients ('enlightened' or otherwise) to realize their work. Academics have (for as long as it lasts) the freedom to explore questions of import without immediately addressing applicability. The relation between theory and practice should become less one of ideological legitimization and more one of mutual exchange. The field of architecture is in need of a change, particularly in how the academic and professional world relate. As long as the ties between the two remain severed, architecture may have some difficulty progressing beyond territorial discussions on stylistic and political differences. Given that there is a component of design craft to the field (and that some architects are better at it than others), and that there are pressing issues to address of spatial planning, architectural design, cultural meaning, sustainable development and countless other issues that only find a partial way into the general discourse, this seems a grand task to work on for the coming years. And it demands something of the critic: to treat the object with care, and to look carefully again.

Although only beginning to break loose from the format, there are a few points one can easily put forward towards a new consideration for architecture. First (perhaps even foremost) is the question of specificity. The discourse of modernism set a goal of attaining universal forms, based on the notion that some things (geometry for example) are universal to all cultures and therefore beyond reprimand. This was simultaneously questioned and reinforced in the 1960s: the introduction of small-scale, realistic, more accurate representations of everyday reality 'as it is' and not as it 'ought to be' helped undermine the universalist visions of late-modern architects, yet the radical appeal to a 'system' of change and flexibility also reinforced the notion that one idea could suit all. The principles of critique became new universal statements. The radical transformation gave us the handhold to understand current architecture but applied it so universally that it defeated its own purpose.

In the end, the divide between practice and theory is perhaps best bridged by Sennett's craftsman – one who has spent so many hours making that his intellectual process has become informed by the knowledge embodied in his hands. This adds a dimension to the idea of 'matters of concern'. For how can we concern ourselves with things until we engage ourselves with them, and how can we engage with them until we spend time studying them, making them, reconstructing them, exploring them? This making must involve all of our senses, not just the intellect. Sennett's craftsman has something tangible to offer the world: beauty (as consolation for the imperfections of our everyday reality) and a hard-earned level of expertise that comes from practice, and the continual learning from mistakes. This learning process requires careful and critical assessment of performance, as well as keeping some form of ideal in mind. The end result is an embodied knowledge that allows us to engage with increasingly difficult and sophisticated questions once the basic skills are mastered.

Within the disciplines founded on craft, be it cooking, technology, music, architecture or any of the other creative fields that employ the work of the hands as well as the intellect, the craftsman can discover new ideas through the collision between his own expertise and the problems that arise from new conditions (new materials that are introduced, new desires of an audience, a rediscovery of old desires that have been latent). This craftsman, by *incorporating* external conditions *within* his own expertise and transforming them into a solidified manifestation of a moment (either as temporary as a theatrical performance, or as permanent as a building), transcends the merely individual and gives voice to a sense of communal value. If architecture has an agency it can appeal to, a sphere of influence that extends beyond the mere fulfilment of spatial requirements, it will not be found in the framework of 'post-critical' architecture, and perhaps not even in 'projective' architecture as long as that remains primarily defined within an intellectual debate. It will be found in the embedding of speculations on fundamental societal questions (sustainability, allowing space for a community to feel 'at home', grounding the spatial experience of those who are overwhelmed by the speed of contemporary society) in the material forms of architecture that allow a multiple reading independent of societal hierarchies and preconceptions. This is the expertise that we may expect from the architect: having incorporated the basic functions of design and spatial composition, to address himself or herself to the task of creating buildings with an embodied sense of what works in the broadest sense: a space that appeals to the cultural imagination as much as the everyday constraints it is created within.

Notes

Introduction
Revisiting the 1960s

1. In the survey books *Architecture Culture: 1943-1968*, edited by Joan Ockman (New York: Rizzoli, 1993) and *Architecture Theory since 1968*, edited by K. Michael Hays (Cambridge, MA: MIT Press, 1998) there is a striking increase in the numbers of philosophers and contributors from other fields than architecture (such as Barthes, Virilio, Derrida and many others). While the early years described are founded primarily on the manifestoes and writings of architects, towards the end of both surveys the contributions from others comprise roughly a quarter of the total. This indicates a gravitation towards more theoretical issues that became prominent, particularly from the 1970s onward.
2. Arthur Marwick postulates an 'extended sixties' from 1958 to 1973-1974. The years I have chosen as boundaries are more directly aligned with the developments in architecture, but I support his argument that developments in the 1950s came to a 'critical point of change' towards the end of the decade, and that the sense of transformation continued into the early 1970s. Arthur Marwick, *The Sixties: Cultural Revolution in Britain, France, Italy, and the United States, c.1958-c.1974* (Oxford: Oxford University Press, 1998), 7.
3. An important exhibition was 'Les Années Pop', held in the Centre Georges Pompidou in Paris in 2001. A little later, the Tate followed suit with 'Art & The 60s: This was tomorrow' (London, 2004).
4. The word *krities* is a phonetic spelling of the traditional Dutch *kritisch*, which means 'critical' in English. Phonetic spelling was initiated in the late 1960s/early 1970s, under the rationale that its phonetic foundation was more accessible and therefore more democratic.

Chapter I
Architecture and the Legacy of the 1960s: Crisis or Opportunity?

1. 'Situativer Urbanismus: Zu einer beiläufigen form des Socialen', *Arch+* 183 (May 2007). Wilfried Houjebek wandered through various cities throughout 2003, including Toronto, London and Dordrecht. On Dordrecht, see: http://www.archined.nl/archined/3512.0.html (11 September 2003).
2. David Robbins, *The Independent Group: Postwar Britain and the Aesthetics of Plenty* (Cambridge, MA: MIT Press, 1990).
3. Sylvère Lotringer, 'The Great Refusal', *Artforum* (May 2008), 302-305. The students 'managed to rouse an entire nation. They stole France, took it for a joyride, and then, just as suddenly, dropped it in a back alley with no more than a few scratches.'
4. Arthur Danto, 'Before the Revolution', *Artforum* (May 2008), 95-100.
5. The notion of some form of crisis in architectural thinking at the end of the twentieth century is visible in many conferences and publications. See for example *Hunch*, Berlage Institute Report 6/7 (summer 2003), which very pointedly asks what architecture can do, and the final

'Any' conference in 2000. Many of the publications also view this form of current stocktaking as an opportunity, as for example a 2003 conference and the resulting book edited by Bernard Tschumi and Irene Cheng, *The State of Architecture at the Beginning of the 21st Century* (New York: The Monacelli Press, 2003), 7-8.

6. 'Rethinking Representation', *Hunch*, Berlage Institute Report 11 (2007), 10-11. To Zaera-Polo, this is then directly correlated with a step *towards* idealism, *away* from realism, and of an ideological position explored through representation. In his sweeping opening statement, he gathers together many issues that, although relevant, need to be dissected carefully if we are to gain any insights from our recent history: the iconic, Utopia, techno-fetishism, resistance, politics and representation, and globalization, to name but a few.
7. Tim Griffin, 'Lessons of '68', *Artforum* (May 2008), 71. Although the mythological character of 1968 is noted, in this issue May 1968 is addressed specifically in relation to contemporary questions 'to discern their lingering, albeit altered, inscription within circumstances now'.
8. As I was finishing this manuscript, a previously unthinkable thing happened: in the wake of the financial crisis of 2008, Americans began to question the limits of individual responsibility and ask what might be seen as communal. There is a potential turnaround in the interest for universal healthcare. Simon Schama noted this turn to the government in his preparations for the book *American History*. Paul Steenhuis, 'De Amerikaanse droom van Schama', *NRC Handelsblad*, 1 November 2008, *Magazine M*, 12-16.
9. Rixt Hoekstra, 'Van tijdgeest tot kwelgeest', *de Architect* 2 (2007), 16-19. Reviewing a conference on Tafuri, Hoekstra clearly delineates the problem with this kind of oppositional thinking that hopes to categorize different kinds of architectural practice in a simple scheme. The problem of 'critique' and the relationship between theory and practice were addressed in the conference, but to Hoekstra nothing was offered beyond a call to arms through the nostalgic device of Tafurian critique. His own work offered a more subtle understanding of architecture, particularly through the juxtapositions of opposing views he analysed in the work of Piranesi.
10. This of course presumes that we would actually want an ideal world and would not find it too stifling in its perfection. We should consider that perhaps we are more suited to maintaining ideals in the face of an imperfect reality, and that our inadequacies make us human. This idea has often been proposed in various forms in science fiction, with a recent example in the film *The Matrix*, where Agent Smith explains that the machines designed a perfect world, but that left people unhappy. In architecture, the early work of Koolhaas explores the underbelly of architecture in part as a response to the rigorously cheerful idealism of his tutors at the Architectural Association in London. See also my essay 'Dreaming the World That Might Still Become', *BEYOND* 1, *Scenarios and Speculations* (2009), 12-17.
11. David Harvey, *The Condition of Postmodernity* (Cambridge, MA: Blackwell, 1990); Jean-François Lyotard, *La Condition Postmoderne: Rapport sur le savoir* (Paris: Minuit, 1979).
12. Jan Willem Duyvendak and Menno Hurenkamp (eds.), *Kiezen voor de kudde: Lichte gemeenschappen en de nieuwe meerderheid* (Amsterdam: Van Gennep, 2004); Menno Hurenkamp and Jan Willem Duyvendak, 'De zware plicht van de lichte gemeenschap', *Krisis* 1 (2008), 1-14.
13. With the events of 2008 rapidly reconfiguring our faith in the endlessness of increasing affluence, it is unclear where the balance will precisely fall between market capitalism and government regulation, but it is clear that a profound shift is taking place along the spectrum of affluence and welfare. Some motions within the consumer society did prefigure the issues confronting us, with an increasing interest in carbon footprints and sustainability.
14. For example, although the Situationist International was only marginally influential beyond its own circle at the height of its activity, it has since been rediscovered and revitalized. First in 1989 with the exhibition 'On the Passage of a Few People through a Rather Brief Moment in Time' in Boston, curated by Elizabeth Sussman; and in the past decade, there has been an enormous amount of situationist writing posted on the Internet, as a logical questioning of the spectacular conditions of the late twentieth century.

15. David Harvey, 'Looking Backwards on Postmodernism', in: *Post-Modernism on Trial, A.D. Profile no. 88* (London: Academy Editions, 1990), 10-12.
16. In this book it is treated as a single transatlantic debate since the exchange of ideas was continuous throughout the twentieth century, ranging from Gropius, Breuer and Mies van der Rohe to Archigram, Venturi and Scott Brown, and Lawrence Alloway. Although there were other voices such as the Metabolists in Japan, the main bulk of the debates was transatlantic.
17. K. Michael Hays (ed.), *Architecture Theory since 1968* (Cambridge, MA: MIT Press, 1998), xiv (introduction).
18. Sarah Whiting and Robert Somol, 'Notes around the Doppler effect and other Moods of Modernism', *Perspecta* 33 (2002), 72-77.
19. Bruno Latour, 'Why Has Critique Run out of Steam? From Matters of Fact to Matters of Concern', *Critical Inquiry* 30 (winter 2004), 225-248.
20. Ibid., 229-230.
21. Ibid., 229.
22. An escape from both media complicity and pure deconstruction is suggested by Jean-François Lyotard's loss of meta-narratives (*La Condition Postmoderne*). Accepting a loss of meta-narratives allows a middle ground between committing entirely to the spectacle in all its forms and resisting the consumer society wholesale, by demanding that each response is to a *specific* condition and *specific* instance.
23. These revisions of course prefigure the slightly later developments of postmodernism in architecture. In postmodernism they were often expressed in a straightforward symbolic manner, which does not preclude their relevance. In this fashion, postmodernism offered a symbolic 'community' construed through traditional forms, high-tech architecture as an expression of technological innovation, and everyday symbolism in a gesture towards mass culture.
24. The problem of uncritical populism lies in its appropriating material from low culture and simply elevating it, providing no critical examination of aesthetics or meaning. In *Media Spectacle* (London: Routledge, 2003), Douglas Kellner suggests that a careful analysis is necessary to understand the position of these images within the spectacle and their social meaning. See pages 12-15.
25. I have been using 'embedded critique' as a shorthand for critique that does not try to reveal a condition of false consciousness in the tradition of the Frankfurter Schule, but rather remains embedded within its societal structure while still reflecting critically on specific conditions within the larger context. The idea is originally indebted to the work of Douglas Rushkoff in his books *Media Virus!: Hidden Agendas in Popular Culture* (New York: Ballantine Books, 1994) and *Children of Chaos: Surviving the End of the World as We Know It* (London: Flamingo, 1997). The phrase may have become somewhat contentious since the advent of 'embedded journalism', but it is still the most accurate description. Lara Schrijver, 'The Power of Lightness: Humor as a Strategy in Architecture and the Visual Arts', in: Martin Nonhoff, Katharina Bunzmann and Johannes Angermüller (eds.), *PostModern Productions* (Hamburg: LIT Verlag, 2001), 147-159.
26. To some extent the dictatorial aspect derives principally from modernism, since it retains an Enlightenment belief in societal transformation through rationality (and by extension, rational architecture). This is different from the idea of being in harmony with the environment in Vitruvius. Moreover, how one 'should' understand space was not questioned to this extent before the analysis of spatial meaning – Gothic churches were not meant to offer multiple meanings, but simply embody and thus convey the spiritual gesture in them.
27. 'Material practices produce new concepts out of the materials and procedures of work itself, and not as a regulating code grafted onto the work from outside.' Stan Allen, *Practice: Architecture, Technique and Representation* (Amsterdam: G+B Arts International, 2000), XVIII.
28. The phrase 'cynical reason' as borrowed from Peter Sloterdijk revolves around the cynicism that ensues when the 'enlightened' rational being is entirely buffered from any impact, any

form of critique thanks to theory. In other words, the senses of both meaning and value begin to fade. This is closely related to the smug position of the critic as addressed in relation to Bruno Latour.

29. Susan Sontag, 'Against Interpretation' (1964), in: Susan Sontag, *Against Interpretation, and Other Essays* (New York: Farrar, Straus and Giroux,1966), 3-14.
30. Martijntje Smits, *Monsterbezwering: De culturele domesticatie van nieuwe technologie* (Amsterdam: Boom, 2002). The book revolves around methods of domesticating new technologies. Smits discusses the notion of purity and danger as a model in cultural anthropology, conceived by Mary Douglas. Following along these lines, Smits positions the ideas of purity and contamination as a productive set of terms in analysing our relationship to technology.
31. Robert Maxwell, 'Reyner Banham – The Man', in: *Sweet Disorder and the Carefully Careless* (New York: Princeton Architectural Press, 1993), 177-182.
32. Alloway already commented on the importance of personal experience of significance in 1958. 'The Arts and the Mass Media', *Architectural Design* (February 1958), 84-85.
33. Latour, 'Why Has Critique Run out of Steam?', op. cit (note 19), 246.

Chapter II
The City: From Modernist Battlefield to Situationist Playground

1. The similarities between transatlantic discourses (here mainly French, English and American) indicate some overarching questions on the place of the city, the position of the metropolitan individual within it, and transformations in public and civic space. At the same time, their differences may help illuminate why the modernist notion of a single universal form to suit the human environment was in the end a failure. The specific distinctions between the cultural discourses will be touched upon, but an extensive study goes beyond the scope of this book.
2. Constant and Jorn were both involved with CoBrA, a group of artists from Copenhagen, Brussels and Amsterdam (1948-1951); the Lettrist International was a group of artists and theorists based in Paris (1952-1957); the International Movement for an Imaginist Bauhaus was founded by Jorn in 1954 to address the place of artists in the machine age, among other things. Here again it becomes clear that the 1960s were not an anomaly with a full-fledged critique of modernity arising from nothing, but rather a critical mass growing from the post-war critiques. For a full genealogy of the Situationist International, see Simon Sadler, *The Situationist City* (Cambridge, MA: MIT Press, 1998), 2-12.
3. Guy Debord, 'Report on the Construction of Situations', translated by Tom McDonough in: Tom McDonough (ed.), *Guy Debord and the Situationist International: Texts and Documents* (Cambridge, MA: MIT Press, 2002), 29-50. This translation will be referred to throughout. Original document: Guy Debord, 'Rapport sur la Construction . . .' (presented at founding conference of Situationist International at Cosio d'Arroscia, July 1957). Reprint: *Internationale Situationniste*, édition augmentée (Paris: Librairie Arthème Fayard, 1997), 689-701.
4. Henri Lefebvre, *Le droit à la ville* (Paris: Éditions Anthropos, 1968).
5. Accounts of the relationship between Lefebvre and the Situationist International vary. The Situationist International accused Lefebvre of stealing situationist theses for his work on the Paris commune, while Lefebvre describes his own work as one of the inspirations for the Situationist International. The accusations of plagiarism are to be found in 'L'historien Lefebvre', *Internationale Situationniste* 10 (1966), 73-75. For Lefebvre's account of his relationship with the Situationist International as unacknowledged mentor of Guy Debord, see Kristin Ross, 'Lefebvre on the Situationists: An Interview', in: McDonough, *Guy Debord*, op. cit. (note 3), 267-283.

6. German text in: *Aufsätze und Abhandlungen*, 1901-8, Bd. 1, 116-131; English translation: 'The Metropolis and Mental Life' by Edward Shils available in: Neil Leach (ed.), *Rethinking Architecture: A Reader in Cultural Theory* (London: Routledge, 1997).
7. Here, other obvious and important references for the architecture discourse are Baudelaire's *flâneur* and Benjamin's discussion of what we can now see as the beginning of mass consumption in the department stores of Paris. The term *Gemeinschaft* derives from Ferdinand Tönnies, implying an interaction between people based on social ties, as found in rural societies. It is opposed to *Gesellschaft*, where interaction is regulated through rules rather than social bonds, as in the anonymous condition of the metropolitan society.
8. The official viewpoint of the Situationist International was that 'situationism' as such did not exist or was conceived by 'anti-situationists', since the -ism implied a doctrine (*Internationale Situationniste* 1 (1958), 13. The word is used here in a common sense, to indicate the general activities and theory of the Situationist International. The emphatic official position of the Situationist International only serves to underline the rigid nature of its principles.
9. Guy Debord. *The Society of the Spectacle*, (NY: Zone Books (MIT Press), 1995), translated by Donald Nicholson-Smith, thesis 34, 24.
10. *Internationale Situationniste* 1 (1958), 13. 'The combined use of arts and techniques as a means of contributing to the construction of a unified milieu.' Translation by Ken Knabb, available online at: http://www.bopsecrets.org/Situationist Interantional/index.htm (accessed 16 November 2004).
11. On the level of theory, Raoul Vaneigem also plays an important role in the Situationist International with his critiques on the banality of everyday life, especially in this later period. However, since his work has been less specifically referenced in the architecture discourse, it remains outside the scope of this study.
12. Debord, *Society of the Spectacle*, op. cit. (note 9), thesis 176, 124.
13. Ibid., thesis 169, 121.
14. For example, Lefebvre himself claims more influence on the events of 1968 in his interview with Kristin Ross. This is plausible when taking into consideration how many students must have attended his lectures, as opposed to the probably smaller circle of the Situationist International. See McDonough, *Guy Debord*, op. cit. (note 3), 267-283. The visibility and the influence of the Situationist International has drastically increased with the availability of situationist texts on the Internet (Bureau of Public Secrets, http://www.bopsecrets.org, http://www.not bored.org, http://www.nothingness.org, situationist international online: http://www.cddc.vt.edu/sionline/).
15. 'Théorie des moments et construction des situations' *Internationale Situationniste* 4 (1960), 10-11. In this piece, the situationists also criticize Lefebvre's idea of moments for being too abstract and general, while their situations involve a creative praxis. The 'everyday' with its implication of habits accrued over time, is more present in the French discourse, while the English and American debates center more on the 'ordinary', which tends more towards an aesthetic.
16. For example in *Internationale Situationniste* 1 (1958), the definition of psychogeography (page 13) implicitly resorts to techniques of social geography, and an image by Paul-Henry Chombart de Lauwe (urban sociologist, 1913-1998) is used to demonstrate the narrow scope of urban experience of a city inhabitant (page 28).
17. As Sadler indicates (*Situationist City*, op. cit. (note 2), 11, ff. 38) all these terms are already used in *Potlatch*. However, it is in Debord's 'Report on the Construction of Situations' at the conference in Arroscio that they begin to circumscribe a coherent theoretical position, then to become the Situationist International. The definitions are reiterated and compiled in the first issue of *Internationale Situationniste* (1958, page 13). The list includes the following definition of the *situation construite*, from which the movement derives its name: 'Moment de la vie, concrètement et délibérément construit par l'organisation collective d'une ambiance unitaire en d'un jeu d'événements.' At the founding of the Situationist International Debord also

presented this as 'the concrete constructions of temporary settings of life and their transformation into a higher, passionate nature'. Debord, 'Report on the Construction of Situations', op. cit. (note 3), 44.

18. Ibid., 45. (see also *Internationale Situationniste* 1 (1958), 13). 'Etude des effets précis du milieu géographique, consciemment aménagé ou non, agissant directement sur le comportement affectif des individus.'
19. Guy Debord. 'Theory of the Dérive', *Internationale Situationniste* 2 (1958). Translation by Ken Knabb, available online at: *http://www.bopsecrets.org/Situationist Interantional/2.derive.htm* (accessed 19 November 2004).
    In *Internationale Situationniste* 1 (1958), page 13, the *dérive* is defined as: 'Mode de comportement expérimental lié aux conditions de la société urbaine: technique du passage hâtif à travers des ambiances variées. Se dit aussi, plus particulièrement, pour désigner la durée d'un exercice continu de cette expérience.'
20. 'Détournement d'éléments esthétiques préfabriqués. Intégration de productions actuelles ou passées des arts dans une construction supérieure du milieu. Dans ce sens il ne peut y avoir de peinture ou de musique situationniste, mais un usage situtationniste de ces moyens. Dans un sens plus primitif, le détournement à l'intérieur des sphères culturelles anciennes est une méthode de propagande, qui témoigne de l'usure et de la perte d'importance de ces spheres.' 'Definitions', *Internationale Situationniste* 1 (1958), 13. Translation by Ken Knabb, available online at: http://www.bopsecrets.org/SI/1.definitions.htm (accessed 14 May 2009).
21. Debord, *Society of the Spectacle*, op. cit. (note 9), thesis 4, 12. Translated by Donald Nicholson-Smith.
22. Ironically, this idea was revived in the Hollywood spectacle of *The Matrix* (1999). One can only speculate as to how Debord would have responded to this mass-entertainment version of his ideas on the spectacle.
23. For a close examination of the full trajectory of the design for New Babylon from a contemporary perspective, see: Mark Wigley, *Constant's New Babylon: The Hyper-Architecture of Desire* (Rotterdam: 010 Publishers, 1998). For a thorough account of Constant's work on New Babylon situated within his working relationships in art and architecture, see Martin van Schaik, 'Psychogeogram of Desire', in: Martin van Schaik and Otakar Mácel (eds.), *Exit Utopia, Architectural Provocations 1956-76* (Lakewood, NJ: Prestel, 2005).
24. *Urbanisme unitaire*: 'Théorie de L'emploi d'ensemble des arts et techniques concourant à la construction intégrale d'un milieu en liaison dynamique avec des expériences de comportement.' (*Internationale Situationniste* 1 (1958), 13).
25. Constant, 'Une autre ville pour une autre vie', *Internationale Situationniste* 3 (1959), 37-40. Constant, 'Description de la zone jaune', *Internationale Situationniste* 4 (1960), 23-26. At this point the project is generally still referred to as the 'Ville Couverte', but he offers the description of the yellow zone as the first 'itinerary' in the 'Promenades à New Babylone', which will become the descriptive guide of the 'island models' that comprise the 'Ville Couverte'.
26. Debord, 'positions situationnistes sur la circulation', *Internationale Situationniste* 3 (1959). This translation from Knabb, as quoted in Sadler, *Situationist City*, op. cit. (note 2), 25.
27. Constant had already written a piece in 1953 on the importance of the situation in relation to the city. See Kristin Ross, *Lefebvre on the Situationists: An Interview*, in: McDonough, *Guy Debord*, op. cit. (note 3), 267-283.
28. Henri Lefebvre, *Writings on Cities*, translated and edited by Eleonore Kofman and Elizabeth Lebas (Oxford: Blackwell, 1996), 148.
29. This problem is most prominent in the opposition between figuration and abstraction, and the emphasis on everyday imagery in the work of Robert Venturi and Denise Scott Brown.
30. William Holford, Arthur Ling and Peter Smithson, 'Planning Today', *Architectural Design* (June 1957), 185.
31. Ibid.
32. Ibid., 186.

33. Debord, *The Society of the Spectacle*, op. cit. (note 9), thesis 173, 122-123.
34. Ibid., thesis 1, 12: 'The whole life of those societies in which modern conditions of production prevail presents itself as an immense accumulation of *spectacles*. All that once was directly lived has become mere representation.'
35. Ibid.,126-127.
36. Pascal Dumontier, *Les Situationnistes et Mai 68: Théorie et Pratique de la Révolution (1966-1972)* (Paris: Éditions Ivrea, 1995), 39. Originally published in 1990 by Éditions Gérard Lebovici, Paris. 'Se différenciant des groupes de l'extrême-gauche, l'Internationale situationniste se distingue particulièrement par la critique radicale et totale du monde moderne qu'elle formule. A travers les ouvrages de Debord et Vaneigem, mais aussi à travers les articles parus dans la revue *Internationale Situationniste*, elle s'attache surtout à critiquer les nouvelles formes de l'aliénation, offrant ainsi une théorie révolutionnaire incontestablement moderne.' This is followed by a quote on the necessity of the *totality* of revolution, from 'Enragés dans l'occupation', indicating further parallels with the universalizing aspect of modernist thought.
37. On this problem, Bruno Latour has proved particularly enlightening when he rigorously attacks the very mechanisms of neo-Marxist critique in 'Why Has Critique Run out of Steam? From Matters of Fact to Matters of Concern', *Critical Inquiry* 30 (winter 2004), 225-248.
38. Jane Jacobs, *The Death and Life of Great American Cities* (New York: Vintage Books (Random House), 1992 [1961]).
39. Ibid., 8.
40. Ibid., 342-345.
41. For example Lefebvre's 'Seen from the Window', in: Lefebvre, *Writings on Cities*, op. cit. (note 28), 219-227.
42. Jacobs, *The Death and Life of Great American Cities*, op. cit. (note 38), 438.
43. Ibid., 3.
44. By Lewis Mumford for example in 'The Sky Line: Mother Jacobs' Home Remedies', *The New Yorker*, 1 December 1962.
45. This is also what situates her within the pragmatic tradition of John Dewey and William James, as noted in a review of her work on CNN, 23 November 2000. Available online at: http://www.cnn.com/2000/books/news/11/23/jane.jacobs.ap/ (accessed 16 November 2004).
46. 'Urban Vitality and the Fallacy of Physical Determinism', originally published in 1962 in: Gans, Herbert, *People and Plans: Essays on Urban Problems and Solutions* (New York: Basic Books, 1968), 25-33.
47. This rests on a common misconception, that the model derived from analysis can be inverted to offer a prescription or a guideline for design. This simple inversion neglects the fact that a model by definition eliminates various characteristics, and thus makes a poor generator of form.
48. The diagram itself is inserted in a 'news item' on the disappearance of Ralph Rumney during a *dérive* in Venice. 'Venise a vaincu Ralph Rumney' (Venice has defeated Ralph Rumney), *Internationale Situationniste* 1 (1958), 28. An extended description and interpretation of the diagram is presented in Guy Debord, 'Théorie de la Dérive', *Internationale Situationniste* 2 (1958), 19-23.
49. Charles Jencks, 'Pop – Non pop (1)', *Architectural Association Quarterly*, vol. 1, no. 1 (1969), 59.
50. The ordinary of the English debate is distinct from the French *quotidienne* or everyday, but the two share some premises. As Paolozzi and Hamilton use ordinary images culled from magazines to undermine the hierarchy between high and low art (also undermining a particularly English class-based hierarchy), so Lefebvre suggests that everyday life is a subversion of the academic understanding of sociology. In both cases, we can see the typical democratization of the 1960s at work: an institution is undermined by introducing the subversive element of 'unworthy' objects, be they in the form of advertising images or street festivals.

51. This idea is borrowed from the 1963 Archigram exhibition 'The Living City', which again bears some resemblance to the fluid and clustered 'ambiances' present in New Babylon (albeit in a much more optimistic, less serious manner). The poster for the exhibition also explicitly uses the word 'situation' to describe the importance of inhabiting the city as opposed to its mere plan.
52. Although this idea may seem paradoxical since I retain the terms *Gemeinschaft* and *Gesellschaft*, I propose that the original connotations of *Gemeinschaft*, referring to the pastoral ideal of a community, may rightfully be applied to the late twentieth-century city with its islands of communal identities.
53. These ideas were widespread at the time. Although the Italian debate lies outside the scope of this study, in *L'architettura della citta* (1966), Aldo Rossi avails himself of psychological metaphors such as memory, and does so primarily through the communal fabric of history and convention.
54. William H. Whyte Jr, 'Are Cities Un-American?', in: Editors of *Fortune, The Exploding Metropolis: A Study of the Assault on Urbanism and How Our Cities Can Resist It* (Garden City, NY: Doubleday Anchor Books, 1957), 1.
55. On the role of imagery in the creation of utopias, see Russell Jacoby, *Picture Imperfect: Utopian Thought in an Anti-Utopian Age* (New York: Columbia University Press, 2005).
56. For an extensive history of Team 10, see: Max Risselada and Dirk van den Heuvel (eds.), *Team 10, 1953-81: In Search of a Utopia of the Present* (Rotterdam: NAi Publishers, 2005).
57. Lawrence Alloway, 'The Arts and the Mass Media', *Architectural Design* (February 1958), 84-85.
58. Guy Debord, *Mémoires* (Paris: Editions Allia, 2004), title page (originally published in Copenhagen in 1958).
59. The intervention remained incomplete, among other reasons because their installation was deemed dangerous by the fire department, and the Situationist International decided to call off the exhibition. 'Die Welt als labyrinth', *Internationale Situationniste* 4 (1960), 6-7. Jeroen Boomgaard notes that its failure appears to have been intentional. 'Het podium van de betrokkenheid', *reflect* 1, *Nieuw engagement in architectuur, kunst en vormgeving* (2003), 98-108.
60. See also Tom McDonough, 'Situationist Space', in: McDonough, *Guy Debord*, op. cit. (note 3), 241-266.
61. See also Libero Andreotti, 'Architecture and Play', in: ibid., 213-240.
62. Constant, 'A Different City for a Different Life', in: ibid., 95-101. Originally published as: 'Une autre ville pour une autre vie', *Internationale Situationniste* 3 (1959), 37-40.
63. Ibid.
64. Jacobs, *The Death and Life of Great American Cities*, op. cit. (note 38), chapters 2 through 4, 29-88.
65. Jacobs offers an urban version of *Gemeinschaft* here, where 'natural' social relations become reintroduced within the smaller urban entity of a neighborhood.
66. In an extensive article on the Robin Hood Gardens housing project, Peter Eisenman defines one of the primary issues driving the Smithsons as a 'concern for a new dwelling-street relationship' as a reaction to the introduction of the motor car. In a succinct formulation, Eisenman argues that this concern becomes manifest in two principal ways: a pedestrian deck and a pedestrian precinct. Peter Eisenman, 'Robin Hood Gardens London E14', *Architectural Design* 9 (September 1972), 557-558, 588-592.
67. Constant, 'A Different City for a Different Life', op. cit. (note 62).
68. Henk Engel specifically notes a transition between their projects for Golden Lane (1951-1952) and Robin Hood Gardens (1966-1972), from treating streets and buildings as separate entities, as Le Corbusier did, to connecting both systems. Henk Engel, 'The Collective in Housing', *OASE* 51, *A Smithsons Celebration* (1999), 34-45.
69. The idea of the 'cluster' is central to their departure from the early CIAM principles, and plays a central role in creating community. Annie Pedret, 'CIAM X: Scales of Association', in: Risselada and Van den Heuvel, *Team 10*, op. cit. (note 56), 52-53.

70. According to Roberto Ohrt, Hauptstadt Berlin was a likely reference for Constant's design for New Babylon, which also allows the different spheres to mingle and become more diffuse. As noted in Libero Andreotti, 'Architecture and Play', in: McDonough, *Guy Debord*, op. cit. (note 3), 213-240.
71. From Baudelaire's *flâneur* in relation to the crowd, to Simmel's metropolitan individual, to the Marxist city analysis of the Situationist International and many more, all these discussions relate to the structure of society as manifest in the city. These stand in contrast to the half acre allotted to each inhabitant of Frank Lloyd Wright's Broadacre City, where the social fabric is reduced to a minimum.
72. Robert Venturi, Steven Izenour and Denise Scott Brown, 'The Home', in: Venturi Scott Brown and Associates, *On Houses and Housing*, Architectural Monographs no. 21 (London: Academy Editions, 1992), 58-65.
73. Anthony Vidler, *The Architectural Uncanny* (Cambridge, MA: MIT Press, 1992), 213.
74. In the end, the three volumes of the *Critique de la vie quotidienne* spanned over 30 years. Henri Lefebvre, *Critique de la vie quotidienne.* Volume 1, *Introduction* (Paris : L'Arche, 1947), volume 2, *Fondements d'une sociologie de la quotidiennité* (Paris: L'Arche, 1961) and volume 3, *De la modernité au modernisme, Pour une métaphilosophie du quotidien* (Paris: L'Arche, 1981).
75. The continuing influence of 1960s' modes of critique is also visible in conferences such as 'Tactics of Resistance' held at the University of Western Ontario in 2007, which explored the contemporary potential of resistance to late capitalism. Conference information and programme available online at: http://www.uwo.ca/theory/Events/Resistance/Home.html (accessed May 14, 2009)
76. Holford, Ling and Smithson, 'Planning Today', op. cit. (note 30), 185-189.
77. For a simplified but illustrative discussion of the speed and extent of urbanization at the time, see Kingsley Davis, 'The Urbanization of the Human Population', in: *Cities: A 'Scientific American' Book* (Middlesex: Penguin Books, 1967). Originally published by Alfred A. Knopf in 1965, 11-32. For example, according to an index of urbanization based on how many people as a proportion of the general population live in cities with more than 100,000 inhabitants, he notes, on page 12, that 'the rate of change [in the USA] from 1950 to 1960 was twice that of the preceding 50 years'.
78. Lawrence Alloway, 'City Notes', *Architectural Design* (January 1959), 34-35.
79. Holford, Ling and Smithson, 'Planning Today', op. cit. (note 30), 186.
80. Ibid.
81. Ibid.
82. Herbert Gans, *Popular Culture & High Culture: An Analysis and Evaluation of Taste*, revised and updated edition (New York: Basic Books, 1999 [1974]), 65-66.
83. Holford, Ling and Smithson, 'Planning Today', op. cit. (note 30), 186.
84. The story goes that Aldo van Eyck even designed the space in which young boys would illicitly smoke their first cigarette. In an interview, Peter Smithson comments on this extreme determinism: 'There was little room left for the children to occupy it somehow so that it became theirs.' (page 132) 'When Aldo built the Orphanage it was highly specified to the children; but the children didn't make the program, *he* made the program.' (p. 136). 'Mart Stam's Trousers: A conversation between Peter Smithson & Wouter Vanstiphout', Crimson: Wouter Vanstiphout and Cassandra Wilkins, Michael Speaks, Gerard Hadders (eds.), *Mart Stam's Trousers: Stories from behind the Scenes of Dutch Moral Modernism* (Rotterdam: 010 publishers, 1999), 120-138.
85. See for a discussion of the morals of architecture: David Watkin, *Morality and Architecture: The Development of a Theme in Architectural History and Theory from the Gothic Revival to the Modern Movement* (Oxford: Clarendon Press, 1977).
86. Vittorio Magnago Lampugnani, 'The City of Tolerant Normality', in: A. Graafland and L.J. Kavanaugh (eds.), *Crossover: Architecture, Urbanism and Technology* (Rotterdam: 010 publishers, 2006), 294-311.
87. This translation from Lefebvre, *Writings on Cities*, op. cit. (note 28), 173.

Chapter III
Technology in Architecture: The Ghost in the Machine

1. Technologies of reproduction are a necessary precondition for the expansion of a mass culture, while a rising mass culture may put forward new demands on technology. This intimate link is explored in the seminal text of Walter Benjamin on 'The work of art in the age of mechanical reproduction', but also in the later work of Marshall McLuhan. Archigram was clearly aware of the work of McLuhan, visible in the occasional specific reference, such as in the 1969 L.A.W.U.N. project No. 1, An Experimental Bottery by David Greene, and Ron Herron's 1972 project 'It's a . . .'. See Peter Cook (ed.), *Archigram* (New York: Princeton Architectural Press, 1999), 113, 137. Their reception of the work is debatable however. As Simon Sadler points out, Warren Chalk takes a rather lighthearted approach with an article titled 'How to Get Involved without Understanding McLuhan', published in *AD* (October 1969). Simon Sadler, *Archigram: Architecture without Architecture* (Cambridge, MA: MIT Press, 2005), 143, ff. 16.
2. This connection with mass culture was quickly understood by Banham, but remains a topic of discussion even today, for example in Joel Sanders, 'Archigram: Designs on the Future' (October 2002): 'Archigram's vision of technology in particular was framed through mass culture', http://www.postmedia.net/02/archigram.htm (accessed 18 September 2004).
3. *A Guide to Archigram, 1961-1974* (London: Academy Editions/Vienna: Kunsthalle Wien, 1994), 27. Originally published as: 'Some Notes on the Archigram Syndrome', *Perspecta*, supplement no. 11 (1967).
4. Here I follow Huyssen's argument of the importance of technologies such as reproduction and seriality for developments in the arts; this is also reminiscent of Benjamin's discussion of the impact of reproduction on the art object. It is precisely the intertwining of expressive technology with the use of (or an instrumental) technology that makes the work of Archigram so rich to discuss. Andreas Huyssen, *After the Great Divide: Modernism, Mass Culture, Postmodernism* (Bloomington: Indiana University Press, 1986), 9.
5. This is also a matter of the 1960s' reception of modernist technology, arguably based on the vast amount of post-war building following the rational (and minimal) requirements of CIAM.
6. Peter Cook (ed.), *Archigram* (New York: Princeton Architectural Press, 1999), 4. Originally published in Basel by Birkhäuser Verlag in 1972. Isozaki draws a comparison with metabolism, which in his opinion ended up subjugated by managerial planning.
7. Ibid., 8.
8. *Archigram* 5, *Metropolis* (November 1964), 12.
9. Martin Heidegger, *Die Technik und die Kehre* (Pfullingen: Klett Cotta, 1962). Although this argument on modern technology does seem nostalgic towards a pre-technological era, its analysis of the forcefulness of modern technology is very precise.
10. Marshall McLuhan, *Understanding Media: The Extensions of Man* (London: Routledge, 2001 [1964]); and Reyner Banham, *Theory and Design in the First Machine Age* (Cambridge, MA: MIT Press, 1980), originally published in London by The Architectural Press, 1960.
11. This issue of control has become even more important with the advent of cybertechnology and biotechnology. These have made a hybrid form of technological life possible, as prefigured in Mary Shelley's *Frankenstein* (1818). This line of argument has become increasingly important as technology has shifted gears from an 'external' industrial mode to a more embedded cybernetic mode.
12. This is one of the main arguments of the Situationist International (and Guy Debord in particular), mainly in relation to capitalism and a consumer-oriented society. Although technology itself retains a liberating potential in his work, this distinction in terms of consumerism and choice is a crucial distinction between the continental European discourse on the one hand, and that of England and America on the other.

13. Ellen Lupton, *Mechanical Brides: Women and Machines from Home to Office* (New York: Cooper-Hewitt National Museum of Design, Smithsonian Institution and Princeton Architectural Press, 1993), 19, 26-27.
14. The issue of cybernetics largely falls outside of the scope of this study, except in those instances where it is directly introduced in the architecture discourse, by Archigram for example.
15. This did not necessarily preclude spirituality (Theo van Doesburg) or poetry (Le Corbusier), yet the reception of the discourse in the 1960s focused on the problems caused by a purely mechanical and functional rationality.
16. Here again, it is important to keep in mind that the critiques of the 1960s were derived from their own perception of modernism: the problem of mechanization was as much a societal problem as it was inherently connected to modern architecture.
17. Denise Scott Brown, 'Little Magazines in Architecture and Urbanism', *Journal of the American Institute of Planners* 34 (July 1968), 223-233.
18. Banham, *Theory and Design*, op. cit. (note 10). Banham wrote his dissertation under Nikolaus Pevsner, reacting strongly to Pevsner's turn to the picturesque. Charles Jencks in turn wrote his dissertation under the supervision of Banham. The complexities of these relationships have been discussed in terms of both personal reactions and shifting values in architecture by Nigel Whiteley in his book *Reyner Banham: Historian of the Immediate Future* (Cambridge, MA: MIT Press, 2003).
19. Alan Colquhoun, 'Symbolic and Literal Aspects of Technology', in: *Essays in Architectural Criticism: Modern Architecture and Historical Change* (Cambridge, MA: MIT Press, 1981), 26-30. Originally published in *Architectural Design* (November 1962), 508-509.
20. Inevitably, their points of view were mutually influenced – the article by Colquhoun appeared two years after Banham's book, but in his specification of symbolic and literal certainly adds to the argument. The two were both present in England in the same circle of the Independent Group, the Institute for Contemporary Arts and Archigram.
21. Banham, *Theory and Design*, op. cit. (note 10), 327.
22. Ulrich Conrads, *Programs and Manifestoes on 20th-Century Architecture* (Cambridge, MA: MIT Press, 1975), 89. In the same piece, he also notes the importance of poetry. Although this love for the poetic is an important part of his work, it is of relatively little consequence to the reception of modernism in the 1960s, and hence remains untreated in this book.
23. CIAM Charter of Athens (1933), in: ibid., 137-145, tenet 90.
24. Mies van de Rohe, 'Technology and Architecture' (lecture for Illinois Institute of Technology, 1950), in: ibid., 154.
25. To Le Corbusier, rationality was one of the most important human characteristics, and the best way to rise above his own shortcomings.
26. Banham, *Theory and Design*, op. cit. (note 10), 153; 327-329.
27. Ibid., 10-12; 328.
28. Ibid., 82-83, 181-184. Johnson and Hitchcock produce a similarly filtered view of the International Style, which is implicitly noted in this passage, but it is mainly Nikolaus Pevsner's history that Banham is aiming to revise. Charles Jencks forms an interesting next step in this line of history and polemic: as a thesis student of Banham's, Jencks responds to his mentor's position by moving towards the surface expression in his espousal of postmodernism, just as Banham moves away from pure progressivist historical revision in response to Pevsner, thus continuously completing the oedipal circle.
29. To some degree his work on pop is more revealing in relation to the work of Venturi and Scott Brown, while the focus on technology is more relevant to the work of Archigram. In particular the work on pop was informed by his travels through America, where he was confronted with the developments that Venturi and Scott Brown would later explore in *Learning from Las Vegas*, and later again in relation to Levittown.

30. What was to become the Independent Group was actively involved, but another key figure of 1960s' architecture, Denise Scott Brown, was also present at these meetings.
31. As an aside, the radical nature of his gesture towards pop culture might be considered a new form of ossification – by preferencing pop and mass culture, high culture is then denied the validity of its place within culture.
32. Walter Benjamin, 'The Work of Art in the Age of Mechanical Reproduction' (1936) in Walter Benjamin, *Illuminations: Essays and Reflections.* Edited and with an introduction by Hannah Arendt. (New York: Schocken, 1969), 217-251, and McLuhan, Understanding Media, op. cit. (note 10). Both works explicitly view new technological developments as not only transformations of the objects we encounter, but posit that they also induce a transformed state of the subject.
33. See for further discussion of Banham's own polemic: Whiteley, *Reyner Banham*, op. cit. (note 18).
34. See especially M. Christine Boyer, *CyberCities: Visual Perception in the Age of Electronic Communication* (New York: Princeton Architectural Press, 1996). Although cybertechnology is an important connection to contemporary conditions, it remains outside of the scope of this study. Its developments and ideas in the 1960s were still relatively young, and did not truly enter the architecture discourse beyond the science-fiction projections of Archigram, which arguably also still hold to an earlier, industrial paradigm of technology, with occasional gestures towards cybertechnology.
35. Banham even distinguishes these as two overarching themes of architecture history: tradition and technology. See 'Stocktaking', *Architectural Review* 127 (February 1960). Reprinted in: Penny Sparke (ed.), *Design by Choice* (London: Academy Editions, 1981), 48-55.
36. In the end, additions and modifications were made to the Plug-In City over a longer period of time, but the design itself is generally dated as produced in 1964.
37. The imagery of the Plug-In City does not fully exploit this individuality, with each pod designed by Cook, but the potential is still clear. Cook already critiques his own early drawings for their architectural consistency. Referring to a section drawn up in 1964, he notes: 'That the central *implication* of the Plug-In City is its open-endedness is at this stage belied. If any occurrence can overlay any other, and the boundaries of taste and use are to be eliminated by individual wishes, then any section must not only be capable of extreme limits of absorption but should try to illustrate them.' Cook, *Archigram*, op. cit. (note 6), 38.
38. Jurjen Zeinstra, 'Houses of the Future', *OASE* 32, *Architectuur en stedebouw in de jaren zestig* (1992), 8-31. Zeinstra argues that 'space' is still important to the Smithsons, while Archigram reduces architecture to little more than a technological intervention between man and environment, neglecting 'space' as part of the craft of architecture.
39. Peter Cook, *Architecture: Action and Plan* (London: Studio Vista, 1967). Cook's arguments are reminiscent of Marshall McLuhan's notes on the complexity of technological influence, see McLuhan, *Understanding Media*, op. cit. (note 10).
40. Ibid., 18.
41. The introduction to *Archigram* 7 gathers a number of earlier ideas in the hope of transforming the more static implications of modernist technology. Referring specifically to 'growth, change, metamorphosis, indeterminacy, anti-zoning, expendability, free-zones, etc.', Peter Cook suggests that 'a much bigger conversation looms (one which could not be imagined when we started Archigram, which is more than the sum of its parts): Does architecture have anything to do with life anymore?'. Peter Cook, 'A Very Straight Description', *Archigram* 7 (1966), unpaginated.
42. According to Archigram, the primary distinction between the two resides in the infrastructure. The Plug-In City incorporates some of the technology in its basic structure, while New Babylon has an infrastructure that is completely neutral and purely about infill. *Archigram* 5 (winter 1964-1965), 12.
43. 'Cluster' is a word also used by Archigram at times, though developed in a different fashion from the more specified 'cluster cities' of the Smithsons.

44. *Archigram* 5 (1964), 3. On the same page, there is a comment that deserves further study: the members of Archigram claim the need for a 'governing structure'. This distinguishes them from both the anarchy of the situationists and the liberalism more common in the USA.
45. Peter Blake, 'A Comment from Peter Blake', Cook, *Archigram*, op. cit. (note 6), 7. The reference to Le Corbusier is to the section on Liners in *Vers une Architecture* (Paris, 1923).
46. Cook, *Archigram*, op. cit. (note 6), 86.
47. Ibid., 88.
48. Ibid., 44.
49. Reyner Banham, 'A Home Is Not a House' (1965), in: William Braham, Jonathan Hale and John Sadar (eds.), *Rethinking Technology: A Reader in Architectural Theory* (London: Routledge, 2006), 168.
50. Cook, *Archigram*, op. cit. (note 6), 51.
51. Ibid.
52. Mike Webb, 'The Cushicle', in: Cook, *Archigram*, op. cit. (note 6), 64.
53. Warren Chalk, 'Housing as a Consumer Product'. Original publication in *Arena*, (March 1966). Reprinted in: Cook, *Archigram*, op. cit. (note 6), 16-17.
54. Cook, *Archigram*, op. cit. (note 6), 51.
55. An even further expansion of this logic may be seen in the later projects of Superstudio. They put forward an expanded urban technological environment, with the possibility of plugging into the grid. More important, through the abstraction of the grid they suggest a complete dissipation of architecture. Superstudio, 'Microevent/ Microenvironment' (1972), in: Braham, Hale and Sadar, *Rethinking Technology*, op. cit. (note 49), 186-194.
56. Of particular note in this might be Katavolos' manifesto on 'organics' in which he literally proposes to 'grow' cities, through new developments in chemistry. These speculations are picked up throughout science fiction, but have rarely entered the domain of architecture discourse. William Katavolos, 'Organics' (1960), in: Braham, Hale and Sadar, *Rethinking Technology*, op. cit. (note 49), 140-142.
57. The obvious exception to this is Kiesler's Endless House, but since it falls outside of the canon discussed here as the source of conflict, it also remains outside of this discussion.
58. David Greene, 'Living Pod', in: Cook, *Archigram*, op. cit. (note 6), 52.
59. This transformation is eminently visible in the film *Barbarella* (1968). Barbarella's spaceship is lined with fur, the walls of the city Sogo have soft tentacles or jagged points, and nearly every scene holds some kind of 'tangible' space, rather than a visual one.
60. Ron Herron, Warren Chalk, David Greene, 'Manzak and Electronic Tomato', in: Cook, *Archigram*, op. cit. (note 6), 124.
61. A PhD is currently being finished on the notion that the image may have initiated a different form of discourse in architecture theory (Emre Alturk, Delft University of Technology). The work of Archizoom and Superstudio certainly attest to this valuation of imagery as critical discourse.
62. On 'little magazines' in the 1960s, see Scott Brown, 'Little Magazines', op. cit. (note 17).
63. From 1960 to 1962, three of the members (Warren Chalk, Dennis Crompton and Ron Herron) worked on the South Bank Arts Centre for the London City Council, and the magazine gave them the opportunity to draw and present the projects otherwise unfulfilled.
64. Banham, *Theory and Design*, op. cit. (note 10), 329-330.
65. *Archigram* 3 (1963), 'Expendability: Towards Throwaway Architecture'.
66. Reprint of the editorial in *Archigram* 3 (1963), in: Cook, *Archigram*, op. cit. (note 6), 16.
67. Ibid.
68. This phrase derives from John Kenneth Galbraith's 1958 book *The Affluent Society*.
69. Although the topic extends beyond the discussion here, the films of the era in particular often reflect a smooth, attractive, highly polished architectural environment (although there are also clearly counterparts to this environment in a more dystopian genre).
70. Cook, *Archigram*, op. cit. (note 6), 68.

71. The notion of control is also present in the situationist definition of a 'situation' which is always 'A moment of life *concretely and deliberately* constructed', (my italics).
72. Chalk, 'Housing as a Consumer Product', op. cit. (note 53).
73. McLuhan, *Understanding Media*, op. cit. (note 10).
74. 'Banham – Historian', in: Robert Maxwell, *Sweet Disorder and the Carefully Careless: Theory and Criticism in Architecture* (New York: Princeton Architectural Press, 1993), 163-176.
75. Hans Achterhuis, et al. (eds.), *Van stoommachine tot cyborg: Denken over techniek in de nieuwe wereld* (Amsterdam: Ambo, 1997). Particularly Achterhuis's introduction and his analysis of the work of Andrew Feenberg argue the usefulness of a pragmatic approach.
76. One of the seminal texts on the issues surrounding industrial technology is by Herbert Marcuse. *One Dimensional Man: Studies in the Ideology of Advanced Industrial Society* (Boston: Beacon Press, 1964). This perception of the power of technology is also present in the 1965 film *Alphaville* by Jean-Luc Godard. Both avail themselves of a 'conspiracy theory' understanding of the mysterious forces of technological domination.
77. Colquhoun, 'The Symbolic and Literal Aspects of Technology', op. cit. (note 19).
78. Ibid.
79. It cannot be emphasized enough how important this observation is, since many of the modernist manifestoes were founded on the notion that the rational and technological society was freed from ideology. In other words, to be technological was to be value-free. Both Colquhoun and Banham clearly argue why this is a (possibly intentional) misrepresentation.
80. Banham argues that this is what Le Corbusier finally produced: a 'machine aesthetic'. To him, Futurism is more interesting, since the futurists express a 'technological aesthetic', but are also very much engaged with the 'actual' ramifications of technology, beyond its aesthetic. Banham, *Theory and Design*, op. cit. (note 10), 150-153.
81. Colquhoun, 'The Symbolic and Literal Aspects of Technology', op. cit. (note 19).
82. Achterhuis, *Van stoommachine tot cyborg*, op. cit. (note 75), 40.
83. Banham, *Theory and Design*, op. cit. (note 10), 321.
84. I largely refrain from using the word 'progress' because the notion of progress implies a forward movement, or a becoming 'better'. The words 'development' and 'transformation' imply that change is involved without arguing the moral quality of that change.
85. Banham, *Theory and Design*, op. cit. (note 10), 329, my italics.
86. Colquhoun, 'Form and Figure', in: *Essays in Architectural Criticism*, op. cit. (note 19), 190-202. Originally published in *Oppositions* 12 (spring 1978), 28-37.
87. McLuhan, *Understanding Media*, op. cit. (note 10), 12.
88. Banham, *Theory and Design*, op. cit. (note 10), 10.
89. McLuhan, *Understanding Media*, op. cit. (note 10), 4.
90. Morality remains a touchy issue in architecture, especially since the modernist discourse. See especially: David Watkin, *Morality and Architecture: The Development of a Theme in Architectural History and Theory from the Gothic Revival to the Modern Movement* (Oxford: Clarendon Press, 1977). This issue returns in the leftist moralizing tendency of the 1960s, where anti-establishment becomes a rigid norm rather than a liberating response.
91. This radicalization is noted throughout Achterhuis, *Van stoommachine tot cyborg*, op. cit. (note 75), not only in relation to Heidegger, but also to Marcuse for example.
92. Ibid., 7, 10-12, 16-17, 29.
93. Banham, *Theory and Design*, op. cit. (note 10), 330.
94. Zeinstra, 'Houses of the Future', op. cit. (note 38).
95. Martijntje Smits, *Monsterbezwering: De culturele domesticatie van nieuwe technologie* (Amsterdam: Boom, 2002), 252-264, 272. Smits builds on the ideas of Mary Douglas on cultural classification. If we understand our cultural order as based on a conceptualization of perceptions that are grouped into categories, we must acknowledge a mutual relation between categories and perceptions: while our perceptions are mediated by our cultural categories, they also sometimes transgress them. Smits notes that in most approaches, anomalies

and innovations are 'judged in terms of existing cultural categories and cultural boundaries are considered more or less as facts. This however prevents new phenomena to reveal their full potential.' She concludes that a pragmatic approach is more fruitful, where anomalies are seen as a 'creative challenge to reconcile new technology and existing categories, by adapting both'. This approach 'regards technological facts as well as cultural categories as social constructs that can be adapted in time'. In other words, both the technologies themselves and their conceptualization are reconfigured, depending on what the issue at hand is. Her discussion of pragmatism parallels a notion of 'contamination' that presumes the mutual dependency between a transcendent idea and its specific application.

96. This positivity had disappeared almost entirely by the mid-1970s. By 1968, Philip K. Dick had published his novel *Do Androids Dream of Electric Sheep?* (Doubleday) with its post-apocalyptic setting populated by androids (the novel would later be filmed as Blade Runner). An earlier foreboding of this quick downturn in the belief in technology is to be found in Rachel Carson's *Silent Spring* (Boston: Houghton Mifflin Co., 1962).
97. Petran Kockelkoren, *Technology: Art, Fairground and Theatre* (Rotterdam: NAi Publishers, 2003).

Chapter IV
Architecture in Its Own Image: Pop Reflections

1. In the 1990s this reaches a new level, as discussed by John Seabrook in his book *Nobrow. The Culture of Marketing the Marketing of Culture* (London: Methuen, 2000).
2. Charles Jencks, 'Pop – Non pop (1)', *Architectural Association Quarterly*, vol. 1, no. 1 (1969), 49.
3. Georg Simmel and Robert Park were important to the early modern period, but did not make practical urban planning suggestions. By the late 1950s, Young and Wilmott as well as Gans were offering more problem-solving comments. Especially in the USA, these urban renewal schemes were critical.
4. Although modernism was not averse to using images from advertisements, the problem with the imagery I am referring to here extends primarily to symbols of pop culture. The images within modernist tracts tended towards the industrial, while those of the 1960s tended towards the popular.
5. Robert Venturi, *Complexity and Contradiction in Architecture* (New York: The Museum of Modern Art Papers on Architecture, 1966), 17.
6. See for example: David Robbins (ed.), *The Independent Group: Postwar Britain and the Aesthetics of Plenty* (Cambridge, MA: MIT Press, 1990); Anne Massey, *Modernism and Mass Culture in Britain, 1945-1959* (Manchester: Manchester University Press, 1995); and Herbert Gans, *Popular Culture & High Culture: An Analysis and Evaluation of Taste*, revised and updated edition (New York: Basic Books, 1999 [1974]).
7. John Kenneth Galbraith, *The Affluent Society* (Boston: Houghton Mifflin, 1958). In this book, Galbraith proposed that economics needed to rethink its premises of scarcity and understand the new logic arising from conditions of affluence.
8. Olav Velthuis, *Imaginary Economics* (Rotterdam: NAi Publishers, 2005); Michael Müller, 'Aestheticization, Culture and Economy', submission for the as yet unpublished book resulting from the conference 'The Projective Landscape', held at Delft University of Technology on 16 and 17 March 2006.
9. This is primarily about the communicative aspect of symbolism, which is central to the work of Venturi and Scott Brown.
10. Although I will be using both the terms 'popular' and 'mass' culture, the preferred term for the 1960s will be mass culture with its connotations of urbanity and mass production.
11. Although the films of Jacques Tati are beyond the scope of this study, they offer a strong example of a general aesthetic and cultural critique of the modern city and its architecture. See for example Iain Borden, 'Material Sounds: Jacques Tati and Modern Architecture', in: Bob

Fear (ed.), *Architecture + Film II* Architectural Design 70: 1 (New York: Wiley, January 2000): 26-31.

12. The work of Wolfe in particular formed a background to the later work of Venturi and Scott Brown – he helped define a connection between the manifestations of low-culture aesthetics and their implications for a reconsideration of their role in (high) culture.
13. This hostility is a legacy of modernism, but in contemporary architecture culture, it may be more accurate to speak of a very intimate relationship that is masked by an affected hostility.
14. Venturi, *Complexity and Contradiction*, op. cit. (note 5), 54-55, 68-69, 104-105.
15. He does have a publication on this topic prior to the publication of *Complexity and Contradiction*: 'A Justification for a Pop Architecture', *Arts and Architecture* (April 1965), 22. This article is a hint of the argument to come in the book.
16. Venturi, *Complexity and Contradiction*, op. cit. (note 5), 104.
17. Lefebvre also uses the word 'reduction' in his critique of architectural representations of space. See excerpts from *The Production of Space*, in: Neil Leach (ed.), *Rethinking Architecture: A Reader in Cultural Theory* (London: Routledge, 1997), 138-146.
18. Venturi, *Complexity and Contradiction*, op. cit. (note 5), 17.
19. The firm they run together now has gone through different phases and names, including Venturi and Rauch, Venturi Scott Brown and now Venturi Scott Brown and Associates. In this book, I primarily address the studios and books they organized and produced together, thus I typically use Venturi and Scott Brown.
20. 'Long before visiting Las Vegas, I was taking snapshots of popular culture and everyday landscapes in Africa, Europe, and England.' Denise Scott Brown, 'Activities as Patterns: Lessons About Architecture from Planning', MetropolisMag.com, February 2003. Lecture given September 2001 (online only). This documents some useful biographical dates. See http://www.metropolismag.com/html/vsba/index.html (accessed 28 July 2004).
21. Venturi, *Complexity and Contradiction*, op. cit. (note 5), 19.
22. In fact, a striking example of this is to be found in C.A. van Eck, 'The Visually Immediate: Sir Christopher Wren on the Corona of the Temple of Peace in Rome', *OASE* 59, *Scratching the Surface* (2002), 6-21. In this article she discusses the distinction Wren made between the ideal form (in plan and in geometry) and the visual perception of his work. In the case discussed, he modified the typical sequence of elements to attain the *visual effect* of perfect geometry.
23. Henri Lefebvre, *The Production of Space*, as excerpted in: Leach, *Rethinking Architecture*, op. cit. (note 17), 144-145.
24. Although this is similar to the 'total experience' of the Situationist International and Lefebvre, it is nevertheless different in its ramifications: where the implication of the situationist 'total experience' was meant to be transformative, the notion of complexity derived more from a pragmatic acceptance of plurality.
25. Herbert Gans, *People and Plans: Essays on Urban Problems and Solutions* (New York: Basic Books, 1968).
26. Venturi, *Complexity and Contradiction*, op. cit. (note 5), 41.
27. Ibid., 42.
28. Ibid., 41.
29. Ibid., 42.
30. Lawrence Alloway, 'City Notes', *Architectural Design* (January 1959), 34-35, and 'The Arts and the Mass Media', *Architectural Design* (February 1958), 84-85. In the latter essay, Alloway even goes so far as to suggest that the fine arts may learn something from Hollywood.
31. Venturi, *Complexity and Contradiction*, op. cit. (note 5), 44.
32. Ibid., 10.
33. Douglas Haskell, 'Architecture and popular taste', *Architectural Forum* (August 1958), 105-109.
34. Alan Colquhoun, 'Sign and Substance: Reflections on Complexity, Las Vegas and Oberlin', *Oppositions* 14 (Fall 1978), 26-37.
35. Scott Brown, 'Activities as Patterns', op. cit. (note 20); Denise Scott Brown, 'Learning from the New Brutalism', in: Robbins, *The Independent Group*, op. cit. (note 6).

36. Robert Venturi in an unpublished interview with the author, June 2003.
37. Some interesting aspects of the work produced in the early 1960s remain undisclosed, or at least underanalysed, in part due to primary attention being given to the role of Venturi. For Scott Brown's own perspective on being the 'silent partner' and how the 'star system' in architecture feeds this (there can, after all, be only one 'star'), see Denise Scott Brown, 'Room at the Top? Sexism and the Star System in Architecture', in: Ellen Perry Berkeley (ed.), *Architecture: A Place for Women* (Washington: Smithsonian Institution Press, 1989), 237-246.
38. Social realism is a term that has been used in diverse contexts – I use it here as it is used in reference to a group of English painters (then usually called kitchen-sink realism) who simply represent their everyday environment in an almost aggressively ordinary way (late 1940s, early 1950s). Since the mid-1990s it has also been used in relation to English cinema with the same attention to gritty everyday detail. Scott Brown uses it as well in relation to New Brutalism in her article 'Activities as Patterns', op. cit. (note 20).
39. Scott Brown, 'Learning from the New Brutalism', op. cit. (note 35). Archigram started a little later than the work of the Independent Group, with their first pamphlet appearing in 1961. This slight difference in time-frame may be historically significant; Denise Scott Brown left England while the Independent Group (with Reyner Banham, who later became a great fan of Archigram) was still the main influence in the sphere of pop-sensibility.
40. Although it is impossible in such a close partnership as that between Venturi and Scott Brown to determine exactly who introduced what, these studio notes are in Denise Scott Brown's handwriting, indicating that at least a significant part of its organization was developed by her.
41. According to Scott Brown, the structure was based on both her pedagogical interests and her planning background. Unpublished interview with author, June 2003.
42. Scott Brown, 'Learning from the New Brutalism', op. cit. (note 35).
43. This introduction of *empirical* sociological research is an important shift, as opposed to the sociological philosophies of Simmel and Robert Park. By using empirical research, the basis of design became quantifiable existing conditions, rather than sociological and philosophical paradigms as a qualitative premise.
44. Moreover, with industrialization and urbanization came the shift from rural, folk culture to an urban mass culture. See Gans, *Popular Culture*, op. cit. (note 6).
45. Brian Wallis, 'Tomorrow and Tomorrow and Tomorrow: The Independent Groups and Popular Culture', in: *Modern Dreams: The Rise and Fall and Rise of Pop* (London: Institute for Contemporary Arts, 1991), 9.
46. Ibid., 9.
47. Ibid.
48. John Habraken, for example, notes a transformation in architecture due to post-war reconstruction; he claims that the transition from the extraordinary to the ordinary should be considered one of the most important transformations in design culture. John Habraken, *Het Alledaagse: Over het ontstaan van de omgeving van alledag*, Inaugural speech, Eindhoven University of Technology, 8 June 1967.
49. Alloway, 'City Notes', op. cit. (note 30).
50. Alison and Peter Smithson, 'But Today We Collect Ads', in: *Modern Dreams*, op. cit. (note 45), 53-55.
51. As noted earlier, the relationship between Lefebvre and Debord was tenuous, with Debord denying (or not discussing) the influences of his former teacher. See especially Kristin Ross, interview with Lefebvre, in: Thomas McDonough, *Guy Debord and the Situationist International: Texts and Documents* (Cambridge, MA: MIT Press, 2002). Peter Wollen also notes that Debord audited a class with Lefebvre, see Elisabeth Sussman (ed.), *On the Passage of a Few People through a Rather Brief Moment in Time: The Situationist International, 1957-1972* (Cambridge, MA: MIT Press and Boston: Institute of Contemporary Art, 1989), 25.
52. Peter Wollen, 'The Art and Politics of the Situationist International', in: ibid., 22. An important source for this is Guy Debord's 'Report on the Construction of Situations', for example

his comment that it was now important to utilize 'all the means of transforming everyday life'. Translation in: McDonough, *Guy Debord*, op. cit. (note 51), 42.

53. Michèle Bernstein, 'The Situationist International', *The Times Literary Supplement*, special issue, September 1964.
54. See for example Guy Debord, *The Society of the Spectacle* (NY: Zone Books (MIT Press), 1995), thesis 6: 'Understood in its totality, the spectacle is both the outcome and the goal of the dominant mode of production'; and thesis 7: 'The language of the spectacle is composed of *signs* of the dominant organization of production – signs which are at the same time the ultimate end-products of that organization.'
55. 'There might be an argument in favor of this point of view if modern society were constructed on medieval or even eighteenth century lines, and if there were a convergence of taste between society as a whole (or its dominant subculture) and the artist whose role it was to interpret its values. But such a situation simply does not exist today.' Colquhoun, 'Sign and Substance', op. cit. (note 34), 29.
56. Dick Hebdige, 'In Poor Taste: Notes on Pop', in: *Modern Dreams*, op. cit. (note 45), 77-85.
57. Beyond his interest in mechanical reproduction, and the Paris warehouses, he also wrote on Mickey Mouse and the Karl May stories.
58. Andreas Huyssen, *After the Great Divide: Modernism, Mass Culture, Postmodernism* (Bloomington: Indiana University Press, 1986); Gans, *Popular Culture*, op. cit. (note 6). Gans notes that mass culture is an urbanized (and commercial) form of folk culture.
59. Avant-garde art here is seen as a vanguard, and the artist has a crucial role in preparing the way for progress. For an analysis of the relation between avant-garde and mass culture see also: Huyssen, *After the Great Divide*, op. cit. (note 58), especially 'The Hidden Dialectic', 5-15.
60. Other sources on the avant-garde include: Renato Poggioli, *The Theory of the Avant-Garde* (Cambridge, MA: Harvard University Press, 1968); Peter Bürger, *Theorie der Avantgarde* (Frankfurt: Suhrkamp, 1974); Matei Calinescu, *Faces of Modernity: Avant-garde, Decadence, Kitsch* (Bloomington: Indiana University Press, 1977); in direct relation to architecture, see: Michael Müller, *Architektur und Avantgarde: Ein vergessenes Projekt der Moderne?* (Frankfurt: Suhrkamp, 1984).
61. Le Corbusier, *Towards a New Architecture* (New York: Dover Publications, Inc., 1986), 19, 102. Originally published as *Vers une architecture* (1927).
62. Patricia Phillips, 'Why Is Pop So Unpopular?', in: *Modern Dreams*, op. cit. (note 45), 118-133.
63. This argumentation is also present today, albeit transformed, in the work of Douglas Rushkoff and Naomi Klein. Both theorists argue that the imagery of mass culture is not only a spectator sport, but can become an active part of new developments in both high art and general culture.
64. Le Corbusier, 'Eyes which do not see', in: *Towards a New Architecture*, op. cit. (note 61), 90-148.
65. Banham was already exploring the tension between commercial design and artistic value by 1955 in 'Industrial Design and Popular Art', *Industrial Magazine* (March 1960), originally published as *Civilta delle Macchine* in November 1955.
66. Lecture, SOMEone conference. Eindhoven University of Technology, April 2001.
67. In 1950, only 9 per cent of the households in the USA owned a television, while in 1960 that was already 87 per cent. Source: US Census Bureau, statistical abstract of the US, http://www.census.gov/statab/hist/HS-42.pdf (accessed 29 July 2004).
68. The main precedent for this use of imagery is Dada, but the Dadaists do not seem to have had much influence on the mainstream of architecture design and theory.
69. In this sense, the Independent Group also arguably introduces an important premise of postmodern architecture: the introduction of 'otherness' as a way to both undermine the rigorous purity of modernism and open it up to the presence of variety.
70. Phillips, 'Why is Pop So Unpopular?', op. cit. (note 62).
71. Richard Hamilton, 'Letter to Peter and Alison Smithson', 16 January 1957. Reprinted in: *Les Années Pop* (Paris: Centre Georges Pompidou, 2001).

72. Alison and Peter Smithson, 'But Today We Collect Ads', op. cit. (note 50).
73. Debord, *The Society of the Spectacle*, op. cit. (note 54), thesis 34.
74. Today, something similar can be seen in the products of 'culture jammers', which utilize the power and the creativity of 'everyman' as well. Culture jamming is about subverting the intentions of well-known capitalist artefacts, and it can be done by anyone, following the classic grassroots principle of the 1960s. The most visible of these projects are t-shirts which transform well-known logos such as 'Lego' and 'Ford' into 'ego' and 'Fuct', within their own recognizable graphics.
75. They often refer to their comment that 'children have always played in monumental fountains'.
76. Robert Venturi and Denise Scott Brown, *Learning from Las Vegas* (Cambridge, MA: MIT Press, 1972), 3.
77. In this view, they are closely aligned with the general interest in 'messy reality' and Lefebvre's distinction between the space of architects and that of users.
78. There is an important distinction between the Situationist International and Venturi and Scott Brown here, in that the situationists were seeking to liberate a creativity they thought was inherent in every individual; yet they saw most of the 'existing environment' as little more than the embodiment of capitalist domination. Venturi and Scott Brown tend more towards folk-art in their desire to examine the symbolism of everyday form.
79. Moreover, the importance of 'being revolutionary' is still emphasized throughout these interventions (the idea of revolution and originality of course in essence modern notions) – the first sentence of *Learning from Las Vegas* is: 'Learning from the existing landscape is a way of being revolutionary for an architect', op. cit. (note 76), 3.
80. Colquhoun, 'Sign and Substance', op. cit. (note 34), 29-30.
81. Ibid., 36.
82. Robert Venturi and Denise Scott Brown, *On Houses and Housing*, Architectural Monographs no. 21 (London: Academy Editions, 1992).
83. Denise Scott Brown, in unpublished interview with author, June 2003.
84. The second film however, *Critique de la Séparation* (1961), already began to explore Debord's future theses on the totality of art and life. Wollen 'The Art and Politics of the Situationist International', op. cit. (note 52).
85. Lara Schrijver, 'The Power of Lightness: Humor as a Strategy in Architecture and the Visual Arts', in: Martin Nonhoff, Katharina Bunzmann and Johannes Angermüller (eds.), *PostModern Productions* (Hamburg: LIT Verlag, 2001), 147-159.
86. De Stijl manifesto, 1922, point 4. As quoted in Ulrich Conrads, *Programs and Manifestoes on 20th-Century Architecture* (Cambridge, MA: MIT Press, 1975), 64.
87. Commentary of Van Doesburg on manifesto V, in: ibid., 67.
88. Huyssen, *After the Great Divide*, op. cit. (note 58).
89. Conceptually, there is a separate discussion underlying all this in terms of the analytic value of text and synthetic value of imagery, as well as the troubled relationship between image and text, which returns throughout this chapter.
90. Denise Scott Brown, 'Team 10, Perspecta 10 and the Present State of Architectural Theory', *Journal of the American Institute of Planners* (January 1967), 42-50.
91. Scott Brown, 'Learning from the New Brutalism', op. cit. (note 35). The book accompanied an exhibition, and contains work by the Independent Group, texts from the time as well as retrospective texts and interviews.
92. Jacquelynn Baas and David Robbins, interview with Denise Scott Brown, in: Robbins, *The Independent Group*, op. cit. (note 6), 203.
93. An important criticism of the work of Venturi and Scott Brown in this context is formulated by Colquhoun. All the 'jokes', transformations and inconsistencies (or complexities) are aimed purely at an in-crowd of architects, regardless of the references made to the 'commonplace' or 'popular culture'. This is a central problem in the 1960s, despite the general desire to

connect or communicate with 'the masses' (or 'the people') – criticism of the modernist forefathers is still so embedded within an architects-only discourse that it appropriates popular imagery to its own ends rather than utilizing it. 'Unlike the music hall comedian, whose jokes are understood by his box-office audience (even if their typology is only appreciated by his fellow actors), Venturi's wit seems to be aimed solely at his fellow architects. The semiological intention of these projects is clearly not to provide the client with what he wants (though an essential part of the joke is that they do so *faute de mieux*) but to draw attention to the absurdity of popular taste.' Colquhoun, 'Sign and Substance', op. cit. (note 34), 29.

94. Lawrence Alloway, 'The Arts and the Mass Media', *Architectural Design* (February 1958), 84-85.
95. The representations of architectural traditions and clichés in television series and films are documented in the results of their 'Learning from Levittown' studio (source: office archives, Venturi and Scott Brown). This is one of the earliest examinations of architectural language on television.
96. For example, discussions on TV-shows like *Buffy the Vampire Slayer* run rampant in academic circles in terms of their intellectual subtext. In point of fact, Buffy did at the time toy with numerous conventions of television, ranging from the lighting styles of film (darker than typical on TV) and genre-blending as well as inverting expectations. Also, media theorist Douglas Rushkoff has offered highly critical insights into the sophistication of contemporary media culture and its use of the image in his books *Media Virus!: Hidden Agendas in Popular Culture* (New York: Ballantine Books, 1994) and *Children of Chaos: Surviving the End of the World as We Know It* (New York: HarperCollins, 1997).
97. In structuralism, the visual was largely treated as analogous to language, consisting of signifiers and signifieds that were only related to one another through agreement. The idea of an unmediated reflection of reality is most prominent in photography. One of the best examples of this is to be found in a *National Geographic* cover showing the Egyptian pyramids: they were moved somewhat closer together in the photograph, to fit on the cover, which prompted an intense public debate on 'lying' to the public in this photograph.
98. Denise Scott Brown, unpublished interview with author, June 2003.
99. Mark Taylor, *Hiding* (Chicago: University of Chicago Press, 1997).
100. Martin Jay 'Cultural Relativism and the Visual Turn', Journal of Visual Culture, vol. 1, no. 3 (December 2002), 274.
101. Le Corbusier, *Towards a New Architecture*, op. cit. (note 61), 87.
102. 'Custom' versus 'natural' reflects the distinction made by Colquhoun on 'form' and 'figure' in his 1977 essay on the two. 'Form and Figure', in: Alan Colquhoun, *Essays in Architectural Criticism: Modern Architecture and Historical Change* (Cambridge, MA: MIT Press, 1981), 190-202.
103. Le Corbusier, *Towards a New Architecture*, op. cit. (note 61), 87. This contains an implication of the unfinished project of modernity as posited by Habermas.
104. Colquhoun, 'Form and Figure', op. cit. (note 102). The essay offers an analysis of modernist architecture as 'form' (transcendent and universal), and postmodern architecture as introducing 'figure' (based on context and tradition). He borrows the notion of figure from rhetoric, and implies something in between Jay's ideas of discursive and figural. Colquhoun's notion of form is closer to Jay's idea of the figural.
105. Le Corbusier, *Towards a New Architecture*, op. cit. (note 61), 127.
106. Jay, 'Cultural Relativism', op. cit. (note 100), 269.
107. Ibid., 271.
108. Ibid.
109. Ibid., 275.
110. Barthes as referred to through a quote of David MacDougall in: ibid., 275.
111. Denise Scott Brown, unpublished interview with the author, June 2003. 'Architecture is always behind – marketing has been handling niches since the 60s.'
112. Phillips, 'Why is Pop So Unpopular?', op. cit. (note 62).
113. *Modern Dreams*, op. cit. (note 45).

Chapter V
A Brave New World: Is Resistance Futile?

1. Jencks argues that the downfall of modernism is exemplified in the demolition of the Pruitt-Igoe building in St Louis in 1972. See *The Language of Post-modern Architecture* (London: Academy Editions, 1977). This housing development was modelled on modernist insights, but the optimistic ideas of Le Corbusier were belied by the vagrancy of the (low-income) residents. Fires were set in the hallways, elevators were used as toilets, and within a little over a decade of its being completed it was essentially uninhabitable. Ironically, the designer of this emblem of the downfall of modernism according to Jencks was Minoru Yamasaki, the same architect who would later design the World Trade Center. The attacks of 11 September 2001 have been noted as the destruction of postmodernism (or late capitalism). This irony is also noted by Anthony Fontenot in 'Planned Destruction: Modern Planning, War and Public Housing', http://www.hatjecantz.de/leseproben/3775717110_06.pdf. Philipp Oswalt (ed.), *Shrinking Cities*, vol. 2, 'Interventions' (Ostfildern: Hatje Cantz Verlag, 2006), 52-61.
2. Sylvère Lotringer, 'A Revolutionary Process Never Ends', interview with Antonio Negri, who identifies 1968 as the end of the modern, and the beginning of the postmodern. *Artforum* (May 2008), 306-309. Charles Jencks situates this transition a little later, in 1972, with the demolition of the Pruitt-Igoe building in St Louis. Jencks, *The Language of Postmodern Architecture*, op. cit. (note 1).
3. An essay that has addressed this problem of discourse coloured by the 1960s directly is by Hans den Hartog Jager. 'Zet die roze bril eens af! Overspannen verwachtingen helpen de beeldende kunst niet', *NRC Handelsblad*, 17 February 2006, Cultureel Supplement, 24. He critiques the conflation of art and politics, and argues that the legacy of the 1960s has made it difficult to discuss art in its own (material) terms.
4. The critique of consumption holds a central place in this debate even through today. In particular, the events of 2008, with its financial turmoil reinforcing the question of whether affluence itself can resolve issues not destined to be addressed through market mechanisms, have recalibrated the relationship to consumption. However, this too is not an easily identifiable question of right and wrong. Even in the midst of the neo-Marxist critiques of the 1960s, Antonio Negri, on looking back, also acknowledges the power of affluence in lightening the burden of everyday life in post-war Europe: 'I always find a strong moralistic and religious side to any attack and critique of consumption, and that has notably been the case in Germany. I would strongly disagree with that. I don't believe that May '68 was a rejection of consumer society. For us, in the postwar years, consumption wasn't oppressive; it was restoring life. Introducing hygiene, bathrooms, toilets in the apartments being built throughout Europe around 1960 [following the destruction caused by the Second World War] – that wasn't negligible. It genuinely changed people's entire way of life.' Sylvère Lotringer, 'A Revolutionary Process Never Ends', interview with Antonio Negri, *Artforum* (May 2008), 309. The grand problem of course arises when this is no longer about addressing needs, but becomes a need in itself. Debord may argue that this is necessarily so with the advent of consumption, and yet it may be more appropriate to address it as an issue in degree rather than in kind.
5. This has been answered in the contemporary tendency of incorporating failure as an inevitable part of artistic production. In doing so, the work maintains its optimism, acknowledging the need for ideals worth aiming at. At the same time, it also acquires humility by allowing for the impossibility of one person's ideal being sufficient to construct an ideal world for everyone. On issues of incorporating failure, see Jeroen Boomgaard, 'Onhaalbaarheid als ideaal', *Open* 5 (2003), 26-31, and 'Het podium van de betrokkenheid', *reflect* 1, *Nieuw engagement in architectuur, kunst en vormgeving* (2003), 98-108. On the need for ideals and their role in architecture, see Lara Schrijver, 'Dreaming the World That Might Still Become', *BEYOND* 1, *Scenarios and Speculations* (2009), 12-17.

6. The relation between film and architecture in the late twentieth century could be an interesting avenue to take in exploring the resonance between architectural ideals and societal reception. There are a number of arguments to be made about an increasingly visually sophisticated audience and its relation to architectural production. The argument on visual sophistication begins with Banham, but has retreated from architectural discourse into the realm of cultural and visual studies.
7. Bruno Latour, 'Why Has Critique Run out of Steam? From Matters of Fact to Matters of Concern', *Critical Inquiry* 30 (Winter 2004), 225-248.
8. Ibid., 231.
9. Ibid.
10. Following this line of reasoning, the social issues that the modernists addressed in their manifestoes, in principle 'matters of concern' were reduced to 'matters of fact' by their tendency to quantify.
11. Lotringer, 'A Revolutionary Process', op. cit. (note 2), 309.
12. Seeing architecture as a battleground seems to be a particularly twentieth-century perception, correlated perhaps to the enormous transformations taking place at the turn of the century. De Tocqueville suggests that the equality of democracy requires a more passionately argued position. Mies van der Rohe, in his inaugural speech for IIT, speaks of architecture as battleground, not playground, not for the weak of spirit.
13. Manuel Gausa, 'Operative Optimism: Toward a New Pragmatic Idealism in Europe', in: Manuel Gausa and Susanna Cros (eds.), *OpOp: Operative Optimism in Architecture* (Barcelona: Actar, 2005), 0.4-0.33. Gausa uses phrases such as a 'propositive ethics', suggesting that these projects aim to 'optimize reality, projecting new qualitative actions on the environment'. His essay indicates many different directions, all tied together by an engagement with reality and a diversity of approaches.
14. Sarah Whiting and Robert Somol, 'Notes around the Doppler Effect and Other Moods of Modernism', *Perspecta* 33 (2002), 72-77.
15. George Baird, 'Criticality and its Discontents', *Harvard Design Magazine*, no. 21 (fall 2004/ winter 2005), 16-21. The article offers a chronological overview of the demise of the critical (and rise of the projective) in the contemporary debate. Available online at: http://www.gsd.harvard.edu/research/publications/hdm/back/21_baird.html.
16. Whether the current era is seen as the postmodernity of David Harvey, the collapse of grand narratives of Jean-François Lyotard, or the space of flows of Castells, each interpretation requires a new approach to our ideas about knowledge, critique and reflection.
17. Scott Lash, 'Informationcritique', in: Deborah Hauptmann and Arie Graafland (eds.), *Cities in Transition* (Rotterdam: 010 Publishers, 2001), 233.
18. This work of Speaks begins with a series of essays for *A+U*. The first is: Michael Speaks, 'Design Intelligence', Part 1: Introduction, *A+U* 387 (2002). He has developed this material in various forums.
19. Lara Schrijver, 'The Power of Lightness: Humor as a Method of Critique in Architecture and the Visual Arts', in: Martin Nonhoff, Katharina Bunzmann and Johannes Angermüller (eds.), *PostModern Productions* (Hamburg: LIT Verlag, 2001), 147-160.
20. Lash, 'Informationcritique', op. cit. (note 17), 233.
21. This is perhaps what Whiting's idea of 'slipping in and out of critical theory' is aiming at: it *combines* the moment of production (specificity) with other moments of reflection (universal context).
22. Sarah Whiting, 'Going Public', *Hunch*, Berlage Institute Report 6/7 (summer 2003), 502. She implies here that critical theory is both useful and limited, and that architectural production itself allows a freedom from (destructive) critique.
23. Kate Nesbitt distinguishes a number of different roles for theory, ranging from analytical to prescriptive, which might help reconstitute and recalibrate the relationship between theory and practice in architecture. Kate Nesbitt (ed.), *Theorizing a New Agenda for Architecture: An*

Anthology of Architectural Theory 1965-1995 (New York: Princeton Architectural Press, 1996), introduction, 16-70.

24. Yet radicalism should not be replaced by all-out fatalism: some level of criticism remains necessary to not fall into pure formalism with no conscience.
25. Authors who similarly address this hybrid of theory and practice or a 'contaminated' or 'realist' condition are Stan Allen, Douglas Kellner, Martijntje Smits and Douglas Rushkoff.
26. See for example Alejandro Zaera-Polo, 'The Hokusai Wave', *Volume* 3 (2005), 32-39.
27. Richard Sennett. *The Craftsman* (London: Allen Lane, 2008), 21-27.
28. Ibid., 50-51, 77-78, 160.
29. Ibid., 10-11, 52.
30. It should be noted here that Sennett also distinguishes between 'absolute quality' and 'quality of practice'. While 'absolute quality' sets a standard that becomes a guideline for subsequent production – Sennett uses the example of the Stradivarius – 'quality of practice' should not be dismissed. Sennett primarily argues against embedding our absolute quality in institutionalized codes of practice. Ibid., 45, 79-80, 159.
31. Whiting, 'Going Public', op. cit. (note 22), 502.
32. Gausa and Cros, *OpOp*, op. cit. (note 13).
33. 'Die Produktion von Präsenz', *Arch+* 178 (2006).
34. On tacit knowledge, which incorporates the many adjustments of craft through trial and error, see Sennett, *The Craftsman*, op. cit. (note 27), 50-51, 79-80. On the importance of the connection between means and ends as ethical reflection implicated in the process of making, see ibid., 287-288, 294-296.
35. Inaugural speech by Pieter van Wesemael, Eindhoven University of Technology.

Selected literature

Achterhuis, Hans, et al. (eds.), *Van stoommachine tot cyborg: Denken over techniek in de nieuwe wereld* (Amsterdam: Ambo, 1997)

Actie, werkelijkheid en fictie in de kunst van de jaren '60 in Nederland, exhibition catalogue (Rotterdam: Museum Boymans-van Beuningen, 1979)

Allen, Stan, *Practice: Architecture, technique and representation* (Amsterdam: G+B Arts International, 2000)

Alloway, Lawrence, 'The Arts and the Mass Media', *Architectural Design* (February 1958), 84-85

Alloway, Lawrence, 'City Notes', *Architectural Design* (January 1959), 34-35

Andreotti, Libero and Xavier Costa (eds.), *Theory of the Dérive and other Situationist Writings on the City* (Barcelona: Museu d'Art Contemporani de Barcelona & ACTAR, 1996)

Les Années Pop, exhibition catalogue (Paris: Centre Georges Pompidou, 2001)

Archigram Group, *Archigram*, journal issues 1961-1970

Arendt, Hannah, *The Human Condition: A study of the central dilemmas facing modern man* (New York: Doubleday Anchor Books, 1958)

Apollonio, Umbro (ed.), *Futurist Manifestos* (London: Viking Press, 1973)

Baird, George, '"Criticality" and its Discontents', *Harvard Design Magazine* no. 21 (fall 2004/winter 2005)

Banham, Reyner, *Theory and Design in the First Machine Age* (London: The Architectural Press, 1960)

Benjamin, Walter, *Illuminations: Essays and Reflections*, edited by Hannah Arendt, with an introduction by Hannah Arendt, translated by Harry Zohn (New York: Schocken Books, 1968)

Benjamin, Walter, *Reflections: Essays, Aphorisms, Autobiographical Writings*, edited by Peter Demetz, with an introduction by Peter Demetz (New York: Harcourt Brace Jovanovich, 1978)

Berting, Jan, Leo d'Anjou and Bram Steijn (eds.), *De tirannie van het beeld: Collectieve voorstellingen en handelen* (Amsterdam: Boom, 1997)

Blake, Peter, *No Place Like Utopia: Modern Architecture and the Company We Kept* (New York and London: W.W. Norton, 1993)

Blazwick, Iwona (ed.), *An Endless Adventure... An Endless Passion... An Endless Banquet: A Situationist Scrapbook* (London: ICA & Verso, 1989)

Boyer, M. Christine, *The City of Collective Memory: Its Historical Imagery and Architectural Entertainments* (Cambridge, MA: MIT Press, 1994)

Boyer, M. Christine, *CyberCities: Visual Perception in the Age of Electronic Communication* (New York: Princeton Architectural Press, 1996)

Bürger, Peter, *Theory of the Avant-garde* (Minneapolis: University of Minnesota Press, 1984), originally published as *Theorie der Avant-garde* (Frankfurt: Suhrkamp Verlag, 1974)

Calinescu, Matei, *Faces of Modernity: Avant-garde, Decadence, Kitsch* (Bloomington: Indiana University Press, 1977)

Cities: A 'Scientific American' Book (New York: Alfred A. Knopf, 1965)

Colquhoun, Alan, 'Symbolic and Literal Aspects of Technology', *Architectural Design* (November 1962), 508-509

Colquhoun, Alan, *Essays in Architectural Criticism: Modern Architecture and Historical Change* (Cambridge, MA: MIT Press, 1981)

Cook, Peter, *Architecture: Action and Plan* (London: Studio Vista, 1967)

Cook, Peter (ed.), *Archigram* (Basel: Birkhäuser, 1972)

Cooke, Lynn, 'Architecture and the Sixties: Still Radical after all these Years', an interview with Rem Koolhaas, *Tate etc.* issue no. 2 (autumn 2004)

Le Corbusier, *Towards a New Architecture* (London: J. Rodker, 1931), translated from the thirteenth French edition of *Vers une Architecture*, 1927

Le Corbusier, *The City of To-morrow and Its Planning* (New York: Dover Books, 1987), translated by Frederick Etchells from the eighth French edition of *Urbanisme* (1929)

Crow, Thomas, *The Rise of the Sixties* (New York: Harry N. Abrams, 1996)

Debord, Guy, 'Rapport sur la construction des situations et sur les conditions de l'organisation et de l'action de la tendence situationniste internationale' (presented at the founding conference of the Situationist International at Cosio, july 1957). Reprinted in: *Internationale Situationniste*, édition augmentée (Paris: Librairie Arthème Fayard, 1997), 689-701

Debord, Guy, structured by Asger Jorn, *Mémoires* (Paris: Jean-Jacques Pauvert, 1993), this publication is the facsimile edition of the original work published in Copenhagen in 1958
Debord, Guy, *La Société du Spectacle* (Paris: Éditions Buchet-Chastel, 1967)
Debord, Guy, *The Society of the Spectacle* (NY: Zone Books (MIT Press), 1995), translated by Donald Nicholson-Smith
DeLong, David G. (ed.), *Frank Lloyd Wright: Designs for an American Landscape 1922-1932* (NY: Harry N. Abrams Publishers, 1996)
Dilthey, Wilhelm, *Einleitung der Geisteswissenschaften: Versuch einer Grundlegung für das Studium der Gesellschaft und der Geschichte* (1914, currently published by Vandenhoeck & Ruprecht)
Doremus, Thomas, *Frank Lloyd Wright and Le Corbusier: The Great Dialogue* (New York: Van Nostrand Reinhold Company, 1985)
Douglas, Mary, *Purity and Danger* (London: Routledge, 1966)
Dumontier, Pascal, *Les Situationnistes et Mai 68: Théorie et Pratique de la Révolution (1966-1972)* (Paris: Éditions Gérard Lebovici, 1990)
Van Eck, Caroline, 'The Visually Immediate: Sir Christopher Wren on the Corona of the Temple of Peace in Rome', *OASE* 59, *Scratching the Surface* (2002), 6-21
The Exploding Metropolis: A Study of the Assault on Urbanism and How Our Cities Can Resist It, edited by the editors of *Fortune* magazine, with an introduction by William H. Whyte (Garden City, NY: Doubleday Anchor Books, 1957)
Fishman, Robert, *Urban Utopias in the Twentieth Century: Ebenezer Howard, Frank Lloyd Wright, and Le Corbusier* (Cambridge, MA: MIT Press, 1982)
Foster, Hal, *Recodings: Art, Spectacle, Cultural Politics* (Seattle, WA: Bay Press, 1985)
Galbraith, John Kenneth, *The Affluent Society* (Boston: Houghton Mifflin, 1958)
Gans, Herbert, *People and Plans: Essays on Urban Problems and Solutions* (New York: Basic Books, 1968)
Gans, Herbert, *Popular Culture & High Culture: An Analysis and Evaluation of Taste* (New York: Basic Books, 1974)
Giddens, Anthony, *Sociology: A Brief but Critical Introduction* (London: The MacMillan Press, 1982)
Graafland, Arie and Jasper de Haan (eds.), *The Critical Landscape* (Rotterdam: 010 Publishers, 1996)
Guiheux, Alain, *Archigram* (Paris: Centre Georges Pompidou, 1994)
A Guide to Archigram, 1961-1974 (London: Academy Editions/Vienna: Kunsthalle Wien, 1994)
Harrison, Charles and Paul Wood (eds.), *Art in Theory. 1900-1990: An Anthology of Changing Ideas* (Oxford: Blackwell, 1992)
Harvey, David, *The Condition of Postmodernity* (Cambridge, MA: Blackwell, 1990)
Hays, K. Michael (ed.), *Architecture Theory since 1968* (Cambridge, MA: MIT Press, 1998)
Hays, K. Michael (ed.), *Oppositions Reader* (New York: Princeton Architectural Press, 1998)
Hertz, Noreena, *The Silent Takeover* (London: William Heinemann, 2001)
Holford, William, Arthur Ling and Peter Smithson, 'Planning Today', *Architectural Design* (June 1957), 185-189
Howell, John (ed.), *Breakthroughs: Avant-garde Artists in Europe and America 1950-1990* (New York: Rizzoli, 1991)
Hunch, Berlage Institute Report 6/7 (summer 2003)
Huyssen, Andreas, *After the Great Divide: Modernism, Mass Culture, Postmodernism* (Bloomington: Indiana University Press, 1986)
International Situationniste, Patrick Mosconi (ed.), édition augmentée (Paris: Librairie Arthème Fayard, 1997), compilation of the 12 issues of the journal *International Situationniste*, published from 1958-1969, earlier compilations: (Amsterdam: Van Gennep, 1970); (Paris: Éditions Champ Libre, 1975)
Jacobs, Jane, *The Death and Life of Great American Cities* (New York: Vintage Books, 1961)
Jameson, Fredric, *Postmodernism, or, the Cultural Logic of Late Capitalism* (London: Verso, 1991)
Jay, Martin, *Downcast Eyes: The Denigration of Vision in Twentieth-Century French Thought* (Berkeley: University of California Press, 1993)
Jay, Martin, 'Cultural Relativism and the Visual Turn', *Journal of Visual Culture*, vol. 1, no. 3, December 2002, 267-278
Jencks, Charles, 'Pop – Non pop (1)', *Architectural Association Quarterly*, vol. 1, no. 1 (1969), 48-64
Jencks, Charles, 'Pop – Non pop (2)', *Architectural Association Quarterly*, vol. 1, no. 2 (April 1969), 56-74
Jencks, Charles, *Modern Movements in Architecture* (London: Pelican Books, 1973)

Jencks, Charles, *The Language of Post-modern Architecture* (London: Academy Editions, 1977)
Jenks, Chris (ed.), *Visual Culture* (London: Routledge, 1995)
Kellner, Douglas, *Media Spectacle* (London: Routledge, 2003)
De Kerckhove, Derrick, *The Skin of Culture: Investigating Electronic Reality* (London: Kogan Page, 1996)
Klein, Naomi, *No Logo* (London: Flamingo, 2000)
Knabb, Ken (ed. and trans.), *Situationist International Anthology* (Berkeley: Bureau of Public Secrets, 1981)
Knabb, Ken, *Bureau of Public Secrets*, website, Berkeley. The revised and updated texts from Knabb's *Situationist International Anthology* are available on http://www.bopsecrets.org/SI/index.htm
Kockelkoren, Petran, *Technology: Art, Fairground and Theatre* (Rotterdam: NAi Publishers, 2003)
Krauss, Rosalind, *The Originality of the Avant-Garde and Other Modernist Myths* (Cambridge, MA: MIT Press, 1986)
Lash, Scott and John Urry, *Economies of Signs and Space* (London: Sage Publications, 1994)
Lasn, Kalle, *Culture Jam: How to Reverse America's Suicidal Computer Binge – And Why We Must* (New York: HarperCollins, 1999)
Latour, Bruno, 'Why Has Critique Run out of Steam? From Matters of Fact to Matters of Concern', *Critical Inquiry* 30 (winter 2004), 225-248
Leach, Neil (ed.), *Rethinking Architecture: A Reader in Cultural Theory* (London: Routledge, 1997)
Leezenberg, Michiel and Gerard de Vries, *Wetenschapsfilosofie voor geesteswetenschappen* (Amsterdam: Amsterdam University Press, 2001)
Lefebvre, Henri, *Critique de la vie quotidienne.* Volume 1, *Introduction* (Paris : L'Arche, 1947); volume 2, *Fondements d'une sociologie de la quotidiennité* (Paris: L'Arche, 1961); and volume 3, *De la modernité au modernisme, Pour une métaphilosophie du quotidien* (Paris: L'Arche, 1981)
Lefebvre, Henri, *Le droit à la ville* (Paris: Éditions Anthropos, 1968)
Lefebvre, Henri, *Writings on Cities*, translated and edited by Eleonore Kofman and Elizabeth Lebas (Oxford: Blackwell, 1996)
Lichtenstein, Claude and Thomas Schregenberger (eds.), *As Found: The Discovery of the Ordinary* (Baden: Lars Müller Publishers, 2001)
Lupton, Ellen, *Mechanical Brides: Women and Machines from Home to Office* (New York: Cooper-Hewitt National Museum of Design, Smithsonian Institution and Princeton Architectural Press, 1993)
Lynch, Kevin, *The Image of the City* (Cambridge, MA: MIT Press, 1960)
Lyotard, Jean-François, *La Condition Postmoderne: Rapport sur le savoir* (Paris: Minuit, 1979)
Marcus, Greil, *Lipstick Traces: A Secret History of the Twentieth Century* (New York: Penguin Books, 1989)
Marcuse, Herbert, *One Dimensional Man: Studies in the Ideology of Advanced Industrial Society* (Boston: Beacon Press, 1964)
Marwick, Arthur, *The Sixties: Cultural Revolution in Britain, France, Italy and the United States, c.1958-c.1974* (Oxford: Oxford University Press, 1998)
Massey, Anne, *Modernism and Mass Culture in Britain, 1945-1959* (Manchester: Manchester University Press, 1995)
Maxwell, Robert, *Sweet Disorder and the Carefully Careless: Theory and Criticism in Architecture* (New York: Princeton Architectural Press, 1993)
McDonough, Thomas (ed.), *Guy Debord and the Situationist International: Texts and Documents* (Cambridge, MA: MIT Press, 2002)
McLuhan, Marshall, *Understanding Media: The Extensions of Man* (New York: McGraw Hill, 1964)
Merrifield, Andy, *Metromarxism: A Marxist Tale of the City* (London: Routledge, 2002)
Michelson, Annette, et al. (eds.), *October: The First Decade* (Cambridge, MA: MIT Press, 1987)
Modern Dreams: The Rise and Fall and Rise of Pop (New York: The Institute for Contemporary Art and MIT Press, 1988)
Mumford, Lewis, *The Culture of Cities* (New York: Harcourt, Brace and Company, 1938)
Mumford, Lewis, *The City in History* (New York: Harcourt, Brace & World, 1961)
Nesbitt, Kate (ed.), *Theorizing a New Agenda for Architecture: An Anthology of Architectural Theory, 1965-1995* (New York: Princeton Architectural Press, 1996)
Obrist, Hans Ulrich and Rem Koolhaas, 'An Interview with Denise Scott Brown and Robert Venturi', in: Chuihua Judy Chung, et al. (eds.), *Harvard Design School Guide to Shopping* (Cologne: Taschen, 2001), 593-617

Ohrt, Roberto, *Phantom Avantgarde: eine Geschichte der Situationistischen Internationale und der modernen Kunst* (Berlin: Lukas & Sternberg, 1997)
De Oliveira, Nicolas, Nicola Oxley, Michael Petry (eds.), with texts by Michael Archer, *Installation Art* (London: Thames and Hudson, 1994)
Papadakis, Andreas C. (ed.), 'Post-Modernism on Trial,' *A.D. Profile* no. 88 (London: Academy Editions, 1990)
Pellegrini, Aldo, *New Tendencies in Art* (New York: Crown Publishers, 1966), translated by Robin Carson
Poggioli, Renato, *The Theory of the Avant-Garde* (Cambridge, MA: Belknap/Harvard University Press, 1968)
Poldervaart, Saskia, 'De paradoxen van de utopie-kritiek', *Feit en fictie. Tijdschrift voor de Geschiedenis van de Representatie*, vol. II, no. 3 (1995), 7-22
Postman, Neil, *Amusing Ourselves to Death* (London: Methuen, 1985)
Robbins, David (ed.), *The Independent Group: Postwar Britain and the Aesthetics of Plenty* (Cambridge, MA: MIT Press, 1990)
Rossi, Aldo, *The Architecture of the City* (Cambridge, MA: MIT Press, 1982), originally published as *L'Architettura della citta* (Padua: Marsilio, 1966)
Ruhe, Harry, *Fluxus: The Most Radical and Experimental Art Movement of the Sixties* (Amsterdam: 'A', 1979)
Rushkoff, Douglas, *Media Virus!: Hidden Agendas in Popular Culture* (New York: Ballantine Books, 1994)
Rushkoff, Douglas, *Children of Chaos: Surviving the End of the World as We Know It* (London: Flamingo, 1997), originally published as *Playing the Future* (New York: HarperCollins, 1996)
Sadler, Simon, *The Situationist City* (Cambridge, MA: MIT Press, 1998)
Sadler, Simon, 'The Brutal Birth of Archigram', in: Elain Harwood and Alan Powers (eds.), *The Sixties: Life: Style: Architecture* (London: The Twentieth Century Society, 2002)
Sadler, Simon, *Archigram: Architecture without Architecture* (Cambridge, MA: MIT Press, 2005)
Sanders, Joel, 'Archigram: Designs on the Future', October 2002. Available online at: http://www.postmedia.net/02/archigram.htm (last accessed August 30, 2004)
Scott Brown, Denise, 'Team 10, Perspecta 10 and the Present state of Architectural Theory', *Journal of the American Institute of Planners* (January 1967), 42-50
Scott Brown, Denise, '"Little Magazines" in Architecture and Urbanism', *Journal of the American Institute of Planners* 34 (July 1968), 223-233
Scott Brown, Denise, 'Room at the Top? Sexism and the Star System in Architecture', in: Berkeley, Ellen Perry (ed.), *Architecture: A Place for Women* (Washington: Smithsonian Institution Press, 1989), 237-246
Schrijver, Lara, 'Reflexivity', *OASE* 52, *Consumption and Territory*, 1999, 2-15
Schrijver, Lara, 'The Power of Lightness: Humor as a Strategy in Architecture and the Visual Arts', in: Martin Nonhoff, Katharina Bunzmann and Johannes Angermüller (eds.), *PostModern Productions* (Hamburg: LIT Verlag, 2001), 147-159
Schrijver, Lara, 'From Public to Publicity ... and Back Again? Collectivity in the Twentieth Century', *OASE* 59, *Scratching the Surface* (2002), 68-79
Simmel, Georg, 'The Metropolis and Mental Life', translated by Edward Shils, in: Neil Leach (ed.), *Rethinking Architecture: A Reader in Cultural Theory* (London: Routledge, 1997)
Smithson, Alison and Peter Smithson, 'But Today We Collect Ads', in: *Modern Dreams: The Rise and Fall and Rise of Pop* (New York: The Institute for Contemporary Art and MIT Press, 1988), 53-55
Smits, Martijntje, *Monsterbezwering: De culturele domesticatie van nieuwe technologie* (Amsterdam: Boom, 2002)
Sussman, Elisabeth (ed.), *On the Passage of a Few People through a Rather Brief Moment in Time: The Situationist International, 1957-1972* (Cambridge, MA: MIT Press and Boston: Institute of Contemporary Art, 1989)
Taylor, Mark C., *Hiding* (Chicago: University of Chicago Press, 1997)
Venturi, Robert, *Complexity and Contradiction in Architecture* (New York: The Museum of Modern Art Papers on Architecture, 1966)
Venturi, Robert and Denise Scott Brown, *Learning from Las Vegas* (Cambridge, MA: MIT Press, 1972)
Venturi Scott Brown and Associates, *On Houses and Housing*, Architectural Monographs no. 21 (London: Academy Editions, 1992)

Vidler, Anthony, *The Architectural Uncanny* (Cambridge, MA: MIT Press, 1992)
Visser, Gerard, *De Druk van de Beleving* (Nijmegen: Uitgeverij SUN, 1999)
Watkin, David, *Morality and Architecture: The Development of a Theme in Architectural History and Theory from the Gothic Revival to the Modern Movement* (Oxford: Clarendon Press, 1977)
Whiteley, Nigel, *Reyner Banham: Historian of the Immediate Future* (Cambridge, MA: MIT Press, 2003)
Wines, James, *De-Architecture* (New York: Rizzoli, 1987)
Wollen, Peter, 'Bitter Victory: The Art and Politics of the Situationist International', in: Sussman, Elisabeth (ed.), *On the Passage of a Few People through a Rather Brief Moment in Time: The Situationist International, 1957-1972* (Cambridge, MA: MIT Press, 1989)

Selected films

Charles Chaplin, director, *Modern Times* (1936)
Richard Fleischer, director, *Fantastic Voyage*, 1966
Terry Gilliam, director, *Brazil*, 1985
Jean-Luc Godard, director, *Alphaville*, 1965
Fritz Lang, director, *Metropolis*, 1927. Based on Thea von Harbou's book *Metropolis* (1926)
W.C. Menzies, director, *Things to Come*, 1936. Based on H.G. Wells' book *The Shape of Things to Come* (1933)
Ridley Scott, director, *Blade Runner*, 1984. Based on Philip K. Dick's book *Do Androids Dream of Electric Sheep?* (1968)
Steven Spielberg, director, *Minority Report*, 2002. Based on Philip K. Dick's short story 'Minority Report' (1956)
Jacques Tati, director, *Les Vacances de Monsieur Hulot*, 1953
Jacques Tati, director, *Mon Oncle*, 1958
Jacques Tati, director, *Playtime*, 1967
Roger Vadim, director, *Barbarella*, 1968
Dziga Vertov, director, *Man with a Movie Camera* (1927)

Illustrations credits

Klaus Pinter: cover (*Downtown Megastructures*, 1971)
Socialfiction.org (2003): 14
TUMULT, Utrecht (2005): 24
Ralph Kämena (2003): 29, 30 (source: www.skor.nl)
Jannes Linders (2005): 33, 34 (source: www.skor.nl)
ARCAM, Amsterdam/Jan Rothuizen (2008): 37
Jean-Luc Godard, director, *Alphaville* (1965): 43
Fritz Lang, director, *Metropolis* (1927): 47t
Jacques Tati, director, *Playtime* (1967): 50t, 153
Frank van der Salm (2004): 61t
TIME'S UP!, New York (1998): 75
Roger Vadim, director, *Barbarella* (1968): 122b
Dziga Vertov, director, *Man with a Movie Camera* (1927): 102 (collage by manchesterurbanscreens.org)
Poster Thunderbirds (1965-1966): 126
Venturi, Scott Brown and Associates Archive (Architectural Archives of the University of Pennsylvania, box VSB.28): 162

Illustrations that have been reproduced from the following publications:
Les Années Pop, exhibition catalogue (Paris: Centre Georges Pompidou, 2001): p.46*(20)*, p.96, p.98*(61.41)*, p.99 *(63.88)*, p.108a*(64.11)*, p.112*(64.16)*, p.113*(68.21, 68.22)*, p.119*(65.63)*, p.121*(57.16)*, p.135*(67.7.1, 67.7.2)*, p.136*(67.46)*, p.148*(56.4)*, p.150*(59.19)*, p.158*(68.5)*, p.186*(67.42)*
Archigram no.5 (1964): p.110a*(p. 6)*, p.110u*(p. 12)*
Archigram no.4 (1964): p.126l, p.127

Archigram no.7 (1966): p.97, p.124
Architectural Design 5 (1960): p.79 *(p.181)*
Architectural Design 6 (1957): p. 65l(p.185)
Architectural Design 7 (1956): p.78*(p. 231)*
Architectural Forum 1 (1962): p.76*(p.102)*
Architectural Forum 9 (1956): p.80*(p.130)*
Archplus 183, Situationist Urbanism – 'towards a casual form of the social'(2007): p.22
Baan, Christine de, et al. (eds.*), Visionary Power, Producing the Contemporary City* (Rotterdam: NAi Publishers, 2007): P.16*(cover)*, p.26*(p.216, p.217)*
Brauer, David E. et al., *Pop Art: U.S./U.K. Connections, 1956-1966* (Houston: The Menil Collection / Ostfildern-Ruit: Hatje Cantz Publishers, 2001): p.13*(p.81)*, p.175a*(p. 141)*, p.175u*(p.179)*
Cook, Peter (ed.), *Archigram* (Basel: Birkhäuser, 1972): p. 66*(p.18)*, p.108*(p 39)*, p.118*(p.64)*, p.117*(p.82)*, p.119*(p. 46)*, p.120*(p. 53)*, p.122*(p.125)*, p.129l*(p. 14)*, 129r*(p. 15)*, p.143*(p.124)*
Le Corbusier, *The City of To-morrow and Its Planning* (New York:Dover Books, 1987), translated by Frederick Etchells from the eighth French edition of *Urbanisme* (1929): p. 42*(p.246, p.247)*, p.183a*(p.242, p.243)*
Crimson Architectural Historians and Felix Rottenberg, *WiMBY! (Welcome into My Backyard!). Future, Past and Present of a New Town* (Rotterdam: NAi Publishers, 2007): p.31a*(p 344)*, p.31u*(p.343)*
Debord, Guy, structured by Asger Jorn, *Mémoires* (Paris: Jean-Jacques Pauvert, 1993): p.55l, p.55r *(n.p.)*
Fishman, Robert, *Urban Utopias in the Twentieth Century: Ebenezer Howard, Frank Lloyd Wright, and Le Corbusier* (Cambridge, MA: MIT Press, 1982): p.181a
Guiheux, Alain, *Archigram* (Paris: Centre Georges Pompidou, 1994): p.100*(p.143)*
Internationale Situationniste 1 (1957): p.64l
Internationale Situationniste 3 (1959): p.49*(p.37, p38)*, p.51(p.6)
Internationale Situationniste 4 (1960): p.57l, p.57r*(p.24)*
Internationale Situationniste 6 (1961): p.65r*(p.35)*
Internationale Situationniste 8 (1963): p.50, p.74*(p.42)*
Internationale Situationniste 11 (1967): p.177*(p.57)*
Internationale Situationniste 12 (1969): p.47u, p.52*(p.102)*, 2.30*(p. 103)*, p.73*(p.103)*, p.178*(p.38)*
Lynch, Kevin, *The Image of the City* (Cambridge, MA: MIT Press, 1960): p.64r*(p.146)*
Milestones of the 20th Century. Annual supplement to Collier's Encyclopedia, Merit Students Encyclopedia, and Young Students Learning Library (New York: Collier's, 1999): p.73u*(p.200)*
Modern Dreams: The Rise and Fall and Rise of Pop (New York: The Institute for Contemporary Art and MIT Press, 1988): p.166*(p.13)*, p.174*(p.55)*
OASE 51: Rearrangements, A Smithsons Celebration (2000): p.181u*(p.56)*
Ottagono, May (2003): p.13r*(Cover)*
Ohrt, Roberto, *Phantom Avant-Garde: A History of the Situationist International and Modern Art* (Hamburg: Nautilus, 1990): p.41*(p.XIV)*
Sadler, Simon, *The Situationist City* (Cambridge, MA: MIT Press, 1998): p.54*(p.79, photo Ralph Rumney)*
Venturi, Robert and Denise Scott Brown, *Learning from Las Vegas* (Cambridge, MA: MIT Press, 1972): p.69*(p.63)*, p.151*(p.62)*, p.190u*(p156)*, p.193*(p.67)*
Venturi, Robert, *Complexity and Contradiction in Architecture* (New York: The Museum of Modern Art Papers on Architecture, 1966): p.155*(p. 54 Photograph Peter Blake)*, p.156*(p 105 Photograph Wallace Litwin)*
Venturi Scott Brown and Associates, *On Houses and Housing, Architectural Monographs no. 21* (London: Academy Editions, 1992): p.131*(p.65)*, p.191*(p.65)*
Wigley, *New Babylon and the hyperarchitecture of desire* (Rotterdam: 010 Publishers, 1989): p.44*(p.119)*, p. 70*(p.184 photo Victor E. Nieuwenhuys)*, p.83*(p.190)*, p.91*(p.207)*
Wines, James, De-Architecture (New York: Rizzoli, 1987): p.61m, p.61u*(p.39)*
Risselada, Max and Dirk van den Heuvel (eds.), *Team 10, in search of a Utopia of the present* (Rotterdam: NAi Publishers, 2005): p.77*(p.52)*, p.183u*(p.33)*
Signs of life: Symbols in the American City. Catalogue for exhibition designed by Venturi and Rauch at the Renwick Gallery of the Smithsonian Institution (New York: Aperture Inc., 1976): p.190a*(p.12)*

Credits

This book was made possible in part by the support of the Netherlands Architecture Fund.

Author: Lara Schrijver
Copy editor: D'Laine Camp
Image cover: *Downtown Megastructures* by Klaus Pinter
Design cover and title page: Zuiderlicht, Maastricht
Design: Studio Tint, The Hague
DTP, printing: Drukkerij Die Keure, Brugge
Paper: Fly White, 115 grs
Production: Marcel Witvoet, NAi Publishers, Rotterdam
Publisher: Eelco van Welie, NAi Publishers, Rotterdam

Stimuleringsfonds voor Architectuur
the Netherlands Architecture Fund

NAi Publishers is an internationally orientated publisher specialized in developing, producing and distributing books on architecture, visual arts and related disciplines.
www.naipublishers.nl

Available in North, South and Central America through D.A.P./Distributed Art Publishers Inc, 155 Sixth Avenue 2nd Floor, New York, NY 10013-1507, tel +1 212 627 1999, fax +1 212 627 9484, dap@dapinc.com

Available in the United Kingdom and Ireland through Art Data, 12 Bell Industrial Estate, 50 Cunnington Street, London W4 5HB, tel +44 208 747 1061, fax +44 208 742 2319, orders@artdata.co.uk

Printed and bound in Belgium
ISBN 978-90-5662-678-5